An International
Anthology of
Women's Experiences
in Sport

C R O S S I N G
B O U N D A R I E S

Susan J. Bandy, PhD
The Hungarian University of
Physical Education

Anne S. Darden, MA
East Tennessee State University
EDITORS

HUMAN KINETICS

Library of Congress Cataloging-in-Publication Data

Crossing boundaries: an international anthology of women's
  experiences in sport / Susan J. Bandy, Anne S. Darden, editors.
      p.   cm.
  Includes bibliographical references.
  ISBN 0-7360-0088-7
      1. Sports—Literary collections. 2. Women athletes—Literary
  collections. 3. Literature—Women authors.   I. Bandy, Susan J.
  II. Darden, Anne S., 1963-   .
  PN6071.S62C76 1999
  808.8'0355—dc21   99-13733
                                                                  CIP

ISBN: 0-7360-0088-7

Copyright © 1999 by Susan J. Bandy and Anne S. Darden

Acquisitions Editor: Steven W. Pope, PhD; **Managing Editor:** Katy M. Patterson; **Assistant Editor:** Chris Enstrom; **Permissions Manager:** Terri Hamer; **Copyeditor:** Anne Mischakoff Heiles; **Proofreader:** Erin Cler; **Graphic Designer:** Stuart Cartwright; **Graphic Artist:** Brian McElwain; **Cover Designer:** Debby Winter/Buerkett Marketing Consultants; **Printer:** United Graphics

Human Kinetics books are available at special discounts for bulk purchase. Special editions or book excerpts can also be created to specification. For details, contact the Special Sales Manager at Human Kinetics.

Printed in the United States of America   10 9 8 7 6 5 4 3 2 1

Web site: http://www.humankinetics.com/

United States: Human Kinetics
P.O. Box 5076
Champaign, IL 61825-5076
1-800-747-4457
e-mail: humank@hkusa.com

Canada: Human Kinetics
475 Devonshire Road Unit 100
Windsor, ON N8Y 2L5
1-800-465-7301 (in Canada only)
e-mail: humank@hkcanada.com

Europe: Human Kinetics, P.O. Box IW14
Leeds LS16 6TR, United Kingdom
+44 (0) 113-278 1708
e-mail: humank@hkeurope.com

Australia: Human Kinetics
57A Price Avenue
Lower Mitcham, South Australia 5062
(08) 82771555
e-mail: humank@hkaustralia.com

New Zealand: Human Kinetics
P.O. Box 105-231, Auckland Central
09-523-3462
e-mail: humank@hknewz.com

Contents

Part III: Woman and Nature: The Bond With the Hunted   113

Part IV: The Contact Imperative   153

Contents

Who knows this woman?
Who knows her breast is full of remembered water!
Who knows what her chest will say to us if only
it keeps up its terrible running . . .

Don't stop, now, chest . . .
Chest that touches no one . . .

Listen . . .

The Runner
Erin Mouré

Prelude

Some years ago we began to collect poems and short stories that women had written about their sporting experiences, in part because we simply wanted to know how much of this type of writing had been published. More importantly, we had a feeling that our own sporting experiences, so different from those portrayed in "mainstream" male sport literature and in the lives of our male friends and colleagues, would be shared by other women and reflected in their writings. It seemed clear to us that while sport for men is often a confirmation of manhood and a journey to a known world, sport for us was certainly not a confirmation of our womanhood; if anything, it called our femininity into question.

In fact, we experienced sport as a new and uncertain world, a place where we could, like men, come to understand the physical demands of athletic performance and the emotional and psychological challenges of competition, but one where we also had to confront, in a uniquely female way, our own perceptions of our bodies and identities. To our surprise and delight, we discovered a profusion of literature written by women from a variety of historical and cultural perspectives. We found that women who are involved in sport, either as athletes or as spectators, believe that sport is more than a rite of passage to a masculine world, more than a rule-dominated substitute for the rigors of the battlefield, more than an outlet for elemental aggression, and more than a win-at-all-cost proposition. It is also more than a commercial product to be fashioned and marketed for public consumption.

Our principal intent in compiling this anthology has been to discover and reveal the depth, variety, and complexity of the female experience in sport. Who are these women who have crossed the boundaries of the most fiercely guarded bastion of masculinity? What do they seek? What have they encountered? What is the nature of their experience? What do female athletes understand about themselves and sport that other women might not?

To address these questions we have intentionally included only works written by women because we believe in the uniqueness of the female experience and the necessity that "woman must write woman," as Hélène Cixous urged some years ago in "The Laugh of the Medusa."[1] We have also intentionally excluded references to male perspectives of sport found in sport literature; to include such references would presuppose the primacy of the male perspective and the secondary and derivative or "other" nature of the female, as de Beauvoir noted many years ago.[2] The male perspective of sport is, after all, well-documented. It seemed important to first explore what women think about their own experiences independent of anything else.

Before we can understand this collective human experience, however, we must first understand the female experience. We hope that this collection of works, the first of its kind, will establish a foundation for future analyses of the androgynous character of sport as it is presented in sport literature.

As we began our search, almost automatically we included literature about play, dance, movement, games, and exercises—activities often considered ancillary or preparatory for the more important activity of sport. Because females have been excluded from sport and relegated to the role of passive spectator for centuries, it was necessary to open our search to those activities in which they *have* participated, even if those activities are not usually considered sports. We also extended our search to countries beyond the Anglo-Saxon world to expand the contemporary perception of sport, which has been fashioned in the West and predominantly by North Americans. Eventually we expanded our search to include all genres of literature: poetry, short stories, prose memoirs, journalistic accounts, plays, and novels, written from ancient times to the present.

By necessity, our methodology was itself unique—as has often been the case when women's works have been collected and anthologized for the first time. Many of these works were dragged from musty archives by librarians in New York, Paris, Münster, Lausanne, Budapest, and many other cities; given to us by our friends and colleagues around the world; ferreted from unknown anthologies and journals; and, on more than one occasion, discovered in used bookstores whose whereabouts would never had been known without the kindness and direction of virtual strangers. In the end, our friends and colleagues translated some of these works into English.

As this literature reveals, women have written about sport throughout the ages in disparate eras and cultures, yet most of their writings remain shrouded in obscurity. Like women themselves, these writings have been ignored and marginalized, their voices drowned out by the dominant male voices in literature. Anthologies devoted to sport, even those purported to be general and inclusive, continue to exclude women's writings, and many of those works that have been published remain on the periphery in little-known journals and magazines or in languages other than English.

Over the course of four years we found more than a thousand pieces of literature written by women from over 20 countries. The works included in

Crossing Boundaries surely reveal our own literary preferences and tastes, yet they also fulfill our goal of representing varied historical periods and diverse cultures. The diversity of these works was often challenging. At times the voices that resonate through the works are angular and separating, at other times, soft and connecting. Characters are old, young, retiring from sport, and taking their first golf lesson. They are spectators and fans, professional basketball players, international amateur runners, and grade school competitors. They are paragliding, playing pool, running laps, or kicking soccer balls. They are in the bleachers, along the Charles, in the locker room, and on the court.

Such diversity seemed to defy order and traditional methods of analysis and presentation. After countless attempts to organize these works into chapters, we realized that what they defy is a linear, restrictive, and segmenting order. As a result, we have again chosen a more "open" approach, by theme, which has allowed ideas to connect, converge, merge, and flow freely one into the other and one from the other. Because some pieces of literature explore several themes, even the thematic organization has at times been problematic and difficult. Ultimately, these multidimensional pieces have helped us connect ideas within and between sections. The renegade works that seemed to fit nowhere have often proved to be the most helpful in refining our ideas about women in sport. This literature led us toward transforming our own thinking, from the linear and restrictive—the limited model within which we began to understand and explore language in the first place—toward the circular and limitless. As our perspectives began to change, we began to see how the themes in these writings liberate sport from the confines of language (definitions), the very structure of language (genres of literature), and the restraints of culture and history, revealing at last the female, perhaps the human, in sport.

Within the complexity and diversity of these works, there is one resounding theme that unites all of the works and their themes: the impulse to be free, to be liberated from the confining expectations of others and the control that those expectations exert over the minds and bodies of women. According to Alicia Ostriker, author of *Stealing the Language: The Emergence of Women's Poetry in America*, this "quest for autonomous self-definition and self-determination . . . [the need] to define oneself as authentically as possible from within" is the principal theme in women's poetry in America. Essentially this is a search for an identity that is personally experienced and defined, rather than an identity created by others. This is the problem of the "outsider," as Colin Wilson proposed in his classic work, *The Outsider*. The outsider lives in another world, another reality, and as a result, the self is a divided self, one that is experienced in both worlds. The problem then is the division and fragmentation of the self. Ultimately, this division provokes what Wilson believes to be the quest of the outsider: to go in search of reconnection, of a genuine identity, of a "way back" to a harmonious and undivided self.

In women's prose, the experience of the outsider and her quest for identity and freedom are common themes. Women have often written literature about outsiders, perhaps because they have recognized themselves in the experiences of their excluded characters. Most of the women who have long been part of the Western literary tradition—George Eliot, Edith Wharton, Flannery O'Connor—address the theme of exclusion. Eliot's Silas Marner, Wharton's Lily Barth and Countess Olenska, and O'Connor's Misfit are all ostracized, marginalized, and alienated in some way from the larger society.

In sport literature the experience of the outsider and her quest for identity and freedom pervade the writings, chronicling the journey women have made from spectators to recreational participants to competitive athletes. As women have crossed those boundaries that once barred their entrance to the sporting world, they have begun to understand sport itself as an expression of the larger quest for female autonomy.

A woman begins her journey into sport as an outsider, peering in. Once she enters sport, she begins a journey similar to the one described by Maureen Murdock.[3] She enters a world in which she has no identity, a world that affirms what she is not, a male. Sport cannot be used to affirm her femininity; if anything, it is a challenge to or even a denial of her femininity and her femaleness. As she continues her journey as a participant, she must, by necessity, reject the female and the feminine, which will lead her to experience the "divided self" so characteristic of the experience of the outsider. And from this split, and the anguish of this split, comes the search for wholeness, a return of the feminine to join the masculine, and the resolution of the divided self. The heroine's journey is circular in nature; it begins with the self and ends with the self. However, a woman is transformed during her journey into an autonomous, whole, and free person, a transformation brought about and fashioned by her own personal experiences.

This identification of the feminine with the circular and its impact on art and culture has been the subject of numerous and quite varied approaches to the subject.[4] With specific regard to language and literature, scholarly analysis of l'écriture feminine—both French and English—suggests that this literature is resistant to hierarchies that are linear in nature, lending itself instead to the multiple perspectives of the circular. According to Alicia Ostriker, the importance of the contact imperative, the need to connect with others, underlies this rejection of the linear "vertical grid." Even in their seemingly linear and singular quest to know and define themselves, women seek unity in the form of mutuality, continuity, connections, identification, and touch, which allows them to escape this vertical grid of dominance and submission.[5]

In *Crossing Boundaries* there is a similar rejection of the linear, as the numerous works emphasizing the contact imperative suggest. Even in the earliest works on exclusion, females attempt to connect with a world that they can neither enter nor know, often seeing themselves as the "neither crowned nor slain" or aligning themselves with nature, frequently with hunted animals. This need to connect resonates through all of the literature, long after women have been allowed entry into sport. Even the literature written about elite athletes, those who must by the very nature of competition and achievement differentiate themselves from others, is replete with the need to connect with something or someone outside of the self. Initially, women make that first critical connection with their own bodies, through which they begin to redefine themselves and the world around them. Their perspectives of nature—the world's body—the animal world, competition, and their own personal encounters both with others and with sport all seem to be either connected to or informed by their connection with their own bodies.

Because women have lived so long on the periphery of the male world, they have learned that to maintain their essential connections with others they must hone their powers of observation and circle around ideas, instead of addressing them directly. Female spectators, yearning to be on the inside, have often accepted their role as outsiders in order to stay connected to sport and to their men. Likewise, female authors have often selected inoffensive and modest themes to stay connected to the male world. In much of women's sport literature, however, authors have not accepted Emily Dickinson's advice to "tell all the truth but tell it slight"; instead, like Dickinson herself, they have used metaphor and abstraction to address truth as directly as possible, given the frailties and confines of language. Muriel Rukeyser once warned that "If one woman told the truth about her life, the world would split open." Nonetheless, the writers included in this anthology have dared to answer Erin Mouré's burning questions: "Who knows this woman? / Who knows her breast is full of remembered water! / Who knows what her chest will say to us if only / it keeps up its terrible running . . ."

Crossing Boundaries is a journey to the center of female identity. It explores the complexities of female experiences as authors and athletes challenge cultural notions of gender, gender roles, and the very nature of femininity and sport. It is a chronology of attitudes, a catalog of experience, a survey of past and present voices—resigned and rebellious, detached and connected, searching and authoritative. The themes of the poems, short stories, prose memoirs, plays, and journalistic accounts in this anthology are utterly and uniquely female. They are the themes of centuries of pain and joy inside and outside the sporting world. These themes have long been addressed in women's literature and have long been overlooked by literary critics: the impact of exclusion, female reactions to exclusion, the centrality of the body, the female identification and merger with nature, the crucial connections women seek with others, the discovery of self, and the very nature of sport. The marvelous pieces of literature in this collection are uniquely significant and connecting. Their themes have come to us over and over again, echoing and reverberating the female experience from the first piece to the last, weaving and knitting the poignancy and joy of that experience into the fabric of sport.

[1] Hélène Cixous, "The Laugh of the Medusa," in Robyn R. Warhol and Diane Price Herndl, *An Anthology of Literary Theory and Criticism* (New Brunswick, NJ: Rutgers University Press, 1991, pp. 334–349).

[2] Simone de Beauvoir, *The Second Sex* (New York: Knopf, 1952).

[3] Maureen Murdock, *The Heroine's Journey* (Boston: Shambala Publications, 1988).

[4] Camille Paglia, in *Sex, Art, and American Culture* (New York: Random House, 1992) offers a unique interpretation of the relation of the feminine and the circular.

[5] Alicia Suskin Ostriker, "In Mind: The Divided Self in Women's Poetry," in Paul Mariani and George Murphy, comp., *Poetics: Essays on the Art of Poetry, a Special Issue of* Tendril Magazine, p. 123.

Acknowledgments

A project of such scope and duration as this one has required the assistance and support of many people whom we wish to gratefully acknowledge. As we began our work, Beth Baron (Interlibrary Loan) and Carol Norris (On-Line Search) of East Tennessee State University Library enthusiastically helped us locate promising fiction, poems, and journalistic accounts for *Crossing Boundaries*. They, together with Mark Ellis and Rita Scher (Reader Services) and Kelly Hensley (Interlibrary Loan), have helped us track down obscure and out-of-print anthologies, assisted us with book loans from libraries across the United States, and located authors and publishers whose permission we needed. Thanks in large part to the encouragement of Dr. Michael Woodruff, Vice-President for Research, and Ms. Ethel Garrity, Director of Sponsored Programs, we applied for a grant from the Research Development Committee at East Tennessee State University and became the first adjunct faculty members to win this award.

Our research in Europe, which was necessary for making this collection international in scope, was aided and enhanced by the hospitality, scholarship, and direction of many friends, colleagues, and kind strangers. Kathryn Seris provided a place to live and work in Paris. Serge Laget, sport journalist at *L'Equipe* and sport literature scholar, provided entrée into many libraries and archives. The assistance of Cécile Roche of I.N.S.E.P. in Paris and Claude Bourgeaud, Ruth Beck-Perrenoud, Patricia Eckert, Yoo-Mi Steffen, and Michelle Veillard of the *Musée Olympique* in Lausanne enabled us to find works in languages other than English. They have continued to receive us graciously in their libraries and offer support throughout the project. In Germany, Renate Nocon spent countless hours searching through anthologies of women's writings and then helped us choose the works from which we could make the final selection. The work of the translators, Stavros Deligiorgis, Ruth Griffiths, Gerald Nixon, Patricia Nolan, and Kathryn Seris, who gave so freely of their time and talents, have made it possible for us to offer several new works, translated into English for the first time, to an audience interested in sport and literature.

In the latter stages of our work, we are grateful to our friends and colleagues of the Hungarian-American Fulbright Commission and the Hungarian University of Physical Education who provided the friendships, material means, and collegial environment so necessary to sustaining such an endeavor. At Human Kinetics, many people helped us see the project to an end and enabled us to have an anthology very much like the one we had envisioned from the onset. Our acquisitions editor, Steve Pope, and managing editor, Katy Patterson, relaxed our deadlines when necessary and also pressed us when necessary to bring the project to a close. Debby Winter at Buerkett Marketing Consultants created an aesthetic design for the cover and Stuart Cartwright created its interior design, both of which beautifully reflect the intent and content of the book. And in the final stages of the book, the meticulous work of Terri Hamer, permissions manager, who helped us secure the necessary permissions, and the exceptional editorial work of Chris Enstrom, assistant editor, were invaluable.

The contributions of others have sustained us throughout the entirety of this project. Dr. Styron Harris, Chair of the Department of English at East Tennessee State University and Ruth Tapp, secretary of the English Department, and Mary Katherine Deaton and Karen Hughes of the Department of Physical Education, Exercise, and Sport Science provided us with a supportive work environment. Ruth Hill and Helen Nicodemus came to our rescue on the several occasions when computer, copier, and fax problems were plaguing us.

To Jack Higgs, our dear friend and advisor extraordinaire, and his wife, Reny, we say thanks for everything—the bibliographies, articles, and advice, and, most especially the deep and abiding friendship they continue to offer to so many in their vast circle of friends. To Steve Darden and Tom McKee, whose love (and fax machines, office equipment, and make-shift courier services) was graciously and consistently given—in spite of our unpredictable work hours, urgent deadlines, and unrelenting mood swings—we give our love and thanks. And, lastly, we would like to thank the many authors who contributed to this anthology, with special gratitude to those who gave so freely of their work with much enthusiasm for the book.

Part I

The Outsiders:
Cheerleaders, Lamenters, and Rebels

We are the women on bleachers
here to cheer for our men:
the screamers, the ardent beseechers
. . . It's why they bring us.

The Players[1]
Kim Roberts

The story of the outsiders in sport begins with the boastful and proud claim of Cynisca, the first female victor in the ancient Olympic Games. The following, inscribed on the base of a monument at Olympia, commemorates Cynisca's second victory in the quadriga race (a race for a four-horse chariot) in 396 B.C.

> I, Cynisca, who descend from Spartan Kings,
>
> Place this stone myself to mark
>
> The race I won with my quick-footed steeds
>
> The only woman in all of Greece to win[2]

Curiously, Cynisca's words telling us of her achievement convey both her connection to the male world of sport and ancient Greek festivals and of her exclusion from them. Of aristocratic birth, Cynisca had the privilege of owning, training, and even entering horses in public festivals—as long as she used male drivers for them. However, like all other females, she was barred from attending and competing in any of the Panhellenic festivals of ancient Greece. Her victory, then, was from a distance, from the outside— the win of the owner, not of the jockey. Cynisca's experience as an outsider, not a participant, foreshadowed the role of spectator that women were to play for centuries in sport.

The roles of spectator and outsider assigned to women informed the perspectives held by the writers of the earliest works to follow Cynisca's brief literary passage. A montage of female writers from a variety of cultures and historic periods found sport an exciting medium for examining the traditions of their cultures and the perplexing themes of their lives. In fact, the first commentary on the role of women in sport is found in the first novel ever written, *The Tale of Genji*,[3] in which Lady Murasaki Shikibu weaves sport into the cultural fabric of 11th century court life in Heian Japan as she chronicles the hunting expeditions, polo games, horse races, and football matches of the upper-class male. At the games of the Royal Bodyguard, the ladies of the court were allowed some "harmless self-display," occasionally winning the attention of one of the young athletes. "Although they had a very imperfect understanding of what was going on, [these ladies] were at least capable of deriving a great deal of pleasure from the sight of so many men in elegant riding jackets hurling themselves with desperate reckless-ness into the fray" (p. 498).

Centuries later Mary Russell Mitford offers similar observations on the role of women in her short story "Lost and Won." The protagonist, Letitia Dale, is a "sparkling beauty" who had delighted the fancy and won the heart of Paul Holton, the best cricketer of the Hazelby Eleven. Such examples of women's early role in sport are rare indeed. In these writings, sport is generally a setting for mating rituals, a place for a man to win a woman with his sporting prowess—and for a woman to win a man with her enthusiasm and appreciation for his sporting prowess. Much of the early women's sport literature makes only oblique references, if any, to women's position in sport; instead it offers chronicles and observations of hunting expeditions involving men with their dogs and horses.[4] However, Margaret Cavendish (the Duchess of Newcastle) in "*The* Hunting *of the Hare*" proffers a blistering commentary on hunting and hunters in the 17th century, a sympathy for and alliance with the hunted that echoes throughout the centuries in women's sport literature.

The perspective of the outsiders begins to change in the late 19th and early 20th centuries, however, as females begin to cross the boundaries of sport. Women's writings become progressively self-reflective as the gaze turns inward, away from observing the male athlete and toward a search for an identity in connection with sport. It is almost as if females begin to ask, "Who are we in this new world?" Their reactions to the new world and their exclusion from it are varied and multidimensional, yet we can discern two definable and constituent stages. Initially women acknowledge that they are excluded; then they react to this knowledge, either by resigning themselves to a prescribed role and accepting that role even as they lament their own acquiescence or by rebelling against the status quo and braving the criticism that follows.

The works of both Muriel Rukeyser and Helen Rosta[5] illustrate the role of most males and females in 20th century sport: males as participants, females as spectators. And once women recognize sport as a male domain, they begin to understand and expose the typical female role in this celebration of masculinity. As we see in U. A. Fanthorpe's "Hang-gliders in January," the spectators who are "wives and mothers" are "loyally watching" their male heroes, as are the women in Lillian Morrison's "The Sprinters." These women know that "It is for us they run!"

In many of these works, women resign themselves to the female role of outsider and observer. As Judith Wright laments in "Smalltown Dance," while women fold sheets, they dance with their arms wide, but they "know the scale of possibility, / the limit of opportunity, / the fence, / how little chance / there is of getting out." It was only in girthood, as Jean Earle and Laura Jensen maintain, that "Other worlds were possible. / Other worlds were likely." As Tess Gallagher's "Women's Tug of War at Lough Arrow" suggests, sport is a temporary world where women are like "girls" again, playing on a "borrowed field," enjoying this freedom until the game is over, until they are "bound again by the arms / of those who held them."

As girls move toward adolescence in this literature, their freedoms are more restricted, and they begin to see themselves as Pauline Stainer sees them—as "the distraught." Sometimes these young female characters rebel, openly and loudly, against such restrictions, becoming instead intriguing, gutsy protagonists. Angela, in Nancy Boutilier's "Hotshot," is a five-foot-eight-inch fifth grader who is respected by her male peers and by her father who sees her not as a "Tomboy" but as a girl who "can play a wizard game of Horse," an "unbeatable 'Round the World,'" and a mean game of five-on-a-side pick-up. Curiously, it is the women in the story—the mother, the grandmother, and the fifth grade teacher—who want Angela to become more ladylike, wear dresses, play hopscotch, and be generally respectable like the other girls.

Often, it is the grown women, chafing against the rigid expectations of others and their unspoken social codes, who, like Angela, also use sport as a form of rebellion and ultimately find freedom in sport. Stephanie Plotin's "Marathoner" rebels against the high-heeled shoes that "gnawed at her toes," the skirt that was a "hobble," and the partner who told her, "Dress Respectably." Leslie Ullman's runner runs to escape the pain of her failed marriage and the thinly veiled pleas of her mother who, at her age, "wanted babies."

Because they have often been rebellious outsiders themselves, women such as Sonia Sanchez understand how it feels to be on the periphery, to play by the rules and still remain an outsider. Often in their literature, women create male characters who are also on the outside. Sometimes the male outcast in women's sport literature is a grown man, sometimes a young, uninitiated boy,[6] and sometimes an animal. Carson McCullers's short story "The Jockey" and Beryl Markham's "The Splendid Outcast" introduce male characters living solitary, marginal lives, away from human companionship and connection. The views of the jockeys are in stark contrast to those of the owners, the trainers, and the bookies in McCullers's story and those of the spectators and prospective buyers in Markham's. McCullers's jockey understands that humans are not dispensable objects, even when they are injured. Markham's jockey understands that "horses are not tamed by whips or by blows" but by "the virtue of simplicity."

These male characters are marginalized because they refuse to play by rules that conflict with their own truths. For women, the brutal reality in sport is that they are marginalized even when they play by the rules, particularly when they compete with men. Janet Guthrie could not find sponsors—not because she refused to play by the rules, not because she lacked the "necessities" for racing, but because she was a woman. Apparently, the double standards in competition start early. Jadene Felina Stevens's young marble player refuses to return the prize marble she won after a "clean win, / fair game" against a neighborhood boy who would not have returned it to her had he won but who is also unlikely to ever forgive her for beating him at his own game. Julia Darling, playing pool with a man and surrounded by other men, also understands that "He'll never live it down / if I win." And that is why she says, "They love me when I lose." Still, the joys of competition bring her back, "ambitious and hot / wanting to beat him."

Competitive athletics are the source of power and identity for many women, but they are often the source of conflict and pain as well. Many of these athletes feel the conflicting tugs of the "divided self." Cynthia Macdonald's "The Lady Pitcher" tries to reconcile her role as a macho softball pitcher with her desire for marriage; she dreams of victories and marriage but knows "she will have them and probably not it." Maria Noell Goldberg didn't dare acknowledge her passion for sport or her passion for women, both of which were "outside the scope of recognition and naming." And Barbara Lamblin, appreciated as a winner and a champion, was also derided as a jock, a dyke, and a bitch. These athletes who have ventured to compete, even in the face of a constant barrage of disapproval and innuendo, are the rebellious outsiders and the real heroes in sport.

[1]"The Players" from *Aethlon: The Journal of Sport Literature,* Spring 1989.

[2]In Tom Dodge, *A Literature of Sports* (Lexington, MA: D.C. Heath and Company, 1980).

[3]Lady Murasaki Shikibu, *The Tale of Genji,* trans. Arthur Waley (Cambridge: Riverside Press, n.d.).

[4]Dame Juliana Berners in her poems "The Companyes of Bestys and Foul" and "The Properties of a Good Greyhound," and in her book *The Boke of Huntying,* records the sporting experiences of the 15th century British aristocracy, a tradition continued in the 17th century work of Katherine Philips in "The Irish Greyhound."

[5]Please refer to Canadian writer Helen Rosta's short story "The Hunter" (*Imagining Women.* Toronto: The Women's Press, 1988, pp. 146-156) which could not be included in this collection.

[6]In "Through the Tunnel," by Doris Lessing, the young male character is temporarily suspended between the world of his mother and the world of men. This story was the first piece of women's sport literature to be published in a sport literature anthology. See Peter Schwed and Herbert Warren Wind, *Great Stories from the World of Sport* (London: Heinemann, 1958).

Lost and Won

Mary Russell Mitford

"Nay, but my dear Letty—"

"Don't dear Letty me, Mr. Paul Holton. Have not the East-Woodhay Eleven beaten the Hazelby Eleven for the first time in the memory of man and is it not entirely your fault? Answer me that, sir! Did not you insist on taking James White's place when he got that little knock on the leg with the ball last night, though James, poor fellow, maintained to the last that he could play better with one leg than you with two? Did not you insist on taking poor James's place, and did you get a single notch in either innings? And did you not miss three catches, three fair catches, Mr. Paul Holton? Might not you twice have caught out John Brown, who, as all the world knows, hits up? And did not a ball from the edge of Tom Taylor's bat come into your hands, absolutely into your hands, and did not you let her go? And did not Tom Taylor after that get forty-five runs in the same innings, and thereby win the game? That a man should pretend to play at cricket and not be able to hold the ball when he has her in his hands. Oh, if I had been there!"

"You! Why Letty—"

"Don't Letty me, sir. Don't talk to me. I am going home."

"With all my heart, Miss Letitia Dale. I have the honour, madam, to wish you a good evening." And each turned away at a smart pace, and the one went westward and the other eastward-ho.

This unlover-like parting occurred on Hazelby Down one fine afternoon in the Whitsun-week between a couple whom all Hazelby, and Aberleigh to boot, had, for at least a month before, set down as lovers—Letty Dale, the pretty daughter of the jolly old tanner, and Paul Holton, a rich young yeoman, on a visit in the place. Letty's angry speech will sufficiently explain their mutual provocation, although, to enter fully into her feelings, one must be born in a cricketing parish, and sprung of a cricketing family, and be accustomed to rest that very uncertain and arbitrary standard, the point of honour, on beating our rivals and next neighbours in the annual match—for juxtaposition is a great sharpener of rivalry, as Dr. Johnson knew, when, to please the inhabitants of Plymouth, he abused the good folks who lived at Dock; moreover, one must be also a quick, zealous, ardent, hotheaded, warm-hearted girl like Letty, a beauty and an heiress, quite unused to disappointment, and not a little in love, and then we shall not wonder, in the first place, that she should be unreasonably angry, or, in the next, that before she had walked half a mile her anger vanished, and was succeeded by tender relentings and earnest wishes for a full and perfect reconciliation.

Reprinted from *Our Village*, by Mary Russell Mitford, 1824.

"He'll be sure to call to-morrow morning," thought Letty to herself: "He said he would, before this unlucky cricket-playing. He told me that he had something to say, something particular. I wonder what it can be!" thought poor Letty. "To be sure, he never has said anything about liking me—but still—and then Aunt Judith, and Fanny Wright, and all the neighbours say—However, I shall know to-morrow." And home she tripped to the pleasant house by the tanyard, as happy as if the East-Woodhay men had not beaten the men of Hazelby. "I shall not see him before to-morrow, though," repeated Letty to herself, and immediately repaired to her pretty flower-garden, the little gate of which opened on a path leading from the Down to the street—a path that, for obvious reasons, Paul was wont to prefer—and began tying up her carnations in the dusk of the evening, and watering her geraniums by the light of the moon, until it was so late that she was fain to return, disappointed, to the house, repeating to herself, "I shall certainly see him to-morrow."

Far different were the feelings of the chidden swain. Well-a-day for the age of chivalry! the happy times of knights and paladins, when a lecture from a lady's rosy lip, or a buffet from her lily hand, would have been received as humbly and as thankfully as the benedicite from a mitred abbot, or the accolade from a king's sword! Alas for the days of chivalry! They are gone, and, I fear me, for ever. For certain our present hero was not born to revive them.

Paul Holton was a well-looking and well-educated young farmer, just returned from the north, whither he had been sent for agricultural improvement, and now on the look-out for a farm and a wife, both of which he thought he had found at Hazelby, where he had come on the double errand of visiting some distant relations, and letting two or three small houses recently fallen into his possession. As owner of these houses, all situate in the town, he had claimed a right to join the Hazelby Eleven, mainly induced to avail himself of the privilege by the hope of winning favour in the eyes of the ungrateful fair one, whose animated character, as well as her sparkling beauty, had delighted his fancy, and apparently won his heart, until her rude attack on his play armed all the vanity of man against her attractions. Love is more intimately connected with self-love than people are willing to imagine; and Paul Holton's had been thoroughly mortified. Besides, if his fair mistress's character was somewhat too impetuous, his was greatly over-firm. So he said to himself—"The girl is a pretty girl, but far too much of a shrew for my taming. I am no Petruchio to master this Katherine. 'I come to wive it happily in Padua'; and let her father be as rich as he may, I'll none of her." And, mistaking anger for indifference—no uncommon delusion in a love-quarrel—off he set within the hour, thinking so very much of punishing the saucy beauty, that he entirely forgot the possibility of some of the pains falling to his own share.

The first tidings that Letty heard the next morning were that Mr. Paul Holton had departed over-night, having authorised his cousin to let his houses, and to decline the large farm, for which he was in treaty; the next intelligence informed her that he was settled in Sussex; and then his relation left Hazelby, and poor Letty heard no more. Poor Letty! Even in a common parting for a common journey, she who stays behind is the object of pity: how much more so when he who goes, goes never to return, and carries with him the fond affection, the treasured hopes, of a young, unpractised heart,

> *And gentle wishes long subdued —*
> *Subdued and cherish'd long!*

Poor, poor Letty!

Three years passed away, and brought much of change to our country maiden and to her fortunes. Her father, the jolly old tanner, a kind, frank, thoughtless man, as the cognomen would almost imply, one who did not think that there were such things as wickedness and ingratitude under the sun, became bound for a friend to a large amount: the friend proved a villain, and the jolly tanner was ruined. He and his daughter now lived in a small cottage near their former house; and at the point of time at which I have chosen to resume my story, the old man was endeavouring to persuade Letty, who had never attended a cricket match since the one which she had so much cause to remember, to accompany him the next day (Whit-Tuesday) to see the Hazelby Eleven again encounter their ancient antagonists, the men of East-Woodhay.

"Pray come, Letty," said the fond father; "I can't go without you; I have no pleasure anywhere without my Letty; and I want to see this match, for Isaac Hunt can't play on account of the death of his mother, and they tell me that the East-Woodhay men have consented to our taking in another mate who practises the new Sussex bowling; I want to see that new-fangled mode. Do come, Letty!" And with a smothered sigh at the mention of Sussex, Letty consented.

Now old John Dale was not quite ingenuous with his pretty daughter. He did not tell her what he very well knew himself that the bowler in question was no other than their sometime friend, Paul Holton, whom the business of letting his houses, or some other cause, not, perhaps, clearly defined even to himself, had brought to Hazelby on the eve of the match, and whose new method of bowling (in spite of his former mischances) the Hazelby Eleven were willing to try; the more so as they suspected, what, indeed, actually occurred, that the East-Woodhayites, who would have resisted the innovation of the Sussex system of delivering the ball in the hands of anyone else, would have no objection to let Paul Holton, whose bad playing was a standing joke amongst them, do his best or his worst in any way.

Not a word of this did John Dale say to Letty; so that she was quite taken by surprise, when, having placed her father, now very infirm, in a comfortable chair, she sat down by his side on a little hillock of turf, and saw her recreant lover standing amongst a group of cricketers very near, and evidently gazing on her, just as he used to gaze three years before.

Perhaps Letty had never looked so pretty in her life as at that moment. She was simply drest, as became her fallen fortunes. Her complexion was still coloured, like the apple blossom, with vivid red and white, but there was more of sensibility, more of the heart in its quivering mutability, its alternation of paleness and blushes; the blue eyes were still as bright, but they were oftener cast down; the smile was still as splendid, but far more rare; the girlish gaiety was gone, but it was replaced by womanly sweetness—sweetness and modesty formed now the chief expression of that lovely face, lovelier, far lovelier than ever. So apparently thought Paul Holton, for he gazed and gazed with his whole soul in his eyes, in complete oblivion of cricket and cricketer, and the whole world. At last he recollected himself, blushed and bowed, and advanced a few steps, as if to address her; but timid and irresolute, he turned away without speaking, joined the party who had now assembled round the wickets, the umpires called "Play!" and the game began.

East-Woodhay gained the toss and went in, and all eyes were fixed on the Sussex bowler. The ball was placed in his hands, and instantly the wicket was down, and the striker out—no other than Tom Taylor, the boast of his parish, and the best batsman in the county. "Accident, mere accident!" of course, cried East-Woodhay; but another, and another followed; few could stand against the fatal bowling, and none could get notches. A panic seized the whole side. And then, as losers will, they began to exclaim against the system, called it a toss, a throw, a trick; anything but bowling, anything but cricket; railed at it as destroying the grace of the attitude, and the balance of the game; protested against being considered as beaten by such jugglery, and, finally, appealed to the umpires as to the fairness of the play. The umpires, men of conscience and old cricketers, hummed and hawed, and see-sawed; quoted contending precedents and jostling authorities; looked grave and wise, whilst even their little sticks of office seemed vibrating in puzzled importance. Never were judges more sorely perplexed. At last they did as the sages of the bench often do in such cases—reserved the point of law, and desired them to "play out the play." Accordingly the match was resumed; only twenty-seven notches being gained by the East-Woodhayians in their first innings, and they entirely from the balls of the old Hazelby bowler, James White.

During the quarter of an hour's pause which the laws allow, the victorious man of Sussex went up to John Dale, who had watched him with a strange mixture of feeling, delighted to hear the stumps rattle, and to see opponent after opponent throw down his bat and walk off, and yet much annoyed at the new method by which the object was achieved. "We should not have called this cricket in my day," said he, "and yet it knocks down the wickets gloriously, too." Letty, on her part, had watched the game with unmingled interest and admiration. "He knew how much I liked to see a good cricketer," thought she; yet still, when that identical good cricketer approached, she was seized with such a fit of shyness—call it modesty— that she left her seat and joined a group of young women at some distance.

Paul looked earnestly after her, but remained standing by her father, inquiring with affectionate interest after his health, and talking over the game and the bowling. At length he said, "I hope that I have not driven away Miss Letitia."

"Call her Letty, Mr. Holton," interrupted the old man; "plain Letty. We are poor folks now, and have no right to any other title than our own proper names, old John Dale and his daughter Letty. A good daughter she has been to me," continued the fond father; "for when debts and losses took all that we had—for we paid to the uttermost farthing, Mr. Paul Holton; we owe no man a shilling—when all my earnings and savings were gone, and the house over our head—the house I was born in, the house she was born in —I loved it the better for that—taken away from us, then she gave up the few hundreds she was entitled to in right of her blessed mother to purchase an annuity for the old man, whose trust in a villain had brought her to want."

"God bless her!" interrupted Paul Holton.

"Ay, and God will bless her," returned the old man, solemnly. "God will bless the dutiful child, who despoiled herself of all to support her old father!"

"Blessings on her dear, generous heart!" again ejaculated Paul; "and I was away and knew nothing of this."

"I knew nothing of it myself until the deed was completed," rejoined John Dale. "She was just of age, and the annuity was purchased and the money paid before she told me; and a cruel kindness it was to strip herself for my sake; it almost broke my heart when I heard the story. But even that was nothing," continued the good tanner, warming with his subject, "compared with her conduct since. If you could but see how she keeps the house, and how she waits upon me; her handiness, her cheerfulness, and all her pretty ways and contrivances to make me forget old times and old places. Poor thing! She must miss her neat parlour and the flower-garden she was so fond of, as much as I do my tanyard and the great hall, but she never seems to think of them, and never has spoken a hasty word since our misfortunes, for all you know, poor thing, she used to be a little quick-tempered."

"And I knew nothing of this," repeated Paul Holton, as two or three of their best wickets being down, the Hazelby players summoned him to go in. "I knew nothing of all this."

Again all eyes were fixed on the Sussex cricketer, and at first he seemed likely to verify the prediction and confirm the hopes of the most malicious of his adversaries, by batting as badly as he had bowled well. He had not caught sight of the ball; his hits were weak, his defence insecure, and his mates began to tremble and his opponents crow. Every hit seemed likely to be the last; he missed a leg ball of Ned Smith's; was all but caught out by Sam Newton; and East Woodhay triumphed and Hazelby sat quaking, when a sudden glimpse of Letty, watching him with manifest anxiety, recalled her champion's wandering thoughts. Gathering himself up, he stood before the wicket another man; knocked the ball hither and thither, to the turnpike, the coppice, the pond; got three, four, five at a hit; baffled the slow bowler, James Smith, and the fast bowler Tom Taylor; got fifty-five notches off his own bat; stood out all the rest of his side; and so handled the adverse party when they went in that the match was won at a single innings, with six-and-thirty runs to spare.

Whilst his mates were discussing their victory, Paul Holton again approached the father and daughter, and this time she did not run away. "Letty, dear Letty," said he, "three years ago I lost the cricket match, and you were angry, and I was a fool. But Letty, dear Letty, this match is won, and if you could but know how deeply I have repented, how earnestly I have longed for this day. The world has gone well with me, Letty, for these three long years. I have wanted nothing but the treasure which I myself threw away, and now, if you would but let your father be my father, and my home your home; if you would but forgive me, Letty."

Letty's answer is not upon record; but it is certain that Paul Holton walked home from the cricket ground that evening with old John Dale hanging on one arm, and John Dale's pretty daughter on the other; and that a month after the bells of Hazelby Church were ringing merrily in honour of one of the fairest and luckiest matches that ever cricketer lost and won.

The **Hunting** *of the Hare*

Margaret Cavendish (Duchess of Newcastle)

Betwixt two *Ridges* of *Plowd-land*, lay *Wat*,
Pressing his *Body* close to *Earth* lay squat.
His *Nose* upon his two *Fore-feet* close lies,
Glaring obliquely with his *great gray Eyes*.
His *Head* he alwaies sets against the *Wind;*
If turne his *Taile*, his *Haires* blow up behind:
Which *he* too cold will grow, but *he* is wise,
And keepes his *Coat* still downe, so warm *he* lies.
Thus resting all the *day*, till *Sun* doth set,
Then riseth up, his *Reliefe* for to get.
Walking about untill the *Sun* doth rise,
Then back returnes, downe in his *Forme he* lyes.
At last, *Poore Wat* was found, as *he* there lay,
By *Hunts-men*, with their *Dogs* which came that way.
Seeing, gets up, and fast begins to run,
Hoping some waies the *Cruell Dogs* to shun.
But they by *Nature* have so quick a *Sent,*
That by their *Nose* they trace what way *he* went.
And with their deep, wide *Mouths* set forth a *Cry,*
Which answer'd was by *Ecchoes* in the *Skie*.
Then *Wat* was struck with *Terrour*, and with *Feare,*
Thinkes every *Shadow* still the *Dogs* they were.
And running out some distance from the *noise,*
To hide himselfe, his *Thoughts* he new imploies.
Under a *Clod* of *Earth* in *Sand-pit* wide,
Poore *Wat* sat close, hoping himselfe to hide.
There long he had not sat, but strait his *Eares*
The *Winding Hornes*, and crying *Dogs* he heares:
Starting with *Feare*, up leapes, then doth he run,

From *Poems and Fancies*, 1653, by Margaret Cavendish.

And with such speed, the *Ground* scarce treades upon.
Into a great thick *Wood he* strait way gets,
Where underneath a *broken Bough he* sits.
At every *Leafe* that with the *wind* did shake,
Did bring such *Terrour*, made his *Heart* to ake.
That *Place he* left, to *Champian Plaines he* went,
Winding about, for to deceive their *Sent*.
And while they *snuffling* were, to find his *Track*,
Poore Wat, being weary, his swift pace did slack.
On his two *hinder legs* for ease did sit,
His *Fore-feet* rub'd his *Face* from *Dust*, and *Sweat*.
Licking his *Feet*, he wip'd his *Eares* so cleane,
That none could tell that *Wat* had hunted been.
But casting round about his *faire great Eyes*,
The *Hounds* in full *Careere* he neere him 'spies:
To *Wat* it was so terrible a *Sight*,
Feare gave him *Wings*, and made his *Body* light.
Though weary was before, by running long,
Yet now his *Breath* he never felt more strong.
Like those that *dying* are, think *Health* returnes,
When tis but a *faint Blast*, which *Life* out burnes.
For *Spirits* seek to guard the *Heart* about,
Striving with *Death*, but *Death* doth quench them out.
Thus they so fast came on, with such loud *Cries*,
That *he* no hopes hath left, nor *help* espies.
With that the *Winds* did pity *poore Wats* case,
And with their *Breath* the *Sent* blew from the *Place*.
Then every *Nose* is busily imployed,
And every *Nostrill* is set open, wide:
And every *Head* doth seek a severall way,
To find what *Grasse*, or *Track*, the *Sent* on lay.
Thus quick Industry, that is not slack,
Is like to Witchery, brings lost things back.
For though the *Wind* had tied the *Sent* up close,

A *Busie Dog* thrust in his *Snuffling Nose*:
And drew it out, with it did foremost run,
Then *Hornes* blew loud, for th' *rest* to follow on.
The *great slow-Hounds*, their throats did set a *Base*,
The *Fleet Swift Hounds*, as *Tenours* next in place;
The little *Beagles* they a *Trebble* sing,
And through the *Aire* their *Voice* a round did ring?
Which made a *Consort*, as they ran along;
If they but *words* could speak, might sing a *Song*,
The *Hornes* kept time, the *Hunters* shout for *Joy*,
And valiant seeme, *poore Wat* for to destroy:
Spurring their *Horses* to a full *Careere*,
Swim Rivers deep, leap Ditches without feare;
Indanger *Life*, and *Limbes*, so fast will ride,
Onely to see how patiently *Wat* died.
For why, the *Dogs* so neere his *Heeles* did get,
That they their sharp *Teeth* in his *Breech* did set.
Then tumbling downe, did fall with *weeping Eyes*,
Gives up his *Ghost*, and thus poore *Wat he* dies.
Men hooping loud, such *Acclamations* make,
As if the *Devill* they did *Prisoner* take.
When they do but a *shiftlesse Creature* kill;
To hunt, there needs no *Valiant Souldiers* skill.
But *Man* doth think that *Exercise*, and *Toile*,
To keep their *Health*, is best, which makes most spoile.
Thinking that *Food*, and *Nourishment* so good,
And *Appetite*, that feeds on *Flesh*, and *Blood*.
When they do *Lions, Wolves, Beares, Tigers* see,
To kill poore *Sheep*, strait say, they cruell be.
But for themselves all *Creatures* think too few,
For *Luxury*, wish *God* would make them new.
As if that *God* made *Creatures* for *Mans meat*,
To give them *Life*, and *Sense*, for *Man* to eat;
Or else for *Sport*, or *Recreations* sake,

Destroy those *Lifes* that *God* saw good to make:
Making their *Stomacks, Graves,* which full they fill
With *Murther'd Bodies,* that in sport they kill.
Yet *Man* doth think himselfe so gentle, mild,
When *he* of *Creatures* is most cruell wild.
And is so *Proud,* thinks onely he shall live,
That *God* a *God*-like *Nature* did him give.
And that all *Creatures* for his sake alone,
Was made for him, to *Tyrannize* upon.

Boys of These Men Full Speed

for Jane Cooper
Muriel Rukeyser

Boys of these men
    full speed across free,
    my father's boyhood eyes.
    Sail-skating with friends
    bright on Wisconsin ice
    those years away.

Sails strung across their backs
    boys racing toward
    fierce bitter middle-age
    in the great glitter of
    corrupted cities.
    Father, your dark mouth
    speaking its rancor.

Alive not yet, the girl
    I would become

stares at that ice
stippled with skaters,
a story you tell.

Boys of those men
call across winter
where I stand and shake,
woman of that girl.

Hang-gliders in January
for C.K.

U. A. Fanthorpe

Like all miracles, it has a rational
Explanation; and like all miracles, insists
On being miraculous. We toiled
In the old car up from the lacklustre valley,
Taking the dogs because somebody had to,
At the heel of a winter Sunday afternoon

Into a sky of shapes flying:
Pot-bellied, shipless sails, dragonflies towering
Still with motion, daytime enormous bats,
Titanic tropical fish, and men,
When we looked, men strapped to wings,
Men wearing wings, men flying

Over a landscape too emphatic
To be understood: humdrum fields
With hedges and grass, the mythical river,
Beyond it the forest, the foreign high country.
The exact sun, navigating downwards

To end the revels, and you, and me,
The dogs, even, enjoying a scamper,
Avoiding scuffles.

It was all quite simple, really. We saw
The aground flyers, their casques and belts
And defenceless legs; we saw the earthed wings
Being folded like towels; we saw
The sheepskin-coated wives and mothers
Loyally watching; we saw a known,
Explored landscape by sunset-light,

We saw for ourselves how it was done,
From takeoff to landing. But nothing cancelled
The cipher of the soaring, crucified men,
Which we couldn't unravel; which gave us
Also, somehow, the freedom of air. Not
In vast caravels, triumphs of engineering,
But as men always wanted, simply,
Like a bird at home in the sky.

The Sprinters

Lillian Morrison

The gun explodes them.
Pummeling, pistoning they fly
In time's face.
A go at the limit,
A terrible try
To smash the ticking glass,
Outpace the beat

That runs, that streaks away
Tireless, and faster than they.

Beside ourselves
(It is for us they run!)
We shout and pound the stands
For one to win
Loving him, whose hard
Grace-driven stride
Most mocks the clock
And almost breaks the bands
Which lock us in.

Smalltown Dance

Judith Wright

Two women find the square-root of a sheet.
That is an ancient dance:
arms wide: together: again: two forward steps: hands meet
your partner's once and twice.
That white expanse
reduces to a neat
compression fitting in the smallest space
a sheet can pack in on a cupboard shelf.

High scented walls there were of flapping white
when I was small, myself.
I walked between them, playing Out of Sight.
Simpler than arms, they wrapped and comforted—
clean corridors of hiding, roofed with blue—
saying, Your sins too are made Monday-new;
and see, ahead

Judith Wright: "Smalltown Dance" from *A Human Pattern: Selected Poems* (ETT Imprint, 1996).

that glimpse of unobstructed waiting green.
Run, run before you're seen.

But women know the scale of possibility,
the limit of opportunity,
the fence,
how little chance
there is of getting out. The sheets that tug
sometimes struggle from the peg,
don't travel far. Might symbolise
something. Knowing where danger lies
you have to keep things orderly.
The household budget will not stretch to more.

And they can demonstrate it in a dance.
First pull those wallowing white dreamers down,
spread arms: then close them. Fold
those beckoning roads to some impossible world,
put them away and close the cupboard door.

Young Girls Running

Jean Earle

Almost, flight . . .

Herons, angling
A tilted grace. Spring twigs,
Taking the awkward wind.

Three-as-one, linked onrush
Mirrored in polished sand,
Light legs

Spattering pools, shells.

'The sea!' they cry, 'the sea!'
Birdlike, birdshape

Breasting the tide
With no breasts, merged
In the thrown wave

Which will rain them
Rosy, swept
Through its firming sting,
Medicinal shock, thrust . . .

They will be women,
Breasted, hipped,
Salted,
When they come out.

Golf

Laura Jensen

It seems always two years ago
no matter which two years
I was a child
thinking I had grown.

Two years ago I was playing
solitaire in the frightening room.
At the center of each card
laid out on a brown table
was a pink ceramic lady.

Outdoors the snow
fell unpardonably.
What a child I was.

I could not speak intelligently
and found cards in the gutter.

And another memory.
My only time on the golf course
we whacked at balls.

I sat on the hill
watching the slope
slope down to the water.

I could not play golf automatically,
and having no other opportunity,
I never did. In the evening light,
no words for it—such a long slope—
to roll down it over
and over, the grass
long, thick, and cool.

What a child I was.
Other worlds were possible.
Other worlds were likely.

Women's Tug of War at Lough Arrow

Tess Gallagher

> In a borrowed field they dig in their feet
> and clasp the rope. Balanced
> against neighboring women, they hold
> the ground by the little gained
> and leaning like boatmen rowing into
> the damp earth, they pull
> to themselves the invisible waves, waters
> overcalmed by desertion
> or the narrow look trained to a brow.
> The steady rain has made girls of them,
> their hair in ringlets. Now they haul
> the live weight to the cries
> of husbands and children, until the rope
> runs slack, runs free
> and all are bound again by the arms
> of those who held them, not until, but so
> they gave.

A Study for the Badminton Game

(after David Inshaw)

Pauline Stainer

> Presentiment even here—
> in the surrealist height of the trees,
> the suspended shuttlecock,
> the windless landscape.

From the observatory
at the top of the tall house,
you can see the bright unease
of banners above the topiary;

the yew-alley
going down to the river;
the pared moon,
the clipped pyramid.

How silently they play,
the girls on the lawn;
a guest clutches her garden-party hat—
Ophelia floats by.

Why is it
we watch the distraught
from the sunlit roof
with such terrible detachment?

Hotshot

Nancy Boutilier

A five-foot-eight-inch fifth grader is probably going to be one of the best basketball players in her school no matter if she's girl or boy. But I happen to be a girl, and pretty good at sticking the "J" too, so don't go challenging me to one-on-one, unless, of course, you don't mind losing. And I'm not gonna play you easy on account of what Mom calls "ego"—especially no "male ego" that some boys got. I don't play easy for any reason or anyone. It's that simple.

Most of life is simple. Too many people want to make stuff way more difficult than it is. Like the time school pictures came back and I was holding a pencil behind Tony Kramer's head so it looked like the pencil grew right out of his ear. Well, Mrs. Kramer goes and calls my teacher and then my mom and we all have to sit down and discuss it. They all try to tell me what a horrible thing I did, messing up the picture and all. And I kept trying to tell them how funny it was—and even Tony thought so too—but no one else was laughing. So I end up feeling bad about something I thought was fun—and I would never have done it to someone like Laurie Strandy or Darius Silvers because I know it would have made them feel bad. But Tony—I knew he could take it.

Oh, well, I guess I'm supposed to be learning the when's and where's of having fun. And what I like most is fun on the basketball court. Shooting, dribbling, rebounding—I can outrun and outjump anyone in the fifth or sixth grade—anyone!

Most of the teachers gave up on trying to make me stay on the girls' side of the hardtop. But old Miss Monzelli, who I call Miss Von Smelly when she can't hear me, sometimes still screeches from behind those pointy glasses with the fake little diamonds for me to get onto the hopscotch side of the blacktop. She says I can't play with the boys because it ain't ladylike. She says I might get hurt. She also says that saying *ain't* ain't ladylike neither, so I do it just to remind her who's boss. We'll see who's going to get hurt.

Truth is, no boy ever hurt me more than I hurt him. Besides, I've had stitches four different times, and not once have I even cried at the blood or the needles. Broke a bundle of bones, too—three fingers, my wrist, both collarbones, and my left ankle—seven all together.

That's how I learned that basketball is in me—it's in my bones. Every time I've been sidelined, I don't mind missing out on a football game, or the roller coaster at the carnival, but not being able to play hoops sets my skin crawling. I know it's in my blood too because my Dad is six-foot-four and played in college. He still plays at the Y, and I get to shoot around at halftime of his games. All the referees there like me. Sure, they have to show off, spinning the ball on their fingers or throwing it to me behind the back, but they all like me. I figure they are jealous of the guys like Dad who get to strut their stuff while they only get to run up and down the court blowing whistles and ticking everyone off.

But at halftime, the refs rebound for me and call me Hotshot.

I'm telling you all this so you can see how some things are born in a girl, even though most people seem to think they're reserved only for boys. And don't go calling me Tomboy unless you can give account of what it means. I'm a girl who can throw a football further and with a better spiral than anyone at Maple Street School, except for Greg Merrit, who is my best friend, and Mr. Leon, the gym teacher. I don't mind that Greg can throw further than me because he's real good and that's just that. I can respect that. Besides, I'm a better free throw shooter than he is, so really, we're even. But don't go saying that I throw like a boy any quicker than you'd say that Greg throws like a girl, which he does, because he throws like me, and I'm a girl. There's nothing Tomboy about it. I'm a girl and I can play a wizard game of Horse, I'm unbeatable at 'Round the World, I hold my own in 21 and you'll want me on your side if we're playing five-on-a-side pickup. I told you, it's that simple.

And I'm not good just because I'm tall. My dad told me not to be worried about being a six-foot girl because he says if any girl is going to dunk in high school it's going to be me. Mom says I slouch too much. I don't think I slouch at all. I just lean kind of forward when I walk and bounce on my toes so I can feel my hightops hugging my ankles. Air Hotshot! I hit the ground and my treads spring me right back up on my toes. I can see that it scares the boys a bit when I stride out onto the court bouncing like I'm the best thing since the hook shot in my black leather Cons. I'll take hightops over high heels any day!

Anyhow, what I'm trying to tell you about is my problem with Miss Monzelli. She's my Social Studies teacher who seems to think she got hired by the school solely to mess with my life. She tries to make me play only with the other girls at recess, and I told her I don't have anything against girls, but I like playing basketball, and it's the boys who play basketball. She says I'm not learning to be a lady if I don't play with girls and held me after school to point out that if I dress like the boys and talk like the boys, I'll find myself in trouble. It seemed to me that the only trouble I was in was with her, but I didn't think I'd score points by telling her so. Instead, I asked her if it was bad for me to be like the boys, why wasn't it bad for the boys to be like boys. After all, I didn't see her making no fuss about what they were wearing or playing.

Miss Monzelli got all red in the face so that her cheeks and neck matched the fire-engine-red lipstick she wears. She chewed me out for being fresh, and then insisted that the boys are supposed to act like boys because they are boys. It didn't make sense to me, so I didn't listen to most of what she was saying until I caught on that she had phoned my mom to say that I was supposed to wear dresses to school unless we were scheduled for gym class. Well, we only have gym twice a week, so Miss Von Smelly was saying that I had to wear a dress every Monday, Wednesday, and Friday! Now, I don't even like wearing dresses when I go to see my grandmother in the city, but that's the deal. And even then I don't like it, but my grandmother does. Gram is worth pleasing for the way she lets me climb on through the attic to the roof. Gram keeps a treasure chest for me in the closet and takes me to the zoo. Her oatmeal cookies are the best on this planet, and I get to lick the batter from the bowl. She even sewed me a pair of pajamas with tiger stripes and a long tail stuffed with nylon stockings. For Gram I will wear a dress.

Mom gave up with me and dresses when I was in the third grade. That's when we agreed that I wouldn't fight over wearing a dress for Sunday mass or for visits to Gram. If I didn't put up a stink on those occasions, I wouldn't have to wear dresses the rest of the whole year. At Gram's house and God's house, it makes Mom happy if I wear a dress, but no way am I wearing no dress for no old Miss Von Smelly—not even if she could bake oatmeal cookies like Gram's. Mom's only other rule was "No hightop sneakers when wearing a dress!" I don't much mind that rule, because hightops just don't look right when you got a skirt flapping around your thighs.

Mom lets me wear low-cut sneakers with my knee socks, so I can still run around, because I wear shorts underneath. I just don't like the idea that when I sprint, jump, fall or wrestle the whole world has a front-row seat to my underwear. And if I wear a dress to school, I have to put up with all Miss Von Smelly's stupid comments to us girls to sit with our knees locked together so our legs get all sore and cramped from trying to keep ourselves all shut up tight under our desks, as if it isn't easier to just tell the boys they got no business looking up our skirts in the first place.

I've never seen Miss Von Smelly in pants, and I feel like telling her how much happier she'd be if she didn't have to pay so much worrytime making sure her underwear ain't on display when she bends over, or reaches up high, or just stands in the wind. She wears all these silly shoes that make her look like a Barbie doll when she walks—stiff-kneed and pointy-toed, scuttering along.

I don't understand Miss Monzelli any better than she understands me, but I don't go telling her that she should be wearing hightop sneakers and jeans, so where does she get off calling my mom to say that I have to dress like her? That's all I want to know.

So anyway, I go home, and at dinner, Mom tells Dad about Miss Monzelli's phone call, and I just about choke on a tomato when Dad says "If that's what the teacher says, I suppose Angela will just have to put up with the rule."

"But Dad, Miss Monzelli is such a witch. She's just making me wear dresses because she knows how much I hate it! She's out to get me!"

"Now, Tiger," Dad calls me "Tiger" when we horse around or when he wants me to think that he's on my side, but he's really not. "I'm sure Miss Monzelli is not out to get you. She is your teacher, and she knows what is best for you and for the school."

"I'm not wearing dresses three times a week!"

"Honey," Mom calls me that when I start getting stubborn, and I can tell it's going to be two against one, three against one if you count Miss Monzelli. "I've let you take responsibility for your wardrobe this year, but maybe it's time that we take another look at what is appropriate attire for a young lady in your school. What do the other girls wear?"

"Mom," I could hear the whine in my voice, which meant that I knew reasoning wouldn't really work, "the other girls in my school play hopscotch at recess, and go to the corner store for Doritos and Coke after school. They don't play basketball or football or even climb on the jungle gym."

"Well, you could come home and change into your play clothes after school if you wanted to. . . ."

"Aww, come on, Mom, I'd never get in the game if I came home while the kids were choosing up teams. Dad . . ." I looked hopefully to my father for support, but he was staying out of this argument for as long as possible.

"Angela," my father said with a mix of sympathy and hesitation in his voice, "your teacher seems to think . . ."

"Dad, my teacher is a witch who waddles around in high heels and can't even hold a football in one hand. She picks it up at arm's length with two hands, like it's a piece of corn on the cob, too hot to bring within three feet of her body."

"Now, that's no way to talk about your teacher."

"Then there's no way she should talk about me as if I have no right to dress as I please."

Both my parents seemed to be defending Miss Monzelli only because she was my teacher, but I could tell that words were not going to convince them of what a jerk Miss Monzelli was being. So I sat quiet, hoping they would just forget about it, and life would go on as usual as I trotted off to school in my hightops and jeans the next morning. Besides, I didn't even own enough dresses to get through a week without repeating, unless I wore the satin dress I had from being the flower girl at my cousin's wedding. That dress puffed out so that I looked like a piece of Double Bubble Chewing Gum wrapped up and twisted in bows at both ends. No way was I stepping out of the house in that thing!

My other two dresses had both been made by Gram. My favorite was yellow with purple and white stripes down the side and a big number 32 on the front. Gram made it special to look like Magic Johnsons's Lakers uniform. For a dress, it's pretty neat, but it's still a dress. None of the other dresses I own fit me because I've been growing too fast for my clothes to keep up with me. The only reason the gum-wrapper dress fits is because an older cousin was supposed to be the flower girl, but she got some mono-disease right before the wedding, and I had to take her place. The dress was too big in the first place.

So Mom and Dad go on as if this conversation is over. I dig into my fish stick as if there's something special about fish sticks, which there definitely is not. I hear my fork scratching my plate, Mom's bracelets knocking against each other, and Dad's jaw cracking the way that it does when he chews. In our family, that's a silent dinner table.

When Mom gets up to clear the table, I leap up to help because I don't want anyone pointing out how much I hate all this housework stuff as if it's because I don't wear dresses often enough. Besides, it helps change the tone of everything for dessert, and we have forgotten the whole conversation enough so that Dad pulls out the weekend football pool that he gets at work. It's the first round of the play-offs, and I'm still hopeful enough to believe that I can bet on the Patriots to make it to the Super Bowl. Dad says that his football sense overrules his loyalty to the home team, so he plays his card differently than I play mine. We argue a bit about whether or not the Patriots can get their ground game going, and then we turn our attention to the chocolate pudding Mom puts in front of us. The silence is broken, and when I go to bed I feel sure no one will notice what I wear to school in the morning.

"Do you have Phys Ed today?" Mom asks as I throw my backpack full of books on the kitchen floor by the backdoor.

"Umm, no. Why?" I pretend innocence and ignorance of Miss Monzelli's mandate.

"Well, because, we agreed that you'd save your jeans for gym days." Mom's trying to be as forgetful of the argument as I am.

"We agreed that I could wear whatever I wanted except for church and for Gram. We never agreed to anything about wearing dresses to school. Miss Von Smelly just poked her nose into something that is not her business." Since this was not one of those times when giving in for the sake of keeping Mom happy was worth it, I made sure not to say *ain't*. I didn't want her to have any dirt on me in any way. Otherwise, I'd be stuck for good. I hoped she'd see this as one of those times when giving in for the sake of keeping ME happy would be worth HER while.

It wasn't.

"Angie, the school has its expectations and standards, and you have to . . ."

"Mom, it's not the school. It's Miss Monzelli! And she's an old witch anyway. Why listen to her?"

Dad walked in and silence returned.

I grew impatient and started pleading. "Mom, watch. No one will say anything's wrong if you just let me keep doing what I'm doing."

"Uh-oh, dresses again, huh? Tiger, why don't you just put on a dress, go to school, and do whatever it is you always do?" offered Dad, trying to be helpful and healing to the conversation.

"Daaadddd," I whined, hoping the tone said more than the word itself.

"Tiger, no one is asking you to change yourself. Nobody is going to stop you from being who you are. It's only your clothes we're asking you to change."

"Well, if it's only clothes, then why is everyone else making such a gigantic deal about what I wear?"

For a moment I grew hopeful when my dad had no answer for me, but then Mom filled the pause. "Because your teacher thinks you ought to dress up a bit more—like the other girls."

"Exactly," seconded Dad. "So why don't you run back into your room, slip those clothes into your backpack for after school, and put on a dress for classes?"

It was more of a commandment than a question, and I knew I wasn't going to get out of the house in my jeans. So I just glared at Dad a bit, then glared even harder at Mom, and stormed back to my room.

I had tried to be honest with my parents, but my honest opinions had gotten me nowhere. I didn't really want to cut school, although that option did come to mind. I figured I could change my clothes as soon as I got around the corner from the house. So, I put on the dress I hated most, the candy-wrapper one from Rico's wedding. It looked really stupid with my sneakers, and I felt like irking my folks because they were siding with Miss Von Smelly. I wore one tube sock with black and orange stripes and one with green and blue stripes, all of which completely clashed with the yellow and red of the dress.

I stomped my way back into the kitchen, no longer hungry for breakfast. I stood in the doorway as defiantly as possible with legs spread wide and arms folded across my chest. Mom and Dad looked at each other, unimpressed by me, and pleased as punch they'd won the argument. I stuffed my jeans and a T-shirt into my backpack as Dad had suggested, but I guess he must've been onto my plan to change before I reached the schoolyard because he offered to drive me to school.

Next thing I know, Dad's dropping me off in the school parking lot, and I'm facing a blacktop filled with my friends who have never even seen me in a dress, let alone in a flower girl gown, and I can't believe it. I'm angry as can be at Mom, Dad, Miss Monzelli, and any kid who dares to look at me. I turn to get back into the car, and when Dad innocently waves "So long, Tiger. See you tonight." I can't believe he's humiliating me this way. I see a few kids pointing toward me, laughing, and I want to punch them all. I don't know where to begin swinging, so I run inside to the girls' room, leap into the second stall, lock the door, and stand up on the seat so that no one can find me.

As I'm catching my breath, I discover that I left my backpack in the car. Everybody has already seen me and I'm weighing my options while perched atop the toilet. Then I hear the bathroom door squeak open. By the clicking of tiny footsteps echoing across the tile, I know Miss Monzelli has stalked me down.

"Hello? Is anyone in here? Hello? Angela? Angela?"

I say nothing, but I think of how stupid I'll feel if she finds me hiding in the stall. I know she knows I'm in here. I quickly and quietly slide my feet down so that it looks like I'm sitting on the toilet, and I drop my underpants down around my ankles. "Yes, Miss Monzelli," in the sweetest voice I can put together. "I'm just, well, ya know, doing what I have to do."

"Oh, Angela, it's you," she says, as if she's surprised I'm here. "I saw someone sneak in, and you know you shouldn't leave the playground without permission. Unless of course it's an emergency. I suppose it's all right this one time if Nature caught you by surprise." She's trying to make me feel better, but it sure as cinnamon ain't working.

"By the way, I thought you looked very pretty when I saw your father drop you off."

That was the final straw. I wanted to scream, punch or puke at her. She sounded so smug in her triumph, like those TV preachers who have saved some stupid sinner from the clutches of the devil. But fighting Miss Von Smelly would be no solution. It would only help prove to her that I behaved unladylike. So I said nothing, and she filled the silence by explaining that she was going back out before the bell rang to line everyone up for homeroom. Again, the bathroom door squeaked and the echoing heel clicks out the door and down the hallway.

I hated the thought of being made a fool of by Miss Monzelli's dumb rules. I needed a way to make her own rules work for me rather than against me. So I sat for a bit, realizing I might as well pee while I was on the toilet. After finishing my piss, I stood and reached to pull my underwear back up. As I turned to flush, a comic vision flashed through my head. I quickly dropped my underwear back to my ankles and stepped out of one leg hole. With my other leg, I kicked it up into the air, then with one arm I reached out to first catch and then slam dunk my underwear into the toilet bowl. A quick kick to the metal bar flushed it all away. No more underwear!

Miss Monzelli could gloat all she wanted over her little victory because I knew I'd have the last laugh. I wasn't thrilled about the razzing I'd have to put up with in the meantime, but it would all be worthwhile.

I returned to the blacktop where everyone was lining up silent and military. Eyes flashed my way, and an occasional head turned, but always at the risk of Miss Monzelli taking away recess period for headturners to practice standing at attention. I always wondered what it was we were supposed to pay attention to.

I held my head high and looked at no one. I had a secret that would teach Miss Monzelli not to mess with my life or my wardrobe so I figured I didn't have to deal with any kid's questions or stares. I just strutted to my place in the back of the line, glad that my last name was Vickery so I was at the end of the alphabetical order that Miss Monzelli organizes her life by. I glared down at Eric Tydings who stood in front of me every time we lined up for anything. He turned with a giggle held under his breath, and I answered his jeering. "If you don't turn around and get rid of that jackass grin, I'm gonna make your teeth permanent fixtures in your stomach."

Eric quickly turned back to the front, and it was a good thing for him, because the line was filing into the school, and Miss Monzelli for sure would have slapped him with some detention time for not paying attention. And no way was she going to blame me for his mischief today. After all, I was wearing a dress, and in Miss Monzelli's book, girls in dresses act ladylike and stay out of trouble.

I spoke to no one all morning except to answer questions with "yes" or "no," because I had nothing much I wanted to say to anyone. We had lots of stuff to do, including a worksheet of word problems, some reading about astronauts, and a spelling test. I pretended not to notice all the attention I was getting—but inside I wasn't missing a single sidelook or whisper. All the while I sat real careful not to let on that I wore nothing beneath my dress. I wanted to be sure that Miss Monzelli could not get word that I had no underwear on. I was determined that the whole school should see for themselves all at the same time, so I waited patiently for morning recess.

The recess bell finally rang at 10:30 just as I was completing an essay about my favorite animal. I had written all that I could think of writing about kangaroos about five minutes earlier, but I added one final sentence to my essay before putting up my pencil and folding my hands together on my desk top the way Miss Monzelli insists we all sit before she will consider allowing us to line up for recess. I wrote, "Kangaroos prove God has a sense of humor, because the only reason kangaroos exist is to jump around and have fun."

I signed my essay the way I always do at the end. Miss Monzelli hates it because she wants my name squished up at the top right corner of the page, neatly printed with her name and the date. She insists we use the "proper heading" on our work, so I do that, but I also let loose in big script letters at the end "by Angela Vickery" like a painter signing a masterpiece.

"All right, children. You may line up quietly in alphabetical order if you would like to go outside for recess." Of course everyone wanted to go out for recess, but Miss Monzelli always made it sound like an option and an invitation all at the same time that it was really, deep down, just another Von Smelly command.

We lined up, with me in the back again, and filed silently down the corridor to the double doors that lead to the playground. Once outside we were allowed to break file, and we scattered ourselves across the blacktop. Kevin Marino was close on my heels asking, "Hey, Angela. What's with the dress?" and I was answering only with an all-out sprint to the basketball court. Tyrone Freeman had the ball, and he was starting a game of 21 rather than choosing up sides for full court. Recess was too short for a game, and 21 gave everyone a chance to play because it's one big half-court game that leaves everyone against everyone scrapping to make a basket. You just have to keep track of your own score, and it's you against everyone any time you get the ball.

So I threw out my elbows the way I always did and made space for myself in the middle of the crowd huddled below the basket. The boys knew me well enough to tell from the scowl on my face that questions or jokes were completely out of order, so we all just settled in to play basketball. When Tyrone missed an outside shot, the rebound went off my fingers, and Stu Jackster came up with the ball. He cleared the ball out past the foul line, and I went out with him to play defense. He drove to my left, but his leg caught my knee, and we both went to the pavement. I landed sitting flat on my fanny with Stu sprawling across my legs. My dress was all in place, and Stu spit at the pavement beside me as he extended a hand to help me up. Meanwhile, the ball had gotten loose, and Greg Merrit had scored on a jump shot.

Greg got to take the ball up top because it's "make it—take it" where you get the ball back after you score a hoop. As Greg went to take a shot from the top of the key, I went back under to rebound. Sure enough, I came up with the ball, and put it straight up for a point of my own. It was my ball, at the top, and I took the ball left, spun around back to the right, and after two dribbles, I put the ball up and off the backboard for another basket.

My ball again. This time Tyrone decides to play me close, and as I move to spin past him, he gets help on the double team from Greg Merrit. BANG! Greg and I collide, and this time I'm on my back with my hightop sneakers looking down at me. Tyrone screams, "She's got no underwear on!" and they're all laughing hysterically. I clench my teeth almost as tightly as my fists and hiss out at them with squinted eyes "Miss Monzelli says I gotta wear a dress. Man, I'm wearing a dress, aren't I? You laugh at her, not at me, Tyrone Freeman. If any of you wanna laugh at me, you gonna have all your faces rearranged!"

Tyrone backed down on account we're friends, but Doug McDermott wasn't so smart. He starts chanting "I see London. I see France. Angela got no underpants." Once Doug gets going, everyone joins him, and I go right for his throat. He lands a half-punch the side of my head, and I throw one he ducks away from. Next thing I know, we're rolling around on the court, neither one of us landing any punches, but my dress is caught up high and my naked butt must be mooning the whole world just as Miss Monzelli arrives at the fight. Her voice is an extra two octaves higher than usual when I hear her scream "Angela Vickery, stop it! Stop this instant. Stop!"

Of course, I'm not stopping. I'm barely listening, but she tells one of the kids to run and get Mr. Stoller, the school principal.

Well, lots of fussing went on about this whole scene. The kids loved it. It was a scandal that had teachers and the principal unsure about what to do. After all, they had brought it on themselves. As Greg Merrit said, "You ask Angie to wear a dress and you gotta expect something crazy!"

Mr. Stoller lectured me a long while about fighting, but he never said anything directly about my lack of underwear. The school nurse gave me a whole lot of nurselike advice about being clean and wearing the proper undergarments. My Mom and Dad had a conference that afternoon with Miss Monzelli, but didn't say much to me about it.

The next day, when I arrived at breakfast in jeans and a Lakers sweatshirt, Mom asked if I wanted Wheaties or Grapenuts and that was that. Even after all the dust settled, Miss Monzelli never brought up the subject of dresses or underwear.

When the weekend arrived, Mom announced that Gram had invited us to the city for the day. I ran back upstairs to my room and happily put on my Magic Johnson dress. When I returned to the kitchen for breakfast, Mom and Dad looked at me, and then at each other, relieved.

I answered their unasked question by quickly turning, bending and lifting my skirt to show them my underwear.

"Looking good, Tiger!" cheered Dad as I turned around to face my smiling parents.

"What are you waiting for? Go on, get dressed. I want to sink my teeth into Gram's oatmeal cookies while they're still warm."

Marathoner

Stephanie Plotin

She started running
on bleached sidewalks;
to the supermarket
the dry cleaners
her office
for she was always
in a hurry;
her heels, little spikes
bit the ground
and gnawed at her toes.
She never realized her skirt was a hobble.
Mornings, she changed her shoes,
freed her legs to
jog through darkened streets
and speak with watching cats.
Days, she'd first run
up the office stairs
before she locked her feet up.
She trotted to the xerox machine
and to the ladies' room
when no one was watching.
But after a while
she did it anyway
and she wriggled her toes
in her running shoes
under her desk.
She discovered tracks,
rolled in the grass—
that was when she realized

feet were better bare.
By the time she found
the forest trails
her soles were her own
sleek leather.
All day her legs
twitch with impatience
to run on powdered dirt
her legs sun-warmed;
when sweat
drips in her eyes
like sweet water
then she feels real.
Twenty-six miles soon
wasn't enough for her—
one hundred almost satisfied her;
she was nearly
getting somewhere.
Soon people got the feeling
she was looking past them
to the next tree in the road.
Her partner told her
Dress Respectably
but her legs were
too strong
to be tied now
and no one can catch her.

Running

Leslie Ullman

i

Lately my neighbor wheezes
pounding dough, her forearms
glazed with sweat and flour.
"At your age," my mother
writes, "I wanted babies
and got pregnant
each time one of you
learned to walk."
I circle the block again
and again, until I run
outside my body.
This time last year
my husband stopped
speaking of the other woman
who slept poorly inside him.

She promised in another town
to give him up. All night she
tossed and tried to speak
until he spoke of his
father, who drank himself
into the cracked
well of his voice
and never touched bottom.
She made him wake sweating
and brooding in the closed
room of his departure
while I ran myself past

"Running" from DREAMS BY NO ONE'S DAUGHTER, by Leslie Ullman, © 1987. Reprinted by permission of the University of Pittsburgh Press.

my neighbor's lawn and plump
loaves settling in their heat
to an early shape of myself.

ii

I'd forgotten the apartment
that stretched like a tunnel,
shapeless and dark
the way my good dress hung
too large, a formal
body outside my body.
The other men drifted
alike behind their drinks
while he stood in one place
and spoke to me of *The Moviegoer*
which spoke, he said, to his very soul.

Sometimes I run in Louisiana
where I've never been,
where the hero saw an egret gather
itself over swamp mist
and settle in a single oak
that rose to meet it.
Later he married his cousin
whose agile mind wandered,
glittering at the family table.
The dense mahogany.
The black butler
wheezed as he passed the beans.
She couldn't sleep, she
said, without pills.
Sometimes she slept for two days.
She promised she could
be like anyone, if he

would tell her each morning
how to pass that day.

That night, my skin
held me like liquid glass.
I wanted to slip
my hand beneath his elbow,
to dance, to see the other women
naked inside their clothes.

iii

Every morning I run
through pollen, late summer
haze, and rain. My husband
is an illness I had
in another country.

The day he left
again and again he said
it wasn't your fault.
I circle the block, pump
and sweat until I run
outside my body.
My ribs ache.
He brushed his hands
gently over them.

Inside my running
I write to him, breaking
the silence we keep
for his new wife:
I saw the sun disappear
into mist as it reached
the horizon. And an egret

airborne, circling all
this time.

The morning bus gathers
husbands and children
and leaves for a moment
a soft rope of exhaust.
I draw breath over breath
as the children

must breath in their sleep.
My neighbor waves
from her doorway, follows my
easy stride: "Your waist,"
she says wistfully,
"fits the dress I wore as a bride."

on watching a world series game

Sonia Sanchez

O say can u see
on the baseball diamond
all the fans
          clappen for they nigger/players
yeah.
          there ain't nothing like a
          nigger playen in the noon/day
          sun for us fun/loving/spectators.
                              sometimes
they seem even human.
          (that is to say
                    every now and then.)

Hooray. hurrah. hooray.

                my. that nigger's

tough on that mound.

             can't git no

batters past him.

            wonder where he

was found

         makes u wonder if

it's still a wite man's game.

              WHO that flexing

his wite muscles.

         oh god yes. another wite hero

to save us from total blk/ness.

            Carl YASTRZEMSKI

yastruski.   YASTROOSKI.

  ya - fuck - it.   yeh.

             it's america's

most famous past time

       and the name

  of the game

         ain't baseball.

The Jockey

Carson McCullers

The jockey came to the doorway of the dining room, then after a moment stepped to one side and stood motionless, with his back to the wall. The room was crowded, as this was the third day of the season and all the hotels in the town were full. In the dining room bouquets of August roses scattered their petals on the white table linen and from the adjoining bar came a warm, drunken wash of voices. The jockey waited with his back to the wall and scrutinized the room with pinched, crêpy eyes. He examined the room until at last his eyes reached a table in a corner diagonally across from him, at which three men were sitting. As he watched, the jockey raised his chin and tilted his head back to one side, his dwarfted[sic] body grew rigid, and his hands stiffened so that the fingers curled inward like gray claws. Tense against the wall of the dining room, he watched and waited in this way.

He was wearing a suit of green Chinese silk that evening, tailored precisely and the size of a costume outfit for a child. The shirt was yellow, the tie striped with pastel colors. He had no hat with him and wore his hair brushed down in a stiff, wet bang on his forehead. His face was drawn, ageless, and gray. There were shadowed hollows at his temples and his mouth was set in a wiry smile. After a time he was aware that he had been seen by one of the three men he had been watching. But the jockey did not nod; he only raised his chin still higher and hooked the thumb of his tense hand in the pocket of his coat.

The three men at the corner table were a trainer, a bookie, and a rich man. The trainer was Sylvester—a large, loosely built fellow with a flushed nose and slow blue eyes. The bookie was Simmons. The rich man was the owner of a horse named Seltzer, which the jockey had ridden that afternoon. The three of them drank whiskey with soda, and a white-coated waiter had just brought on the main course of the dinner.

It was Sylvester who first saw the jockey. He looked away quickly, put down his whiskey glass, and nervously mashed the tip of his red nose with his thumb. "It's Bitsy Barlow," he said. "Standing over there across the room. Just watching us."

"Oh, the jockey," said the rich man. He was facing the wall and he half turned his head to look behind him. "Ask him over."

"God no," Sylvester said.

"He's crazy," Simmons said. The bookie's voice was flat and without inflection. He had the face of a born gambler, carefully adjusted, the expression a permanent deadlock between fear and greed.

"Well, I wouldn't call him that exactly," said Sylvester. "I've known him a long time. He was O.K. until about six months ago. But if he goes on like this, I can't see him lasting another year. I just can't."

"It was what happened in Miami," said Simmons.

"What?" asked the rich man.

Sylvester glanced across the room at the jockey and wet the corner of his mouth with his red, fleshy tongue. "A accident. A kid got hurt on the track. Broke a leg and a hip. He was a particular pal of Bitsy's. A Irish kid. Not a bad rider, either."

"That's a pity," said the rich man.

"Yeah. They were particular friends," Sylvester said. "You would always find him up in Bitsy's hotel room. They would be playing rummy or else lying on the floor reading the sports page together."

"Well, those things happen," said the rich man.

Simmons cut into his beefsteak. He held his fork prongs downward on the plate and carefully piled on mushrooms with the blade of his knife. "He's crazy," he repeated. "He gives me the creeps."

All the tables in the dining room were occupied. There was a party at the banquet table in the center, and green-white August moths had found their way in from the night and fluttered about the clear candle flames. Two girls wearing flannel slacks and blazers walked arm in arm across the room into the bar. From the main street outside came the echoes of holiday hysteria.

"They claim that in August Saratoga is the wealthiest town per capita in the world." Sylvester turned to the rich man. "What do you think?"

"I wouldn't know," said the rich man. "It may very well be so."

Daintily, Simmons wiped his greasy mouth with the tip of his forefinger. "How about Hollywood? And Wall Street—"

"Wait," said Sylvester. "He's decided to come over here."

The jockey had left the wall and was approaching the table in the corner. He walked with a prim strut, swinging out his legs in a half-circle with each step, his heels biting smartly into the red velvet carpet on the floor. On the way over he brushed against the elbow of a fat woman in white satin at the banquet table; he stepped back and bowed with dandified courtesy, his eyes quite closed. When he had crossed the room he drew up a chair and sat at a corner of the table, between Sylvester and the rich man, without a nod of greeting or a change in his set, gray face.

"Had dinner?" Sylvester asked.

"Some people might call it that." The jockey's voice was high, bitter, clear.

Sylvester put his knife and fork down carefully on his plate. The rich man shifted his position, turning sidewise in his chair and crossing his legs. He was dressed in twill riding pants, unpolished boots, and a shabby brown jacket—this was his outfit day and night in the racing season, although he was never seen on a horse. Simmons went on with his dinner.

"Like a spot of seltzer water?" asked Sylvester. "Or something like that?"

The jockey didn't answer. He drew a gold cigarette case from his pocket and snapped it open. Inside were a few cigarettes and a tiny gold penknife. He used the knife to cut a cigarette in half. When he had lighted his smoke he held up his hand to a waiter passing by the table. "Kentucky bourbon, please."

"Now, listen, Kid," said Sylvester.

"Don't Kid me."

"Be reasonable. You know you got to behave reasonable."

The jockey drew up the left corner of his mouth in a stiff jeer. His eyes lowered to the food spread out on the table, but instantly he looked up again. Before the rich man was a fish casserole, baked in a cream sauce and garnished with parsley. Sylvester had ordered eggs Benedict. There was asparagus, fresh buttered corn, and a side dish of wet black olives. A plate of French-fried potatoes was in the corner of the table before the jockey. He didn't look at the food again, but kept his pinched eyes on the centerpiece of full-blown lavender roses. "I don't suppose you remember a certain person by the name of McGuire," he said.

"Now, listen," said Sylvester.

The waiter brought the whiskey, and the jockey sat fondling the glass with his small, strong, calloused hands. On his wrist was a gold link bracelet that clinked against the edge of the table. After turning the glass between his palms, the jockey suddenly drank the whiskey neat in two hard swallows. He set down the glass sharply. "No, I don't suppose your memory is that long and extensive," he said.

"Sure enough, Bitsy," said Sylvester. "What makes you act like this? You hear from the kid today?"

"I received a letter," the jockey said. "The certain person we were speaking about was taken out from the cast on Wednesday. One leg is two inches shorter than the other one. That's all."

Sylvester clucked his tongue and shook his head. "I realize how you feel."

"Do you?" The jockey was looking at the dishes on the table. His gaze passed from the fish casserole to the corn, and finally fixed on the plate of fried potatoes. His face tightened and quickly he looked up again. A rose shattered and he picked up one of the petals, bruised it between his thumb and forefinger, and put it in his mouth.

"Well, those things happen," said the rich man.

The trainer and the bookie had finished eating, but there was food left on the serving dishes before their plates. The rich man dipped his buttery fingers in his water glass and wiped them with his napkin.

"Well," said the jockey. "Doesn't somebody want me to pass them something? Or maybe perhaps you desire to reorder. Another hunk of beefsteak, gentlemen, or—"

"Please," said Sylvester. "Be reasonable. Why don't you go on upstairs?"

"Yes, why don't I?" the jockey said.

His prim voice had risen higher and there was about it the sharp whine of hysteria.

"Why don't I go up to my god-damn room and walk around and write some letters and go to bed like a good boy? Why don't I just—" He pushed his chair back and got up. "Oh, foo," he said. "Foo to you. I want a drink."

"All I can say is it's your funeral," said Sylvester. "You know what it does to you. You know well enough."

The jockey crossed the dining room and went into the bar. He ordered a Manhattan, and Sylvester watched him stand with his heels pressed tight together, his body hard as a lead soldier's holding his little finger out from the cocktail glass and sipping the drink slowly.

"He's crazy," said Simmons. "Like I said."

Sylvester turned to the rich man. "If he eats a lamb chop, you can see the shape of it in his stomach a hour afterward. He can't sweat things out of him any more. He's a hundred and twelve and a half. He's gained three pounds since we left Miami."

"A jockey shouldn't drink," said the rich man.

"The food don't satisfy him like it used to and he can't sweat it out. If he eats a lamb chop, you can watch it tooching out in his stomach and it don't go down."

The jockey finished his Manhattan. He swallowed, crushed the cherry in the bottom of the glass with his thumb, then pushed the glass away from him. The two girls in blazers were standing at his left, their faces turned toward each other, and at the other end of the bar two touts had started an argument about which was the highest mountain in the world. Everyone was with somebody else; there was no other person drinking alone that night. The jockey paid with a brand-new fifty-dollar bill and didn't count the change.

He walked back to the dining room and to the table at which the three men were sitting, but he did not sit down. "No, I wouldn't presume to think your memory is that extensive," he said. He was so small that the edge of the table top reached almost to his belt, and when he gripped the corner with his wiry hands he didn't have to stoop. "No, you're too busy gobbling up dinners in dining rooms. You're too—"

"Honestly," begged Sylvester. "You got to behave reasonable."

"Reasonable! Reasonable!" The jockey's gray face quivered, then set in a mean, frozen grin. He shook the table so that the plates rattled, and for a moment it seemed that he would push it over. But suddenly he stopped. His hand reached out toward the plate nearest to him and deliberately he put a few of the French-fried potatoes in his mouth. He chewed slowly, his upper lip raised, then he turned and spat out the pulpy mouthful on the smooth red carpet which covered the floor. "Libertines," he said, and his voice was thin and broken. He rolled the word in his mouth, as though it had a flavor and a substance that gratified him. "You libertines," he said again, and turned and walked with his rigid swagger out of the dining room.

Sylvester shrugged one of his loose, heavy shoulders. The rich man sopped up some water that had been spilled on the tablecloth, and they didn't speak until the waiter came to clear away.

The Splendid Outcast

Beryl Markham

The stallion was named after a star, and when he fell from his particular heaven, it was easy enough for people to say that he had been named too well. People like to see stars fall, but in the case of Rigel, it was of greater importance to me. To me and to one other—to a little man with shabby cuffs and a wilted cap that rested over eyes made mild by something more than time.

It was at Newmarket, in England, where, since Charles I instituted the first cup race, a kind of court has been held for the royalty of the turf. Men of all classes come to Newmarket for the races and for the December sales. They come from everywhere—some to bet, some to buy or sell, and some merely to offer homage to the resplendent peers of the Stud Book, for the sport of kings may, after all, be the pleasure of every man.

December can be bitterly cold in England, and this December was. There was frozen sleet on buildings and on trees, and I remember that the huge Newmarket track lay on the downs below the village like a noose of diamonds on a tarnished mat. There was a festive spirit everywhere, but it was somehow lost on me. I had come to buy new blood for my stable in Kenya, and since my stable was my living, I came as serious buyers do, with figures in my mind and caution in my heart. Horses are hard to judge at best, and the thought of putting your hoarded pounds behind that judgement makes it harder still.

I sat close on the edge of the auction ring and held my breath from time to time as the bidding soared. I held it because the casual mention of ten thousand guineas in payment for a horse or for anything else seemed to me wildly beyond the realm of probable things. For myself, I had five hundred pounds to spend and, as I waited for Rigel to be shown, I remember that I felt uncommonly maternal about each pound. I waited for Rigel because I had come six thousand miles to buy him, nor was I apprehensive lest anyone should take him from me; he was an outcast.

Rigel had a pedigree that looked backward and beyond the pedigrees of many Englishmen—and Rigel had a brilliant record. By all odds, he should have brought ten thousand guineas at the sale, but I knew he wouldn't, for he had killed a man.

He had killed a man—not fallen upon him, nor thrown him in a playful moment from the saddle, but killed him dead with his hooves and with his teeth in a stable. And that was not all, though it was the greatest thing. Rigel had crippled other men and, so the story went, would cripple or kill still

Beryl Markham, 1944, 1987, *The Splendid Outcast*, (San Francisco: North Point Press). Reprinted by permission of Laurence Pollinger Limited and the Estate of Beryl Markham.

more, so long as he lived. He was savage, people said, and while he could not be hanged for his crimes, like a man, he could be shunned as criminals are. He could be offered for sale. And yet, under the implacable rules of racing, he had been warned off the turf for life—so who would buy?

Well, I for one—and I had supposed there would not be two. I would buy if the price were low enough, because I had youth then, and a corresponding contempt for failure. It seemed probable that in time and with luck and with skill, the stallion might be made manageable again, if only for breeding—especially for breeding. He could be gentled, I thought. But I found it hard to believe what I saw that day. I had not known that the mere touch of a hand, could in an instant, extinguish the long-burning anger of an angry heart.

I first noticed the little man when the sale was already well on its way, and he caught my attention at once, because he was incongruous there. He sat a few benches from me and held his lean, interwoven fingers upon his knees. He stared down upon the arena as each horse was led onto it, and he listened to the dignified encomiums of the auctioneer with the humble attention of a parishioner at mass. He never moved. He was surrounded by men and women who, by their impeccable clothes and by their somewhat bored familiarity with pounds and guineas, made him conspicuous. He was like a stone of granite in a jeweler's window, motionless and grey against the glitter.

You could see in his face that he loved horses—just as you could see, in some of the faces of those around him, that they loved the idea of horses. They were the cultists, he the votary, and there were, in fact, about his grey eyes and his slender lips, the deep, tense lines so often etched in the faces of zealots and of lonely men. It was the cast of his shoulders, I think, the devotion of his manner that told me he had once been a jockey.

A yearling came into the ring and was bought, and then another, while the pages of catalogues were quietly turned. The auctioneer's voice, clear but scarcely lifted, intoned the virtues of his magnificent merchandise as other voices, responding to this magic, spoke reservedly of figures: "A thousand guineas . . . two thousand . . . three . . . four! . . ."

The scene at the auction comes to me clearly now, as if once again it were happening before my eyes.

"Five, perhaps?" The auctioneer scans the audience expectantly as a groom parades a dancing colt around the arena. There is a moment of silence, a burly voice calls, "Five!" and the colt is sold while a murmur of polite approval swells and dies.

And so they go, one after another, until the list is small; the audience thins and my finger traces the name, Rigel, on the last page of the catalogue. I straighten on my bench and hold my breath a little, forgetting the crowd, the little man, and a part of myself. I know this horse. I know he is by Hurry On out of Bounty—the sire unbeaten, the dam a great steeplechaser—and there is no better blood than that. Killer or not, Rigel has won races, and won them clean. If God and Barclays Bank stay with me, he will return to Africa when I do.

And there, at last, he stands. In the broad entrance to the ring, two powerful men appear with the stallion between them. The men are not grooms of ordinary size; they have been picked for strength, and in the clenched fists of each is the end of a chain. Between the chain and the bit there is on the near side a short rod of steel, close to the stallion's mouth—a rod of steel, easy to grasp, easy to use. Clenched around the great girth of the horse, and fitted with metal rings, there is a strap of thick leather that brings to mind the restraining harness of a madman.

Together, the two men edge the stallion forward. Tall as they are, they move like midgets beside his massive shoulders. He is the biggest thoroughbred I have ever seen. He is the most beautiful. His coat is chestnut, flecked with white, and his mane and tail are close to gold. There is a blaze on his face—wide and straight and forthright, as if by this marking he proclaims that he is none other than Rigel, for all his sins, for all the hush that falls over the crowd.

He is Rigel and he looks upon the men who hold his chains as a captured king may look upon his captors. He is not tamed. Nothing about him promises that he will be tamed. Stiffly, on reluctant hooves, he enters the ring and flares his crimson nostrils at the crowd, and the crowd is still. The crowd whose pleasure is the docile beast of pretty paddocks, the gainly horse of cherished prints that hang upon the finest walls, the willing winner of the race—upon the rebel this crowd stares, and the rebel stares back.

His eyes are lit with anger or with hate. His head is held disdainfully and high, his neck an arc of arrogance. He prances now—impatience in the thudding of his hooves upon the tanbark, defiance in his manner—and the chains jerk tight. The long stallion reins are tightly held—apprehensively held—and the men who hold them glance at the auctioneer, an urgent question in their eyes.

The auctioneer raises his arm for silence, but there is silence. No one speaks. The story of Rigel is known—his breeding, his brilliant victories, and finally his insurgence and his crimes. Who will buy the outcast? The auctioneer shakes his head as if to say that this is a trick beyond his magic. But he will try. He is an imposing man, an experienced man, and now he clears his throat and confronts the crowd, a kind of pleading in his face.

"This splendid animal—" he begins—and does not finish. He cannot finish.

Rigel has scanned the silent audience and smelled the unmoving air, and he—a creature of the wind—knows the indignity of this skyless temple. He seems aware at last of the chains that hold him, of the men who cling forlornly to the heavy reins. He rears from the tanbark, higher and higher still, until his golden mane is lifted like a flag unfurled and defiant. He beats the air. He trembles in his rising anger, and the crowd leans forward.

A groom clings like a monkey to the tightened chain. He is swept from his feet while his partner, a less tenacious man, sprawls ignobly below, and men—a dozen men—rush to the ring, some shouting, some waving their arms. They run and swear in lowered voices; they grasp reins, chains, rings, and swarm upon their towering Gulliver. And he subsides.

With something like contempt for this hysteria, Rigel touches his fore-hooves to the tanbark once more. He has killed no one, hurt no one, but they are jabbing at his mouth now, they are surrounding him, adding fuel to his fiery reputation, and the auctioneer is a wilted man.

He sighs, and you can almost hear it. He raises both arms and forgoes his speech. "What," he asks with weariness, "am I offered?" And there is a ripple of laughter from the crowd. Smug in its wisdom, it offers nothing.

But I do, and my voice is like an echo in a cave. Still there is triumph in it. I will have what I have come so far to get—I will have Rigel.

"A hundred guineas!" I stand as I call my price, and the auctioneer is plainly shocked—not by the meagerness of the offer, but by the offer itself. He stares upward from the ring, incredulity in his eyes.

He lifts a hand and slowly repeats the price. "I am offered," he says, "one hundred guineas."

There is a hush, and I feel the eyes of the crowd and watch the hand of the auctioneer. When it goes down, the stallion will be mine.

But it does not go down. It is still poised in midair, white, expectant, compelling, when the soft voice, the gently challenging voice is lifted. "Two hundred!" the voice says, and I do not have to turn to know that the little jockey has bid against me. But I do turn.

He has not risen from the bench, and he does not look at me. In his hand he holds a sheaf of bank notes. I can tell by their color that they are of small denomination, by their rumpled condition that they have been hoarded long. People near him are staring—horrified, I think—at the vulgar spectacle of cash at a Newmarket auction.

I am not horrified, nor sympathetic. Suddenly I am aware that I have a competitor, and I am cautious. I am here for a purpose that has little to do with sentiment, and I will not be beaten. I think of my stable in Kenya, of the feed bills to come, of the syces to be paid, of the races that are yet to be won if I am to survive in this unpredictable business. No, I cannot now yield an inch. I have little money, but so has he. No more, I think, but perhaps as much.

I hesitate a moment and glance at the little man, and he returns my glance. We are like two gamblers bidding each against the other's unseen cards. Our eyes meet for a sharp instant—a cold instant.

I straighten and my catalogue is crumpled in my hand. I moisten my lips and call, "Three hundred!" I call it firmly, steadily, hoping to undo my opponent at a stroke. It is a wishful thought.

He looks directly at me now, but does not smile. He looks at me as a man might look at one who bears false witness against him, then soundlessly he counts his money and bids again, "Three fifty!"

The interest of the crowd is suddenly aroused. All these people are at once conscious of being witnesses, not only before an auction, but before a contest, a rivalry of wills. They shift in their seats and stare as they might stare at a pair of duelists, rapiers in hand.

But money is the weapon, Rigel the prize. And prize enough, I think, as does my adversary.

I ponder and think hard, then decide to bid a hundred more. Not twenty, not fifty, but a hundred. Perhaps by that I can take him in my stride. He need not know there is little more to follow. He may assume that I am one of the casual ones, impatient of small figures. He may hesitate, he may withdraw. He may be cowed.

Still standing, I utter, as indifferently as I can, the words, "Four fifty!" and the auctioneer, at ease in his element of contention, brightens visibly.

I am aware that the gathered people are now fascinated by this battle of pounds and shillings over a stallion that not one of them would care to own. I only hope that in the heat of it some third person does not begin to bid. But I need not worry; Rigel takes care of that.

The little jockey has listened to my last offer, and I can see that he is already beaten—or almost, at least. He has counted his money a dozen times, but now he counts it again, swiftly, with agile fingers, as if hoping his previous counts had been wrong.

I feel a momentary surge of sympathy, then smother it. Horse training is not my hobby. It is my living. I wait for what I am sure will be his last bid, and it comes. For the first time, he rises from his bench. He is small and alone in spirit, for the glances of the well-dressed people about him lend him nothing. He does not care. His eyes are on the stallion and I can see that there is a kind of passion in them. I have seen that expression before—in the eyes of sailors appraising a comely ship, in the eyes of pilots sweeping the clean, sweet contours of a plane. There is reverence in it, desire—and even hope.

The little man turns slightly to face the expectant auctioneer, then clears his throat and makes his bid. "Four eighty!" he calls, and the slight note of desperation in his voice is unmistakable, but I force myself to ignore it. Now, at last, I tell myself, the prize is mine.

The auctioneer receives the bid and looks at me, as do a hundred people. Some of them, no doubt, think I am quite mad or wholly inexperienced, but they watch while the words "Five hundred" form upon my lips. They are never uttered.

Throughout the bidding for Rigel, Rigel has been ignored. He has stood quietly enough after his first brief effort at freedom; he has scarcely moved. But now, at the climax of the sale, his impatience overflows, his spirit flares like fire, his anger bursts through the circle of men who guard him. Suddenly, there are cries, shouts of warning, the ringing of chains and the cracking of leather, and the crowd leaps to its feet. Rigel is loose. Rigel has hurled his captors from him and he stands alone.

It is a beautiful thing to see, but there is terror in it. A thoroughbred stallion with anger in his eye is not a sight to entrance anyone but a novice. If you are aware of the power and the speed and the intelligence in that towering symmetrical body, you will hold your breath as you watch it. You will know that the teeth of a horse can crush a bone, that hooves can crush a man. And Rigel's hooves have crushed a man.

He stands alone, his neck curved, his golden tail a battle plume, and he turns, slowly, deliberately, and faces the men he has flung away. They are not without courage, but they are without resource. Horses are not tamed by whips or by blows. The strength of ten men is not so strong as a single stroke of a hoof; the experience of ten men is not enough, for this is the unexpected, the unpredictable. No one is prepared. No one is ready.

The words "Five hundred" die upon my lips as I watch, as I listen. For the stallion is not voiceless now. His challenging scream is shrill as the cry of winter wind. It is bleak and heartless. His forehooves stir the tanbark. The auction is forgotten.

A man stands before him—a man braver than most. He holds nothing in his hands save an exercise bat; it looks a feeble thing, and is. It is a thin stick bound with leather—enough only to enrage Rigel, for he has seen such things in men's hands before. He knows their meaning. Such a thing as this bat, slight as it is, enrages him because it is a symbol that stands for other things. It stands, perhaps, for the confining walls of a darkened stable, for the bit of steel, foreign, but almost everpresent in his mouth, for the tightened girth, the command to gallop, to walk, to stop, to parade before the swelling crowd of gathered people, to accept the measured food gleaned from forbidden fields. It stands for life no closer to the earth than the sterile smell of satin on a jockey's back or the dead wreath hung upon a winner. It stands for servitude. And Rigel has broken with his overlords.

He lunges quickly, and the man with a bat is not so quick. He lifts the pathetic stick and waves it in desperation. He cries out, and the voice of the crowd drowns his cry. Rigel's neck is outstretched and straight as a sabre. There is dust and the shouting of men and the screaming of women, for the stallion's teeth have closed on the shoulder of his forlorn enemy.

The man struggles and drops his bat, and his eyes are sharp with terror, perhaps with pain. Blood leaves the flesh of this face, and it is a face grey and pleading, as must be the faces of those to whom retribution is unexpected and swift. He beats against the golden head while the excitement of the crowd mounts against the fury of Rigel. Then reason vanishes. Clubs, whips, and chains appear like magic in the ring, and a regiment of men advance upon the stallion. They are angry men, brave in their anger, righteous and justified in it. They advance, and the stallion drops the man he has attacked, and the man runs for cover, clutching his shoulder.

I am standing, as is everyone. It is a strange and unreal thing to see this trapped and frustrated creature, magnificent and alone, away from his kind, remote from the things he understands, face the punishment of his minuscule masters. He is, of course, terrified, and the terror is a mounting madness. If he could run, he would leave this place, abandoning his fear and his hatred to do it. But he cannot run. The walls of the arena are high. The doors are shut, and the trap makes him blind with anger. He will fight, and the blows will fall with heaviness upon his spirit, for his body is a rock before these petty weapons.

The men edge closer, ropes and chains and whips in determined hands. The whips are lifted, the chains are ready; the battle line is formed, and Rigel does not retreat. He comes forward, the whites of his eyes exposed and rimmed with carnelian fire, his nostrils crimson.

There is a breathless silence, and the little jockey slips like a ghost into the ring. His eyes are fixed on the embattled stallion. He begins to run across the tanbark and breaks through the circle of advancing men and does not stop. Someone clutches at his coat, but he breaks loose without turning, then slows to an almost casual walk and approaches Rigel alone. The men do not follow him. He waves them back. He goes forward, steadily, easily and happily, without caution, without fear, and Rigel whirls angrily to face him.

Rigel stands close to the wall of the arena. He cannot retreat. He does not propose to. Now he can focus his fury on this insignificant David who has come to meet him, and he does. He lunges at once as only a stallion can— swiftly, invincibly, as if escape and freedom can be found only in the destruction of all that is human, all that smells human, and all that humans have made.

He lunges and the jockey stops. He does not turn or lift a hand or otherwise move. He stops, he stands, and there is silence everywhere. No one speaks; no one seems to breathe. Only Rigel is motion. No special hypnotic power emanates from the jockey's eyes; he has no magic. The stallion's teeth are bared and close, his hooves are a swelling sound when the jockey turns. Like a matador of nerveless skill and studied insolence, the jockey turns his back on Rigel and does not walk away, and the stallion pauses.

Rigel rears high at the back of the little man, screaming his defiant scream, but he does not strike. His hooves are close to the jockey's head, but do not touch him. His teeth are sheathed. He hesitates, trembles, roars wind from his massive lungs. He shakes his head, his golden mane, and beats the ground. It is frustration—but of a new kind. It is a thing he does not know— a man who neither cringes in fear nor threatens with whips or chains. It is a thing beyond his memory perhaps—as far beyond it as the understanding of the mare that bore him.

Rigel is suddenly motionless, rigid, suspicious. He waits, and the grey-eyed jockey turns to face him. The little man is calm and smiling. We hear him speak, but cannot understand his words. They are low and they are lost to us—an incantation. But the stallion seems to understand at least the spirit if not the sense of them. He snorts, but does not move. And now the jockey's hand goes forward to the golden mane—neither hurriedly nor with hesitance, but unconcernedly, as if it had rested there a thousand times. And there it stays.

There is a murmur from the crowd, then silence. People look at one another and stir in their seats—a strange self-consciousness in their stirring, for people are uneasy before the proved worth of their inferiors, unbelieving of the virtue of simplicity. They watch with open mouths as the giant Rigel, the killer Rigel, with no harness save a head collar, follows his Lilliputian master, his new friend, across the ring.

All has happened in so little time—in moments. The audience begins to stand, to leave. But they pause at the lift of the auctioneer's hand. He waves it and they pause. It is all very well, his gestures say, but business is, after all, business, and Rigel has not been sold. He looks up at me, knowing that I have a bid to make—the last bid. And I look down into the ring at the stallion I have come so far to buy. His head is low and close to the shoulder of the man who would take him from me. He is not prancing now, not moving. For this hour, at least, he is changed.

I straighten, and then shake my head. I need only say, "Five hundred," but the words won't come. I can't get them out. I am angry with myself— a sentimental fool—and I am disappointed. But I cannot bid. It is too easy— twenty pounds too little, and yet too great an advantage.

No. I shake my head again, the auctioneer shrugs and turns to seal his bargain with the jockey.

On the way out, an old friend jostles me. "You didn't really want him then," he says.

"Want him? No. No, I didn't really want him."

"It was wise," he says. "What good is a horse that's warned off every course in the Empire? You wouldn't want a horse like that."

"That's right. I wouldn't want a horse like that."

We move to the exit, and when we are out in the bright cold air of Newmarket, I turn to my friend and mention the little jockey. "But he wanted Rigel," I say.

And my old friend laughs. "He would," he says. "That man has himself been barred from racing for fifteen years. Why, I can't remember. But it's two of a kind, you see—Rigel and Sparrow. Outlaws, both. He loves and knows horses as no man does, but that's what we call him around the tracks—the Fallen Sparrow."

Why Aren't Women Racing at Indy? Janet Guthrie Knows

Tracy Dodds

It was 10 years ago, in 1977, that Janet Guthrie became the first woman to drive in the Indianapolis 500. She's proud that she has the distinction of being the first. But she's piqued that she still has the distinction of being the only.

Why is Guthrie no longer driving Indy cars? And why have no other women followed her lead to Indy?

"The stick-and-ball sports editors who suggested that you ask me that question are probably the same guys who are still puzzling over the question of why there are no black managers in baseball," Guthrie said.

Guthrie keeps answering the question, though. She's been doing it for years. And every time she does, she suffers the consequences.

She explains about the high cost of racing, the dependency on multi-million-dollar corporate sponsorship, the good ol' boy network that keeps racing very male—and then the good ol' boys explain that women can't race.

It's kind of like saying that women don't have the "necessities" for racing.

"Get ready for the knee-jerk reaction," Guthrie said. "I'll talk to you about this, and I'll guarantee what the reaction will be because I've been through this 14 dozen times. It will be written off by men who will say that women can't compete and more specifically, that Janet Guthrie wasn't competitive.

"I know that this is not true. I stand on my record . . . But it's hard to have your reputation kicked around again and again."

Guthrie, 49, lives in Aspen, Colorado, and is busy working on an autobiography that she hopes will show the "passion and complexity" of the world of auto racing. She is engaged to Warren Levine, a United Airlines pilot. And she still does a lot of traveling and speaking.

Guthrie would be in Indianapolis racing today if she could get the sponsorship. "Obviously there is money available to sponsor racing because the race fields remain full of sponsored men," Guthrie said. "Sponsors supposedly put up that money because they want to sell products, but a lot of those products are used by both men and women—beer, for example. But what I especially notice are the sponsors like Tide, Crisco, Folgers and Haines pantyhose who are putting their money behind men.

"Men are getting sponsorship and women can't. That sounds unfair. But who cares about unfair? What counts is the bottom line. Sponsors want the publicity that racing brings. But a successful woman driver will get 10 times the attention that a man will get. So now what really is important?

From Tracy Dodds, May 24, 1987. Reprinted by permission of *Los Angeles Times Syndicate*.

"It keeps coming back to the good ol' boy network. A lot of corporations are spending a lot of tax deductible dollars to sponsor male racing drivers."

And the only way to justify passing over a driver like Guthrie is to say that she can't drive.

"I would like to point out that when I was racing, there were some very good teams that would have had me, and that I would have given my eye teeth to work with—Bignotti for example, McLaren for example—but I had to bring the sponsorship with me, and I was being told that there was no sponsorship available," Guthrie said.

The way it's retold in Gasoline Alley, she didn't really merit sponsorship.

A quick review:

Janet Guthrie did not show up at Indy in 1976 as a publicity stunt. She was a 38-year-old woman who had a degree in physics and had worked as an engineer for Republic Aviation.

She learned to fly planes when she was 13. She had been racing sports cars for more than 10 years and was able to take the engine of her Jaguar XK-120 apart and put it back together.

Guthrie was quite serious about wanting to race cars.

She conducted herself in a calm professional manner at all times, enduring constant scrutiny as she went through some frustrating setbacks with her cars and some cutting remarks from other drivers.

She failed to qualify her first year at Indy because her car was not fast enough. A.J. Foyt was curious enough about her ability to let her take his backup Coyote out to see if she could get a good car up to qualifying speed. She could. But he couldn't afford to go handing out his backup car, so she ended up driving in the World 600 stock car race on the day of the Indy 500.

In 1976 she was in the running for rookie of the year on the NASCAR circuit.

In 1977 she was back at Indy with a car that was good enough to make the field—barely. She qualified 26th and finished 29th after spending more time in the pit than on the track.

After taking on a full load of fuel, the heat of the day and the heat of the car caused the fuel to expand and spill over into her lap. She wore that methanol fuel-soaked suit for hours before she was able to get it off and find some water to rinse away the burning chemical. There was then just one shower in Gasoline Alley, so she had to have her crew construct a makeshift shower stall for her.

She commented to the reporters shadowing her and recording her every word that one shower was hardly adequate.

In 1978, she qualified 15th and finished 9th. Not bad at all for a second try. And, she points out that she did that with a budget that was about five percent of what the top teams were spending that year. She had $120,000 while the Penske team had about $2.3 million.

So did her cohorts herald her arrival and proclaim her worthy of promotion? No, but they couldn't say that she was scared or dangerous or didn't know the sport or didn't know cars. So they said that she ran just to finish. That she didn't challenge the leaders.

To that, she says, "Horsefeathers."

In 1979 she was back in a car that lasted just three laps. It was the car that didn't want to challenge the leaders. And she hasn't been back in the race since.

She would still like to race with a top team so that she would have the wherewithal to challenge.

There were, in her early days in Indy cars, some drivers who showed her respect. Foyt, for one, was willing to give her a chance. After a race at Trenton, Johnny Rutherford acknowledged that she had made a quick transition from sports cars and said, "It's a shame she didn't have a better car." Tom Sneva said, "She ran as fast as the car would run."

But others continued to say that she was just trying to finish, not trying to win.

She's heard it all over the years, about how women don't have the strength, endurance or courage for this sport.

Ever the intellectual, Guthrie counters each point with evidence: "Okay, let's talk about strength. How about the 115-pound woman power lifter who [can] lift 352 pounds? Endurance? What about the ultra-marathon runners and triathletes? The record for the English Channel swim is held by a woman. Courage? Downhill skiers risk terrible injury. A gymnast doing a triple back flip on a balance beam constantly risks breaking her neck. How about Betty Cook, a world champion in power boat racing?

"How about all of those things and more, all in one? The Iditarod [a dogsled race of more than 1,000 miles in Alaska]. In each of the last three years, that's been won by a woman. I have a T-shirt that says, 'Alaska. Where men are men and women win the Iditarod.'

"Women just can't do it? Horsefeathers. I find that highly offensive."

Guthrie is convinced that it's the system that is keeping women from developing into top drivers. She cites examples dating back to the early 1900s in which women of independent wealth successfully ran sports cars.

And she cites the WASPs as examples of how men will strive to deny the history of women who succeed on their turf. The Women Air Force Service Pilots flew planes to and from the war theaters. Thirty-nine were killed in the line of duty during World War II. But they didn't win veterans benefits until 1977 because the military was so determined to keep them classified as civilians.

"We can go all the way back to hot air balloonists in the 1700s to find examples of how women's history has been deliberately suppressed or denied."

So Guthrie is not at all surprised that her efforts of 10 years ago not only have failed to lead to greater opportunities for women, but are shrugged off as an experiment by someone who was not competitive.

"Am I surprised that there haven't been other women at Indy in the last few years? Guthrie asked. "I'm distressed.

"There have been some great natural talents emerge, like Kathy Rude [who survived a terrible racing accident four years ago] and there will be others. Whether they get the chance to drive at Indy is a matter of funding.

"Me? I keep hoping that one of these days, somewhere in Aspen, I'll run into a multi-zillionaire who wants to go racing.

"I'd love to have the money behind me for the car, the team, the testing program that it takes to be competitive."

A Marble Game in 1955

Jadene Felina Stevens

> *Oh, Roger Jones! Oh, Roger Jones!*
> *Oh, Prince! O, Knight! Ah me!*
> *We used to play at keeping house,*
> *Beneath an old oak tree.*
> —Nathalia Crane 1924

The day you asked me if I wanted to play marbles
in your yard,
(a game for "keepsies," you said)
I had just returned from a party,
wore a Swiss dot dress my mother had sewn by hand,
cut from a pair of old curtains.
You dug a cup-sized hole in the ground,
we drew a circle around it,
picked pebbles from the dust.

Reprinted, by permission, from J. F. Stevens, 1989, "A Marble Game in 1955," *Kalliope, A Journal of Women's Art* 11 (1).

We each had a bag of marbles,
loosened draw-strings,
started to roll.
Some days you're on,
some days not.
Kneeling in the hot sun, knuckling down,
knocking one aggie after another into the hole,
until you only had your lucky red shooter left;
an off-round, cranberry red cat's-eye
which looked magical gleaming in the palm of your hand—
when it was over
I pulled the draw-strings tight,
the denim bag bulging.
"Hey! Give 'em back!" you said,
your words heavy and precise.
"I will not!" (I drew the strings tighter.)
"It wasn't for 'keepsies!' It was 'funsies!' Give 'em back!"
You yelled, your face red, eyes full
of the sting of tears.
"Give 'em back, or get out of my yard!" your voice low now,
hatred rising from a cup-sized hole.
I left, your words filling the afternoon air behind me—
"Don't come back . . . EVER!"

I suppose here, I should show some compassion,
say I gave back his marbles,
or at least his Christmas-red shooter,
but I didn't—
knowing he wouldn't have given mine
back to me.
Feeling good in a clean win,
fair game,
I tossed those marbles all over my bed that night,
set the red cat's-eye carefully on the sill.

Playing Pool

Julia Darling

We all know
what we're talking about.

The silver is on the table.
The triangle of coloured spheres
will break.

Me or him.
He'll never live it down
if I win.

That's why I'm ambitious and hot
wanting to beat him
black, purple and blue,
playing pool like a boy
with my eyes down
in the low shabby spotlight
of a yellow room.

Me or him.

The male chorus
gurgling on Guinness
hangs from the ceiling.

Balls roll, like the eyes
peering at my arse
as I bend and squint,
arch over backwards

with professional
amateur dramatics.

And pocket mouths
close and twist
as we click on
desperately.

Me or him.

The last ball hangs like smoke,
snookered, caught in its blind trap.

And how they love me when I lose.
They love me when I lose.

The Lady Pitcher

Cynthia Macdonald

It is the last of the ninth, two down, bases loaded, seventh
Game of the Series and here she comes, walking
On water,
Promising miracles. What a relief
Pitcher she has been all year.
Will she win it all now or will this be the big bust which
She secures in wire and net beneath her uniform,
Wire and net like a double
Vision version
Of the sandlot homeplate backstop in Indiana where
She became known as Flameball Millie.

She rears back and fires from that cocked pistol, her arm.
Strike one.
Dom, the catcher, gives her the crossed fingers sign,
Air, but she shakes it off and waits for fire.
Strike two.
Then the old familiar cry, "Show them you got balls, Millie."
But she knows you should strike while the iron is hot
Even though the manager has fined her
Sixteen times for disobeying
The hard and fast one:
A ball after two strikes.
She shoots it out so fast
It draws
An orange stripe on that greensward.
Strike three.

In the locker room they hoist her up and pour champagne
All over her peach satin, lace-frilled robe.
She feels what she has felt before,
The flame of victory and being loved
Moves through her, but this time
It's the Series and the conflagration matches
The occasion.

In the off-season she dreams of victories and marriage,
Knowing she will have them and probably not it.
Men whisper, in wet moments of passion,
"My little Lowestoft," or, "My curvy Spode," and
They stroke her handle, but she is afraid that yielding means
Being filled with milk and put on
The shelf;
So she closes herself off,
Wisecracking.

When she is alone again she looks at the china skin
Of her body, the crazing, the cracks she put there
To make sure
She couldn't
Hold anything for long.

Change-Ups

Maria Noell Goldberg

When it came to sports, I was one of those girls who gave girls a bad name. My throwing arm traced its trajectory along a course best suited, not to propelling baseballs, but to swatting flies. Balls sailing toward me were treated with the same caution any sensible person uses when an object careens through space in her direction. I ducked. Or stepped sideways and glanced casually into the sky as if a particularly interesting species of bird had just flown overhead on its way to a more hospitable neighborhood.

I grew up during the fifties and sixties, on a small island surrounded by water and trees you couldn't see over the tops of. Like the circumscribed view from our house, societal definitions of sports and love were so limited they left much of my own experience outside the scope of recognition and naming. Sports meant balls and teams to me; love meant boys and men. My friends and I recognized no other kind of sport, no other kind of love. Given the narrowness of these definitions, no matter how feverishly we played, our activities were never sport; no matter how much yearning we directed toward each other, our longing was never love.

While my brothers faced off on the lawn and sent balls sizzling through the air at each other, my best friend Cathy and I stood on the end of the dock trying to master our hula hoops. Once spinning, it took the subtlest hip thrust to keep the hoop moving, circling our waists, orbiting around the planets of our bodies. My brothers and most of the other boys we knew were hopeless when it came to the hula hoop. They'd step into the circle of bright plastic, raise it to their waists and give it a confident spin, then watch it falter and drop to the grass. Synchronizing the spin with the movement of their bodies seemed to require a patience and a particular kind of focus they were unwilling or unable to master. After another attempt or two, when their awkward gyrations failed to keep the hoop aloft, they'd drop it, disdainfully step outside its embrace, and go back to more manly and rewarding pursuits.

Although a few boys mastered the hula hoop well enough to turn it into an endurance test or to fantasize about setting a new world's record, boys had no use for them. Their rejection made it largely a "girl's game." Like my brothers, they preferred practicing the small skills that would eventually lead them to baseball and basketball teams. They faced off as combatants armed with mitts and balls aimed at testing each other while Cathy and I practiced skills that would lead nowhere as we perfected variations in hula hoop speed, rhythm, and orbit. We faced each other, not as combatants, but as mirrors in whose surfaces we saw shining back at us the easy pleasure we took in one another's company. In our difference, we also saw the possibilities of what a girl might be.

Cathy was my best friend through grade school, high school, and the first years of college. Her legs were solid and strong, her thighs as big around as her waist. From the hips down, she was as muscular as her older brother. Proud of his strength, he used his burly thighs to steal bases and charge across basketball courts to shoot lay-up after lay-up. Cathy used hers to ride her bike to my house around curving roads that skirted deep wooded ravines, calling me before she jumped on her Schwinn so I could clock her and chart the seconds she shaved off her arrival time. She did cannonballs off the end of the dock, climbed trees, raced the neighborhood dogs. She used those sturdy legs to ski on snow and water, jumping above earth and wave and seeming, for all her muscle and the pull of gravity, to fly.

I ran. Small and light, I imagined myself a girl from the Haida or Kwakiutl tribe as I cut a fast, silent path over the crumbling layers of the forest floor. I could swim across the lake and back, hold my breath under water longer than any of my brothers, carry the rocks we used for the foundations of the forts and dams we built, and shoot holes into the center of every Spaghetti-O that dotted the cans we shot off stumps in the woods with our B-B guns. I nourished these skills out of a fantasy of survivalism. I knew I did not want to depend on anyone to keep me whole, and that even in the 1950s, the world was not such a safe place for girls. I ran to escape boys chasing me to pull up my dress during recess, perfected my marksmanship and tracking ability should I ever decide to live alone in the woods, and practiced holding my breath and stilling my body out of a sense that a cloak of invisibility might be a more useful garment than a party dress.

Whatever images of femaleness Cathy and I tried on, it never occurred to us to envision ourselves as athletes. The potential for athleticism may have been there, but the models necessary for shaping and directing whatever skill, speed, focus, and endurance we possessed were not. The pictures presented to us about what it meant to be female (read feminine) did not include images of women in sports. To my knowledge, Donna Reed never chucked the family dinner in favor of a few games of tennis. Emily Post and Betty Crocker hovered over our childhood and adolescence with advice on cooking and courtesy, but had nothing to say about running full out to a finish line. And while Ike spent a lot of time on the golf course, Mamie Eisenhower always looked dressed for a tea party in heels, white gloves, and hats the size of salad bowls.

The notion of women in sports was largely an oxymoron since sport and the determination, competitiveness, and sense of agency that sport entails were not included in the territory of womanhood. More specifically than just balls and teams, sports meant males. As a child, even one with brothers, I paid little attention to what the boys were doing, preferring the gestures and sounds of other girls, but I did recognize that most of what the boys played were called "sports"; most of what the girls played were called "games."

I was dimly aware of a handful of women who were doing more than playing "games." Maureen Connolly, in spite of the diminutive "Little Mo," did win a grand slam in 1953, and Tenley Albright became the world figure skating champ in the same year. I knew about Florence Chadwick from a few fifteen minute radio spots which marked her swims across the English Channel in 1951, '53, and '55. She swam. I swam. So I remembered.

But even swimming was never framed for me as a sport, a pleasurable challenge in which I could test the measure of myself or participate in the making of myself. Swimming, too, was about survival. I complained just once as my mother dropped my brothers and me off at the beach club for our lesson in the rain. "We'll get sick," I said as I climbed from the car in the chill drizzle. "We'll get terrible colds." I gave a few preliminary sniffs as if already in the grip of an incipient virus. "A cold is better than a drowning," my mother answered, rolling up the window against the damp grey day. "I don't want to look outside some afternoon and see one of you floating on top of the lake."

The fact that the beach club had a swim team and that I could have been on it was blotted out by the shadow of drowning that now entered my mind each time I entered the water. Cathy was on the swim team until the boys began snickering and teasing her about the size of her legs. "Here come the tree trunks," they'd shout, making chain-saw noises, cutting her down to size. From that summer on, Cathy, instead of using those glorious strong legs to propel her through the water she loved, tried to diet them out of existence.

In the conversion of play to sport, the stakes get higher. In the conversion of child to girl and girl to woman, the stakes are higher still. Cathy learned it first but I soon caught on that just as one has to learn the rules and develop the talents that make one a winner in a particular sport, we had to learn to be girls. From television, from the comics and romance novels we hungrily devoured and the plaintive songs of heartbreak we heard on the radio, we breathed in the directives and expectations about what was required of girls, the rigid codes of appearance and behavior we could not afford to ignore. If you failed at a sport, you were a loser on a particular playing field, but if you failed at being a girl you were—in all quarters—an outcast.

Cheryl appeared in our school in the tenth grade, her hair slicked back into a DA that resembled Elvis's. She wore a pleated grey skirt every day and the same white short-sleeved shirts the boys wore, her sleeves rolled up to expose the lean wiry muscles of her arms. She wore undershirts instead of bras, and we knew from watching her change into her greying gym shorts at two o'clock every day that she never wore a girdle—that important symbol of maturing womanhood—like we all did.

No one ever spoke to her, even in gym class where our natural tendency to huddle, touch, and lean into one another broke down some of the barriers of cliquish hierarchy that existed in the halls. We whispered about her though, stunned and outraged by her difference, her refusal to comport herself in the "appropriate" fashion of the day.

Gym class in high school was the location of the greatest tension between what young women were physically capable of and what we were allowed. Cheryl's presence among us seemed, in the brief year she attended our school, to heighten that tension. Our gym teacher, the lanky Miss Stokes, may have gotten a few of us to move our feet and run, take aim at a basket and shoot, but most of us were expert at feigning the vapors and waiting for the bell to ring. Even those who played hard enough to need a shower at the end of the period, never played basketball or soccer after class was over. Physically, we may have tested and stretched our limits when we were younger, but now the fever to give our all to something had been deflected into the full-time job of dressing and acting the part of a girl.

Cheryl alone was determined to use that hour for all it was worth. She stole basketballs from our unresisting hands and did push-ups long after the rest of us had given up, refusing to stop until Miss Stokes tenderly leaned over her and lifted her shoulders off the cold shiny floor. She hit home runs and ran the bases twice, never looking at any of us, making us feel that for all our obvious talk about her, she didn't know we existed. While I know our condemnation must have pained her, she seemed to have carved out a unique self that no amount of our hissing could shake.

We understood, though Cheryl did not, that in order to succeed as girls, any athletic success girls like Cathy had known as children, could not follow them into lives bound by the necessity to be feminine. Even my mother, a tough, funny, and troubled resister in her own diminished life, taught me that a woman's strength must not be displayed in public. She loved gardening and thought nothing of digging up and moving young trees from one corner of the yard to another. She learned carpentry and added rooms to our house. She dug a ditch the length of a football field from the hilltop behind our house to the lake below, filled it with gravel and lined it with French drains to divert the rainwater that regularly flooded our basement bedrooms. But these were private acts, part of the secret life of our family that arose out of necessity because my father was not "handy around the house." When she went to the grocery store or church, my mother's cracked gardening hands were neatly covered in white gloves, her slim muscular arms hidden inside pearl-buttoned cardigans. When asked to help carry a box, boat, or lumber for a neighbor in need—acts of which she was supremely capable—she anxiously scanned the horizon for a man.

I had my own secrets, facts of my existence that, having no name, were hidden even from myself. I was blind to my own desire, blind to the lesbian selves Cheryl and the lonely, dignified Miss Stokes most likely were. My careful study of them, of Cathy and all the girls and women on whom I had crushes, was belied by the amount of time I spent courting the favor of males. I preened for them, dated them, and because I'm a slow learner, even married a couple, all the while failing to notice that it was women to whom my attention was drawn, women who inspired and consoled me, women who helped me shape and know my Self.

By the time my brothers and I were young adults, they were still practicing change-ups, signaling one kind of pitch then executing another as they tried to fake each other out. I was engaged in another, deeper form of deception, one from which I awakened slowly and late.

Like my mother and Cathy, I had access to skills and strengths which could have been used in the service of sport but which seemed so charged with the possibilities of life and death I kept them hidden like a small arsenal of secret weapons. I never swam during the day, but only at night, hugging the shore while mastering ever increasing distances, and I never asked for help, whether moving an overpacked suitcase, a television set, or a boulder. While sport demands a public display of skill, I nourished my endurance, speed, and strength in secret so that I might pass as an acceptable young woman.

Yet these qualities—strength, physical and mental determination, the hard-won comfort that has come with living and loving fully from the heart of my body, the willingness to dig deep into my body's power in moments of love, work, and life—these have survived their time underground. They are not secrets anymore. In the absence of a particular sport to call my own, I live out my strength just as I live out my love of women—openly. The disowned longings for love and public strength were fed, not consciously but mercifully, by springs deep within me that slowly, patiently, and finally worked their way to the surface.

first peace

Barbara Lamblin

"i hope they realize that the olympics are dead"

anais nin, her clear eyes into mine,
and so finally after years of silence
i begin to speak out

so much crowding into my head to say, to vomit up
to scream, to cry quietly
and finally to accept and breathe deep
and feel the weight of it gone
and free at last

i have been insane the past years of my life
and am just now coming into my own self,
my own voice

i was the all american girl, the winner, the champion,
the swell kid, good gal, national swimmer,
model of the prize daughter bringing it home for dad
i even got the father's trophy

i was also jock, dyke, stupid dumb blond
fridgid castrating domineering bitch,
called all these names in silence,
the double standard wearing me down
inside

on the victory stand winning my medals
for father and coach

and perhaps a me deep down somewhere
who couldn't fail because of all the hours
and training and tears
wrapped into an identity of muscle and power
and physical strength
a champion,

not softness and grace

now, at 31, still suffering from the overhead
locker room talk, from the bragging and the swaggering
the stares past my tank suit
insults about my muscles
the fears, the nameless fears
about my undiscovered womanhood
disturbing unknown femininity,
femaleness

feminine power

Part II

Dear Body . . .

The body's radiance
Like the points of a constellation
Beckons to insight.

Conversation by the Body's Light[1]
Jane Cooper

In Greek mythology Gaea, the Earth, came out of darkness cloaked in mystery, the first of the gods, the creative and generative force. Through her body all life came into being, and in her body were the seeds of all that is and all that can be. In the goddess religions of India, the female body is time and space itself, the creative potential of the universe, the mystery beyond pairs of opposites, and the energy that animates consciousness. In women's writings about sport, the female body is the source of dark and light forces. It is the origin of female confinement and control, of repulsion and abuse. Paradoxically, it is also a harbinger of a new, powerful, and harmonious feminine identity and freedom.

The exclusion of women from all of public and creative life, sport and literature included, has been inextricably bound to their bodies—to their procreative role in society and to societal perceptions of their relative physical, intellectual, and emotional inferiority and frailty. As women have attempted to free themselves from the shackles of traditional confinements, they have gone in search of an identity, an autonomous self, and this search has begun with the body. Seeking the freedom to express themselves through writing, they have concurrently struggled to gain freedom for their bodies. Often these struggles seem inextricably connected. In the view of the French feminists, the body is the source of knowledge. Hélène Cixous insists that "Woman must write her body . . . her body must be heard."[2] And Madeleine Gagnon argues that "All we [women] have to do is to let the body flow, from the inside," to move from a state of unconscious excitation directly to a written female text.[3]

The language of the female body has inspired a vast array of attitudes and perceptions in women's literature, ranging from rejection to ambivalence, and to affirmation of the body as a source of power.[4] Women's complex and varied writings about the body in sport literature are filled with conflicts and contradictions, revealing as well a rejection of, ambivalence toward, and, finally, an affirmation of the female body. This evolutionary pattern parallels the historical and chronological role of the female in sport from that of spectator to recreational participant to elite athlete. As the literature reveals, a woman's view of the body is informed, even fashioned it seems, by the experiences of the protagonist, her level of competition, and the intensity of her engagement in sport.

Sometimes it is the excluded spectator, the one not allowed to play, who offers up the most vitriolic assessments of the female body, often rejecting it entirely—beating it up, so to speak, for being the weak vessel she has come to believe it is. In 1969, when women were still largely excluded from the sporting world, Deena Metzger wrote her poem "Little League Women," a brutal rejection of her own femininity as personified in the female spectators at Little League baseball games. She describes the women as "Jap cows" whose "flanks ripple with fat / above thin hoofs" as "They sweat under their breasts." Hers is the rage of the excluded outsider manifested in a rejection of the female body. Anne Rouse's rejection of the female body in "Athletic" is similarly harsh. Her heart—power, "not love," its new priority—is "red and rude to the egg's melancholy, / Sacrificing her gladly." For her, stripping down to the "clean athletic" means becoming the "arrogant boy" who knows only one thing: how to destroy.

Others, such as the weightlifter in Diane Ackerman's "Pumping Iron," internalize Susan Sontag's assertion that "beauty is indeed a form of power" and attempt to control the look of their bodies through exercise. They don't want the "bunchy look / of male lifters" but" a trim waist / two hands might grip / as a bouquet."[5] For Monica Wood's obese character in "Disappearing," controlling her body for the sake of beauty is not the objective; instead, she swims and starves herself in order to wrest control of her body from an abusive husband. Nancy Boutilier's dancer is similarly obsessed. In her youth she pirouetted, flew, and whirled, yet was strapped, laced, and sculpted; now in middle age she sees "herself grow broader, bloated," until "she explodes. / Vomiting anger. . . . wanting to dissolve or, at least, disappear." Both "Disappearing" and "The Dancer" express a disembodied helplessness, an attempt to gain control of one's body either through systematic suicide or frenetic self-flagellation. Diane Wakoski's "Belly Dancer" is freer, yet she too recognizes the control over their bodies that women seek and the role that men play in female bondage.

Once women begin to enter sport as participants, in search of their own identity as athletes, the body seems to be the first connection that they make in this search. By assertively claiming physical space in gyms, swimming pools, arenas, courts, and pool halls, these women contradict anachronous notions of feminine passivity and stasis. As deliberately strong and muscular women, they disturb predominant notions of femininity, gender, and sexuality. It is, as Susan McMaster tells us in "Learning to Ride," a "curious new world / of body direct," in some ways a threatening world where a woman must anxiously ask, as Tobey Kaplan does, "what if I become a body builder?" Most of the sporting protagonists come to understand what many feminists have failed to recognize: the body is not merely a device for gaining control nor simply a mode of transportation or a vehicle for sex.

Instead, as Maxine Silverman asserts, it is a powerful, pounding source of self-discovery and joy.

A woman's body is also a source of reconnection with her self, which is often divided between the need to conform and the need to be free. Ulla Kosonen explains in "A Running Girl: Fragments of My Body History" that it took her many years to understand the nature of her disconnection in childhood. She was an athlete, born an athlete, encouraged in athletics by her parents and brothers. Nonetheless, outside her family, she had to choose between "the rules of the game of a highly appreciated masculine culture—even to the point of scorn for women" and the rules of the game of the feminine culture—"backcombing" her hair, "wearing high-heel shoes and tight skirts, sitting in bars, smoking and flirting with the boys." These were her alternatives: "to behave as a girl or as a boy." Only through sport did she begin to see herself as "an active agent" in the painful "process of constructing [her] own life."

The swimmer in Lorna Crozier's poem wonders too if this role conflict, this division between being a woman and being an athlete can be resolved. In the water, she finds unity as "she becomes one with her body." But the question remains: "If she climbs from the pool / will she become an ordinary woman"?

The intimate bond that athletes have with their bodies becomes yet another source of reconnection for many athletes. Grace Butcher, both a poet and runner, captures the link among sport, body, and identity in her poem "Runner Resumes Training After an Injury." Returning to her routine allows her body to draw "in upon itself," while "old rhythms restore themselves. / Harmonies reappear." As Butcher's poem suggests, this intimate connection with the body is perhaps most profound and disconcerting for injured and aging athletes whose sense of self is so inextricably tied to the body's ability to perform. When their bodies begin to falter, these athletes fear, perhaps, becoming "ordinary women" once again, excluded from the sporting world, forsaken by their own bodies. Judith Hougen's retrospective, "'Muscles' Hougen Comes Out of Softball Retirement" is at once a lament and a commitment to endure for the sake of the unequaled joy of sport as is Barbara Smith's "Late Bloomers," a poem about women coming to softball, their "lifelong joy," later in life, "After biceps and metatarsal joints / Are long past reshaping."

The athlete's sense of her own body as the source of a powerful identity helps her make connections outside of herself with nature—the world's body—one that is continuous with her own. The natural world becomes another source of being and becoming, instead of an alien entity to subdue and control. In "Antarctica Considers Her Explorers," Diane Ackerman identifies with the land region itself, imagining the feverish desire of the explorers who meet with her chilled defiance. For Linda Rose Parkes, it is a limestone cavern, "close" and "dark," that exhilarates her imagination, her connection with all that is "primal" and "new," as "backbone" joins "rockbone." Jean Monahan's "quick breath" is "spiced with the new-mown grass" as she bikes at dusk along the Charles. And Grace Butcher's runner, in "Runner at Twilight," moves "shining, over dim hills," her hair "heavy with fog," her breathing "the force / that spins the universe."

Through sport the body merges with the elements, as the poems on swimming, which conclude this section, reveal. The swimmers, "sweatless / and weightless," temporarily lose "all / their loneliness" in their intimate union with the sea. Nature becomes the gentle lover who embraces the "sweet intrusion" of the female.

[1]"Conversation by the Body's Light" from *Early Ripening: American Women's Poetry Now*, edited by Marge Piercy, 1987 (New York: Pandora).

[2]Hélène Cixous, "The Laugh of the Medusa," in Robyn R. Warhol and Diane Price Herndl, *An Anthology of Literary Criticism* (New Brunswick, NJ: Rutgers University Press, 1991, pp. 334-349).

[3]Madeleine Gagnon, as quoted in Ann Rosalind Jones, "Writing the Body: Toward an understanding of *l'écriture féminine*," in Warhol and Herndl, p. 367.

[4]Alicia Suskin Ostriker, *Stealing the Language: The Emergence of Women's Poetry in America* (Boston: Beacon Press, 1986, p. 97).

[5]Ironically, in attempting to control their bodies through exercise, females have also objectified and sexualized their own bodies.

Little League Women*

Deena Metzger

The women are larger than I
fed on beefsteak and beer
guzzled from nippled bottles
like Jap cows
in a film I saw once.
Their flanks ripple with fat
above thin hoofs.
The women take it from the earth first.
The juices flow up and make milk
to dribble in one and another
goat red mouth.
Yet the kids are thin
as stalks and corn blond.
The women grow
beyond comfort,
nimble only when surprised.
There is nothing sympathetic about them
They sweat under their breasts
and swat flies.
Herding in dumb bulk,
the women are cows
eating grass and men.
What cud there is
once chewed
is spit.

This poem was written in 1969 at a time when I was still afflicted with the self-hate which is a product of the general devaluation of women in our society. At that time, it was difficult to establish the self without dissociating oneself from other women and women's roles. Rather than experiencing sympathy or empathy, I had absorbed the anger, the stereotypes which are directed at women and mothers in order to maintain us in the inferior female role. Since that time, I have come to see that the women whom I portrayed so cruelly were victims, and that the poem is a lie. Now I honor their efforts, my efforts, to survive by whatever means we found in a society which denied us almost all meaningful participation.

I could pretend that the poem was not written, or could write another (I may, someday) but I think it more honest and appropriate to let the poem stand as a sign of my own ignorance and pain at that time. I am pleased that times have changed and the daughters of these women are now playing ball in Little League and that, hopefully, the fathers are selling hot dogs and standing by the sidelines. In time, I expect we will advance sufficiently so that no one is on the sidelines and everyone plays.

Athletic

Anne Rouse

I've stripped down to the clean athletic.
Even blood relatives fall away. Their trace
Is a spidery map of obligations,
And a compass needle, flitting towards normalcy.
I have my deadlines; my coldwater diet.
The early freshness has burned off,
Although the heart works double time.
Power is its priority, not love.
It is red and rude to the egg's melancholy,
Sacrificing her gladly. My face fits me,
These days, like a glove of pig leather,
And hides the arrogant boy
With the fear of long meetings.
The one thing he knows how to do is destroy.

Anne Rouse, *Sunset Grill* (Bloodaxe Books, 1993).

Pumping Iron

Diane Ackerman

> She doesn't want
> the bunchy look
> of male lifters:
> torso an unyielding love knot,
> arms hard at mid-boil.
> Doesn't want
> the dancing bicepses
> of pros.
> Just to run her flesh
> up the flagpole
> of her body,
> to pull her roaming flab
> into tighter cascades,
> machete a waist
> through the jungle
> of her hips,
> a trim waist
> two hands might grip
> as a bouquet.

Reprinted from JAGUAR OF SWEET LAUGHTER: NEW AND SELECTED POEMS, Diane Ackerman, Random House, 1991.

Disappearing

Monica Wood

When he starts in, I don't look anymore, I know what it looks like, what he looks like, tobacco on his teeth. I just lie in the deep sheets and shut my eyes. I make noises that make it go faster and when he's done he's as far from me as he gets. He could be dead he's so far away.

Lettie says leave then stupid but who would want me. Three hundred pounds anyway but I never check. Skin like tapioca pudding, I wouldn't show anyone. A man.

So we go to the pool at the junior high, swimming lessons. First it's blow bubbles and breathe, blow and breathe. Awful, hot nosefuls of chlorine. My eyes stinging red and patches on my skin. I look worse. We'll get caps and goggles and earplugs and body cream Lettie says. It's better.

There are girls there, what bodies. Looking at me and Lettie out the side of their eyes. Gold hair, skin like milk, chlorine or no.

They thought when I first lowered into the pool, that fat one parting the Red Sea. I didn't care. Something happened when I floated. Good said the little instructor. A little redhead in an emerald suit, no stomach, a depression almost, and white wet skin. Good she said you float just great. Now we're getting somewhere. The whistle around her neck blinded my eyes. And the water under the fluorescent lights. I got scared and couldn't float again. The bottom of the pool was scarred, drops of gray shadow rippling. Without the water I would crack open my head, my dry flesh would sound like a splash on the tiles.

At home I ate a cake and a bottle of milk. No wonder you look like that he said. How can you stand yourself. You're no Cary Grant I told him and he laughed and laughed until I threw up.

When this happens I want to throw up again and again until my heart flops out wet and writhing on the kitchen floor. Then he would know I have one and it moves.

So I went back. And floated again. My arms came around and the groan of the water made the tight blondes smirk but I heard Good that's the crawl that's it in fragments from the redhead when I lifted my face. Through the earplugs I heard her skinny voice. She was happy that I was floating and moving too.

Lettie stopped the lessons and read to me things out of magazines. You have to swim a lot to lose weight. You have to stop eating too. Forget cake and ice cream. Doritos are out. I'm not doing it for that I told her but she wouldn't believe me. She couldn't imagine.

Looking down that shaft of water I know I won't fall. The water shimmers and eases up and down, the heft of me doesn't matter I float anyway.

He says it makes no difference I look the same. But I'm not the same. I can hold myself up in deep water. I can move my arms and feet and the water goes behind me, the wall comes closer. I can look down twelve feet to a cold slab of tile and not be afraid. It makes a difference I tell him. Better believe it mister.

Then this other part happens. Other men interest me. I look at them, real ones, not the ones on TV that's something else entirely. These are real. The one with the white milkweed hair who delivers the mail. The meter man from the light company, heavy thick feet in boots. A smile. Teeth. I drop something out of the cart in the supermarket to see who will pick it up. Sometimes a man. One had yellow short hair and called me ma'am. Young. Thin legs and an accent. One was older. Looked me in the eyes. Heavy, but not like me. My eyes are nice. I color the lids. In the pool it runs off in blue tears. When I come out my face is naked.

The lessons are over, I'm certified. A little certificate signed by the redhead. She says I can swim and I can. I'd do better with her body, thin calves hard as granite.

I get a lane to myself, no one shares. The blondes ignore me now that I don't splash the water, know how to lower myself silently. And when I swim I cut the water cleanly.

For one hour every day I am thin, thin as water, transparent, invisible, steam or smoke.

The redhead is gone, they put her at a different pool and I miss the glare of the whistle dangling between her emerald breasts. Lettie won't come over at all now that she is fatter than me. You're so uppity she says. All this talk about water and who do you think you are.

He says I'm looking all right, so at night it is worse but sometimes now when he starts in I say no. On Sundays the pool is closed I can't say no. I haven't been invisible. Even on days when I don't say no it's all right, he's better.

One night he says it won't last, what about the freezer full of low-cal dinners and that machine in the basement. I'm not doing it for that and he doesn't believe me either. But this time there is another part. There are other men in the water I tell him. Fish he says. Fish in the sea. Good luck.

Ma you've lost says my daughter-in-law, the one who didn't want me in the wedding pictures. One with the whole family, she couldn't help that. I learned how to swim I tell her. You should try it, it might help your ugly disposition.

They closed the pool for two weeks and I went crazy. I went there anyway, drove by in the car. I drank water all day.

Then they opened again and I went every day, sometimes four times until the green paint and new stripes looked familiar as a face. At first the water was heavy as blood but I kept on until it was thinner and thinner, just enough to hold me up. That was when I stopped with the goggles and cap and plugs, things that kept the water out of me.

There was a time I went the day before a holiday and no one was there. It was echoey silence just me and the soundless empty pool and a lifeguard behind the glass. I lowered myself so slow it hurt every muscle but not a blip of water not a ripple not one sound and I was under in that other quiet, so quiet some tears got out, I saw their blue trail swirling.

The redhead is back and nods, she has seen me somewhere. I tell her I took lessons and she still doesn't remember.

This has gone too far he says I'm putting you in the hospital. He calls them at the pool and they pay no attention. He doesn't touch me and I smile into my pillow, a secret smile in my own square of the dark.

Oh my God Lettie says what the hell are you doing what the hell do you think you're doing. I'm disappearing I tell her and what can you do about it not a blessed thing.

For a long time in the middle of it people looked at me. Men. And I thought about it. Believe it, I thought. And now they don't look at me again. And it's better.

I'm almost there. Almost water.

The redhead taught me how to dive, how to tuck my head and vanish like a needle into skin, and every time it happens, my feet leaving the board, I think, this will be the time.

The Dancer

Nancy Boutilier

> She had been a dancer too long.
> Laced in silken slippers,
> wrapped in leotards and
> legends of handsome princes
> who admired supple arms and
> sculpted
> thinness.

Strapped in her own grace and beauty,
everyday flying, whirling, eyeing herself
in a thousand mirrored flashes of flesh and limb
across wooden floor, reflecting back
wrist, neck, thigh, spine-erect and head held high.
She was everything, everywhere,
beautiful.

Recitals and curtain calls behind,
years later, she camouflages thickened thighs
in tents of floral patterns and tie-dyes.
Battling female form, hiding Rubenesque shape,
torturing herself with store fronts,
she pretends to admire new fashions,
while mannequins mock her
with their posed perfection.
Searching for styles,
she tries on clothes
three times the size she wore
when she kept herself starved
and rib-caged
and beautiful.

She pirouettes before changeroom mirrors,
cursing the color, the cut, the fit.
Folding arms to cover breasts
she never asked for.
Wanting to smooth the cottage cheese flesh
that has stolen away the lines
of muscular length.
Not able to undress
far enough.
She buys nothing;
no one is selling

what she
wants.

False solace in an ice cream sundae,
followed by a piece of double-chocolate layer cake,
and later still, a dozen oatmeal cookies.
Returning to her bare apartment
where bathroom mirror tells her
the room is empty no longer.
Too full.
Seeing herself grow broader, bloated,
her imagination steals away sight.
She visions a thin self
leashed in a body
not her own.

Alien costume
constricting
further,
until
she explodes.
Vomiting anger.
Retching between hope and none.
Alternating silence and echoing cough,
as if to rid her of herself,
her imperfection,
her self.
Purging to the point of hollowness,
wanting to dissolve or, at least, disappear,
the dancer slowly lifts her head,
leans forward on ceramic sink
and sees her flushed face steadying
before her on the shelf.
Washing residue from lip,

she sees in the mirror
that she is
still
there.

Belly Dancer

Diane Wakoski

Can these movements which move themselves
be the substance of my attraction?
Where does this thin green silk come from that covers
    my body?
Surely any woman wearing such fabrics
would move her body just to feel them touching every
    part of her.

Yet most of the women frown, or look away, or laugh stiffly.
They are afraid of these materials and these movements
    in some way.
The psychologists would say they are afraid of
    themselves, somehow.
Perhaps awakening too much desire—
that their men could never satisfy?

So they keep themselves laced and buttoned and made up
in hopes that the framework will keep them stiff enough
    not to feel
the whole register.
In hopes that they will not have to experience that
    unquenchable desire for rhythm and contact.

If a snake glided across this floor
most of them would faint or shrink away.
Yet that movement could be their own.
That smooth movement frightens them—
awakening ancestors and relatives to the tips of the
    arms and toes.

So my bare feet
and my thin green silks
my bells and finger cymbals
offend them—frighten their old-young bodies.
While the men simper and leer—
glad for the vicarious experience and exercise.
They do not realize how I scorn them:
or how I dance for their frightened,
unawakened, sweet
women.

Learning to Ride

Susan McMaster

This, then
to let go,
let the body
move the hands.
drag the brain
without holding on
to words, language,
the ways I've learned
so well to define
and subdue

"Learning to Ride" reprinted from *Learning to Ride* by permission of Quarry Press Inc.

the twang of nerve ends,
pulse of arteries,
clench and release
of the bundles of fiber
I name to myself *muscle*,
as if the word alone
brings into being
the smooth working humps
under unregarded skin
that carry me,
have carried me
through every single day
unnoticed, till now—

Before I entered this
curious new world
of body direct
it was naming alone
that stood for all else,
the flap of the tongue,
labile and strong,
the only muscular motion
I'd learned to control.
Held thus, at tongue's length,
the world made sense,
a black and white tale
patterned in words
I could stand back to read.
Tear them up, pull them away,
rip them into tendrils
coiling underfoot
and find—

A steady pulsing region
of thick grounded motion,
a shadowed wildland
of caverns, valleys,
always changing footing,
where I move like a tracker
from childhood tales,
like a cat
like a deer,
to the beat of tissues
flex of sinews
spring of limbs
loose, aware,
learning to learn
a whole new language,
of heat and sweat
power and flow
of pushing the body
till it trembles, groans,
learning to discard
the ancient metaphors
of love and soul
and existential pain,
for the uncoded strophes
of pulse and breath

Learning to ride
the muscular heart
the solid bone

So the mind learns to fly
to match the heart's leap
so the heart soars at last
across the mind's divide

what if I become a body builder?

Tobey Kaplan

1 my body the tree
2 my body the jar
3 my body the saving grace
4 my body the dancing flesh
5 my body well-defined
6 my body looks mean
7 my body the tight belly they want
8 my body rippling flesh
9 my body carries around a tape measure
10 my body with barbells in the trunk of the car
11 my body one nice hunk of a lady
12 my body the prize winner
13 my body the object
14 my body deformed
15 my body redefined
16 my body in the flash of light bulbs
17 my body the champion
18 my body feel my biceps
19 my body the crowd ogles
20 my body well-oiled
21 my body loud smell
22 my body I take home
23 my body this strong woman
24 my body curls up alone
25 my body carries the weight of dreams

Hard-Hitting Woman: Winning the Serve

Maxine Silverman

Whereas before the body was useful for conveying one
through town, or for lying down beside another one,
I have found a new use for mine.
It was there all the time, Platonic,
waiting. Volleyball.
Still, no one was more surprised
at the strength pounding down my powerline arm,
the ball blasted over the net.

There is pleasure standing at the baseline.
I bounce the ball once or twice—the large white roundness
against the golden gym floor, the taut sound on the court.
I look over the crouched bodies
of my teammates through the net to their raised arms,
their tense faces, to the place
I will aim. Pleasure
in bending slightly,
stepping into the serve, running up for the return.
My hands are clasped, a double fist.
I want them to blast it back. I want to hit it
over, blast after blast of this right good fist,
set it leap spike dive keep it up up over.

The red shirt sticks darkly down the spine, rank under the arms.
Wipe the brow, ah, living proof of hard hitting, the blood
flush under the skin, the muscles quivering, cooling down.
Laid bare, the torso gleams the belly the thighs
to stand there in glowing fatigue,
warm water sliding down the sweaty ribs,

Reprinted, by permission, from Maxine Silverman, 1984, "Hard-Hitting Woman." First published in *Atalanta*, Sandra Martz, editor. Papier Mache Press.

the hand flexing to a fist, to a hand, the soap
white and smooth,
the mind returning to the body, the body.

A Running Girl: Fragments of My Body History

Ulla Kosonen

Once upon a time there was a running girl. She lived in Central Finland in a middle-class family; it was the 1960s. This is the story of that girl—who is me.

I have always had an identity of a runner. Sometimes I have been proud of it, sometimes I have tried to deny it and to forget it. Today, I am not quite sure what a running girl represents. Am I a subject or object of my own life? How should I listen to myself, to everything that happened in our court-yard; how do I cope with all the contradictions and conflicts that were instilled in me by the environment, my brothers and my parents?

The discovery of the research method that is known as memory work[1] made me realize the great importance of childhood events in the identity-formation of the sexual human being. The body is a central point in this process. Looking back at my running period, at the emotions involved, and particularly at the tensions and contradictions between my own experiences and the social expectations concerning the body of a girl or a woman, I think I can shed some light on the question: What is the social process of growing up to be a woman? What is the role and meaning of sport in this process?

My childhood's courtyard: "Big Iita" and my brothers.

We lived in a terraced house on the lake, surrounded by the woods. The road ended in our front yard. In the middle of the yard we had a swing and a sand pit. It was an ideal place for outdoor sports and games. In the winter, we used to ski to school, or we went skiing on self-made tracks; we also went skating on the lake, and built our own ski-jumps. In the summer we arranged swimming competitions—the winner was who swam most often during the day. We used to play ten sticks, baseball, cops and robbers, ball games; we also did athletics.

I began to take it all more seriously at the stage where we started listening to sports commentaries on the radio. Uprights appeared in our yard and a long and triple jump were fixed next to the sand pit. Starting holes were dug out in the road. We even set up our own sports club; it was called the *Resistance.* I was the author of the club flag. We all worked together to make membership cards, and the Board members (who had their meetings in the boiler room) were all properly elected.

The most important (and as far as I remember the only) function of the *Resistance* was to organize the top event of the summer: the athletics competition among the different courtyards. Our team consisted of my two brothers, a boy from the neighbourhood, and myself. I was the only girl in the Games. It was really an exciting event, a class struggle par excellence within a small industrial community: we were the bosses' puppies, our opponents represented the workers' brats. As Norbert Elias would have it,[2] we coped with all the aggression very nicely in a civilized way by means of sport.

I was a shark in the sprint and long jump, beating almost all the boys in the neighbourhood. To me this was nothing special; I was used to playing with the boys. I criticized my younger brother for "running like a woman," his arms waving on the side. I was our yard's *Voitto Hellsten*. [3] At that time there were no female sportsmen who could have served as a young girl's idol. Therefore she adopted the rules of the game of a highly appreciated masculine culture—even to the point of scorn for women. How would I have looked on my brothers if they had taken on some "feminine" hobby, such as knitting?

The purpose of the factory race was to do away with class differences and create a sense of solidarity: "We all are the members of the same *Valmet* family."[4] Running competitions were usually the top event of our small community. Perhaps it was because it was I who won the whole class. I remember some of the races very well. Once I came in second. That would have been perfectly alright if it hadn't been for my father's explanations as to why his daughter was such a disappointment; she had been eating too much sweets. For the first time in my life I understood the importance of outer appearances. I was too fat. Fat people are supposed to be ashamed of themselves.

I left the world of innocence and entered the world of social norms. My body was no longer neutral; it had become a seedbed of sexual codes. I became more and more sensitive to comments concerning my body, especially those that came from my brothers. I was called "Big Iita," "Fairy the Fat" or "Tamara Press." Well, I must admit that I was big for my age, but those nicknames made me even bigger. And worst of all, my behaviour did nothing to lessen the impression. In the rough and harsh sort of way that I had learned from the boys, I tried to hide my embarrassment about my body.

"Chest out stomach in!"

My posture was absolutely terrible. There had to be more than a physical explanation. I felt I was too big and too clumsy, so I tried to make myself smaller. And on top of everything else I was ashamed of my breasts that were now beginning to grow. It took a long time before I agreed to wear a bra, in spite of my mother's insistence. Many of my friends at school were in exactly the opposite situation: they were stuffing their sweaters and bras with all sorts of padding just to make their breasts look bigger.

I have now recognized myself in the studies of Birgit Palzkill, [5] who is concerned with the development of the identity of sporting women. These women have usually solved their contradictions of identity in girlhood— i.e., they have coped with the fact that they were to be made for men—by choosing a hobby in which they could retain their manlike characteristics for as long as possible.

However, not wearing a bra created another problem. I could no longer remain *sexless*. As my breasts were getting bigger they were also attracting more and more attention, although that I certainly did not want. I remember once when I was walking in the street in town and a man sitting in his car pointed at my breasts and made a paunchy gesture; I felt dirty.

Looking at old pictures from those days, I can remember the past and the forgotten 'me-thinks,' events and feelings. They also bring back some painful memories. I still blush when I see the picture of "Big Iita," aged ten. I can still hear the comments about the "old maid," the mischievious laughter. What's so funny about the picture? Beyond all the comments and laughter, the information about the set of measures given to the girl's or woman's body is revealed, as Frigga Haug and her research team [6] have observed. We all know what is appropriate and what is inappropriate.

The picture of the Resistance provides a characteristic model of the male and female posture. According to *Marianne Wex*, [7] the most distinctive characteristics of the female posture are: legs tightly together, feet pointing forward and arms close along the body. The male posture is characterized by a broader position of legs, feet pointing outwards and arms off the body. Along with sex role behaviour, posture expresses power or weakness; it is a distinguishing sex phenomenon. The female body expresses smallness, subordination, harmlessness, apology, quietness, hiding.

My father was a sportsman.

My father was a runner; his event was the 400 metres. When we were young, my father used to take us along to the running track where he did his training or took part in the races. Later, I remember being immensely proud of my father taking part in our yard's baseball matches as a pitcher. He used to wear his old faded sweat suit that dated back to his good old sporting days. We used to go together to the races and baseball matches and to listen to the radio commentaries. We were all sports crazy. However, I was the only one who had actually become a competing athlete.

Towards the end of the 1960s when I started rebelling, it was mostly against my father. I mocked his "holy sports." I began my studies at the Faculty of Sport and Health Sciences, and for the first time the values of competitive sports were subjected to open criticism. Afterwards I realized that I was trying to win my father's approval by keeping up the running.

Being a girl, I have never managed to become as smart as the boys; but I was definitely better at running.

I also used to keep my father company when he went fishing. My brothers weren't at all keen on net fishing. I was still quite young when I realized that fishing was not a suitable hobby for a girl. It is impossible to keep clean when you're fishing. This is perhaps why I always tried to tell everyone in different situations how good I was at fishing. I didn't want to be a weak fine lady. I had been living under a spell of self-delusion for a long time and I imagined that the boys I used to fall for would not have liked all those ladylike tricks; they would have liked my sprightly and honest being. As far as I was concerned all other girls were just acting; I was the only honest one.

I deprived myself of something feminine by failing to understand that not everything "feminine" was mere acting. There is a lot that can be precious and good in "being feminine." It took me several decades to understand this. In the search for my own feminine ego I had to recall my childhood, particularly those events that had elicited in me a sort of disrespect for everything that was feminine.

I have to admit that my father had always appreciated my vigour. But I had never been able to win the boys. As far as professions were concerned my father expected that his sons would become something like physicians or engineers or lawyers; as for me, professions didn't really matter. A P.E. teacher would have been just fine because that way I could also have taken care of the home. Was this why I dropped out of teacher training to become a researcher instead?

Was I a tomboy? American women's studies [8] have made critical observations of tomboyism as the main factor of "unfeminine behaviour." In the 1970s, the number of sporting women in America suddenly increased by a phenomenal 700%, implying a serious threat to the position of men. Sporting women were labelled as abnormal, unfeminine, lesbian. Experiments carried out to prove that their "abnormality" was due to their childhood when they were allowed to play with boys. However, tomboyism has always been more acceptable than girlish behaviour in boys. Boys have never had the second choice that I was given: shall I wear trousers or a skirt?

Towards men's sport, with help from my mother.

It was my mother who brought us into contact with the real world of sport; it was she who took us to the school that was organized by a sports club. Rather than playing games or engaging in sports we were now given systematic training; our skills were systematically evaluated and classified according to a national table. From the very outset they put the talented in one group and the non-talented in another group. The talented took part in the competitions organised by the sports clubs.

My dreams were fulfilled. First, I had become a member of the club; then I got my first real track shoes as well as the club tracksuit, and on top of everything else I was nominated to represent the club in the competitions. I remember the first time we travelled out of town to compete for the club, some 20 km away. We had our own bus. A representative of the club gave us instructions, telling us to represent the colours of the club with honour. It was great to belong to the party. I felt important.

There were not very many members in the club, but I did get to know some other girls whom I met in training. I enjoyed being at the sports ground; it was a nice place, and it made our own yard seem ridiculous. I also met some other young people at the sports ground, and even saw real sportsmen practicing. They were men of course; we, girls, swarmed around our idols like flies, trying to get some attention. My mother encouraged me, even urged me to go in for sports. She never came down to the sports ground like my father often did to do the timing, but she became my mental trainer. I remember one particular occasion that betrayed my mother's expectations. I didn't want to go to our weekend training camp because I had my period. I didn't say anything to my mother; "that" was something you never mentioned. She blamed me for being lazy. In any case I didn't go; but later I felt guilty because I had failed to fulfill my mother's expectations.

My mother was a tough woman. She always said that if you wanted something hard enough you can get it, no matter what the obstacles in the way. But could athletics be suitable for a girl? She has never managed to express a single protest against her own role of a full-time mother. Who knows, perhaps she found some compensation through her athletic daughter.

What sort of memories do I have of my sporting days? I was 12-17 years old. Our training camps took us hundreds of kilometres away from home, creating a definite sense of freedom in the life of a young girl. I felt I was privileged when I was allowed to take time off from school. The pain in the muscles after hard training was a fantastic sensation. But the training camps were more than that; they were a meeting place for young people. We also used to go dancing in the village nearby. Dancing was scaring and tempting at one and the same time. I was awfully shy. In the winter our weekly training sessions were held in an indoor hall. The smell of soil in the hall was familiar and safe. I was proud of having all these goings-on.

Travel to the competitions was an escape from everyday routine; it was just like a picnic. The feeling of excitement was quite overwhelming. Then, on the way back, the feeling of release and relaxation, a boisterous feeling. The bus full of young, energetic people. In spite of these many pleasant memories, there is also one incident I remember that through my eagerness caused me considerable embarrassment. It was during the autumn athletic games that were held at my own home ground. There was just one participant in the women's 100 m sprint—me. I was asked whether I'd like to run. First, I interpreted the question as a request. I thought that the event must be an important part of the programme, so I agreed to run. What an absurd situation! A competition with one participant! That 100 metres seemed to last for ages.

Competency through sport—impossible for a girl?

In the third form I had to change my friendly little country school for an elite school in town. I felt childish, clumsy and stupid amongst my adult looking classmates. I used to be the best in our class, but now I was just average. My running skills became even more important to me.

My P.E. teacher soon recognized my talent and enthusiasm and put my name down for the school competition. From that moment on, my whole life centered on that single event: this was my chance to show my classmates! Well, I got the attention I wanted, but it was not exactly what I had expected. Women's sports were not appreciated, and girls going in for sports had always been something of an oddity. I often found myself engaged in discussions on whether or not sports were suitable for women. Somewhere beneath the surface, there still persisted the old prejudices that sport had detrimental effects on the female organism. And then there were the masculine effects of sport; a sporting girl becomes masculine and undesirable. [9]

In those days the image of an ideal woman was changing quite profoundly from the model of Marilyn Monroe to the skinny model of Twiggy. Muscles were not tolerated in either case. In the school competitions, I also wanted to make an impression on the boy who was idolized by all girls in our class. But he just laughed at me; what do I, Tamara Press, really want . . .
Our old math teacher Aatu used to award a silver candle holder to the school's best sportsman. At the same time, moved to tears, he used to give a speech, the prize in his shaking hands:
"This candle holder is like a man. When empty, it is just a cold object, like the human shell. But when you put a candle in it and light the candle, a man comes to life. Sport does the same thing; it is a flame of life."
This used to be the greatest moment of my life, but I had to hide my feelings; everyone else was laughing at this old fool.

From a sporting girl to a woman.

I am not linking together my physical memories of running with my history of running. I don't know whether I actually enjoyed moving; in fact I think I don't really know what was going on in my body. The body is usually not appreciated; it is thinking that counts. However, running brought to my mind all that I had experienced as a girl and a woman compared to the social norms.

I emphasized my sport-mindedness. I underestimated (but secretly envied) the girls of my same age who were making themselves up, backcombing their hair, wearing high-heel shoes and tight skirts, sitting in bars, smoking and flirting with the boys. When they were running after boys, I was running with the dog. To strengthen my self-assurance, I would polish my prizes that were on show in the bookshelf.

The situation began to change in grammar school. I started to behave like the other girls. I had two close girlfriends with whom I used to spend most of my spare time. We used to go dancing or for a walk in town. We talked about clothes and slimming. In grammar school slimming became a major project for me; I no longer wanted to be "Big Iita." I stopped running for a while.

Legs are not vehicles.

For a runner, and for me as well, legs are the most important part of the body. I have always liked beautiful socks and I have also knitted long lace stockings. Reports on the 'leg project' by the research team led by Frigga Haug[10], touched me in a very special way. They had recalled my own experiences.

We all know what beautiful legs look like, what the requirements are. Well, my legs met almost all of those requirements. But there was one problem: I had black hair on my legs. Since I was a teenager I had been shaving my legs with my father's razor and using all sorts of lotions. But one experience made me seriously consider whether there was any point in suffering for the sake of beauty—as my mother used to say.

I was 20. My parents were celebrating their 50th anniversary, and we were going to have a big party. Once again, my attention was drawn to the disgusting hair that showed through my stockings. I decided to get rid of the problem once and for all and arranged for an appointment with a chiropodist. I had heard that specialists used certain agents that could possibly keep leg hair away for some while. What actually happened was this: a thick layer of sticky wax was spread all over my legs, covered with a long tissue stocking, and a strip of cloth was pulled off. The removal of a sticking plaster when I was a child just didn't begin to compare with the pain; I clenched my teeth but I couldn't complain. After the operation my legs were virtually on fire burning red and swollen. Finally, I have accepted my leg hair. It is difficult to admit that it happened just because I wanted to be beautiful.

The body of a running girl.

When sprinting I had no time to think about my body—do I have a potbelly, are my breasts bouncing? When I was running fast, I felt light. I was not big and clumsy, but I was a fairy, the part I could never have got in the school play. Many woman friends of mine have admitted that they, too, have suffered pretty much from their role of goblin at school. Afterwards it seems strange that I was distressed by the idea of having to walk in town with legs that felt like blocks of wood, but then was perfectly comfortable running in front of thousands of people. No wonder that I am still looking for that runner-girl who may be hidden somewhere inside me.

My revolt by means of sport against the restrictions and standards imposed on the woman's body now seemed to make sense, even though I was constantly confused during my sporting days. At that time I had but two alternatives: to behave as a girl or as a boy. Many woman researchers have shown that the dressing and moving of girls according to the norms often prevents them from finding all the potential of their own body, even from breathing at full capacity. [11] However, this does not help when we are aware of the fact that for hundreds of years men have wanted to keep women under control, one form of which is represented by prescriptions concerning women and movement. We are attached to the past, to the situations in which we have become members of society, by means of countless fibres. Those fibres form part of our personality, and the deconstruction and reconstruction of them may become a life-time's work.

These memories were a starting-point for my better understanding of how I had become a sexual human being through my own body. By telling this story I have become aware of the fact that I am not only an object but an active agent in the process of constructing my own life.

Notes

[1] *Haug*, 1983.

[2] *Elias*, 1986.

[3] *Voitto Hellsten* was a famous Finnish sprinter in the 1950s.

[4] *Valmet* was a major state-owned engineering company.

[5] *Palzkill*, 1990.

[6] *Haug*, 1983.

[7] *Wex*, 1979.

[8] See e.g. *Lenskyj*, 1987.

[9] In the 1970s the focal concern of women's studies in physical culture was to undo these myths, see the chapter *"Physiology and Social Attitudes"* in *Twin*, 1979, pp. 5-75, *Oglesby*, 1978, and *Boutilier and SanGiovanni*, 1983.

[10] *Haug*, 1983.

[11] See e.g. *Wex*, 1979; *Young*, 1989.

References

Elias, N., Dunning, E., *Quest Of Excitement Sport and Leisure in Civilizing Process*. Oxford, 1986.

Boutilier, M., SanGiovanni, L., (Eds.), *The Sporting Woman*, Champaign, 1983.

Haug, F. (Ed.), Frauenformen 2. Sexualisierung der Körper, in: *Argument*, Sonderband. A S 90, Berlin, 1983.

Lenskyj, H., Female Sexuality and Women Sport, in: *Women's Study International Forum*. 1987/4, p. 381-393.

Oglesby, C.A. (Ed.), *Women and Sport: From Myth to Reality*, Philadelphia, 1978.

Palzkill, B., *Zwischen Turnschuh and Stöckelschuh. Die Entwicklung lesbischer Identität im Sport*, Oldenburg, 1990.

Twin, S.L., (Ed.), *Out of the Bleachers*, New York, 1979.

Wex, M., *"Weibliche" und "Männliche" Körpersprache als Folge Patriarchalischer Machtverhältnisse*, Hamburg, 1979.

Young, I., Throwing like a Girl. A Phenomenology of Feminine Body, in: A. Jeffner I. Young, (Eds.), *The Thinking Muse. Feminism and Modern French Philosophy*. Bloomington and Indianapolis, 1989, p. 51-70.

The Swimmer

Lorna Crozier

In the solarium pool
she separates like milk
into what is heavy and what is not,
splits like sunlight
passed through a prism.

On the bottom,
dolphin-grey and graceful
her shadow swims.
Eyes closed,
it knows only one thing,
something she can't articulate
but it has to do with motion.

On the ceiling made of glass
her reflection looks back at her,
not with recognition
but with slight surprise
as her head, arms and legs
form the five points of a star.

In between, the part of her
that feels the warmth of water,
her muscles' stretch and pull,
repeats the strokes
she learned as a child.

She wonders how she'll bring
these parts back together.

Inventing the Hawk by Lorna Crozier, 1992. Used by permission, McClelland & Stewart, Inc. The Canadian Publishers.

If she climbs from the pool
will she become an ordinary woman
with children waiting, her darkness
folded like a scarf and tucked away,
her reflection moving to the bathroom mirror?

She hesitates to swim to the ladder,
feel the steel rungs
press against her soles. Maybe
this is how a woman drowns,
raising her arm three times,
not a call for help
but a gesture of acknowledgement,
of recognition

as she becomes one
with her body,
one with her shadow,
one with her drifting star.

Runner Resumes Training After an Injury

Grace Butcher

When I run, my body
draws in upon itself,
hones down.
My bones are within reach;
old rhythms restore themselves.

Harmonies reappear.
I sing my own comeback.
Each rise and fall of breath

has so many notes
like a chord of music.

Something in me tunes in
on my own clearest frequencies;
something resonates with a.clarity,
the high perfect sound
a crystal bell might make.

I am inside this fine body,
tending to the miles as they pass.
I fit perfectly inside my skin;
nothing is left over. Nothing!
The miles become perfect as I finish them.

I can run only where I am,
each step a new place of its own.
Nothing is more right than this:
the grass, the sky, and my body
in between, moving and beautiful.

"Muscles" Hougen Comes Out of Softball Retirement

Judith Hougen

Years ago, I was so lovely
at second, diving for the fly in the ninth
kneecaps pounding packed infield in a hard
tumble, raising a pregnant glove above
my grimed-out body. A play so solid, you could
display it on a coffee table in your head
for days. My left hand is again an elephant

ear of old leather, a second set of hot dog
bun fingers shined dark and smooth in spots from
a thousand line drives to right snagged
on the bounce or plucked like an overdue apple
from flight. These days, it's difficult to cash in
my body for trophies. The nights are long
hot baths and "Liniment" Hougen
smells more and more like my true name.
With my knees two small sloshing buckets
of pain, I stalk the second base line, spit
for effect, crouch down with palms against
patella and wait the play at second
that's still second nature. Left foot
on the bag, left arm stretching
for the grass-streaked splendor of the ball
swacked to left, I brace for it
lean every bone towards the catch
the chance for one thick
leather hand to reach into that much beauty.

Late Bloomers

Barbara Smith

Some have three strikes before they begin,
Being offspring of farmers or portfolios
Rather than famous first basemen,
Being allergic to competition and grass,
Being women instead of men,
Thus coming late to your lifelong joy
After biceps and metatarsal joints
Are long past reshaping,

Body and soul growing closer and closer
While body and spirit go separate ways.
Being three times past Olympic condition,
They still share your championship joy
And every day, every game, the same good intentions.

Antarctica Considers Her Explorers

Diane Ackerman

I
Brash as brash ice, they flock to me
though I chill and defy them;
keen as migrating birds they come,
all white like the kelp goose,
and too hot, too frail, too soft-skinned—
to put it bluntly, too *animal*—
for my small eternities of ice.

They come to me by water, by sled,
by sky, over seas heaving like frightened children.
I have seen them rip apart the tight skirts
of the rain, and plunge through ice packs
dense as thunder. Yet they come to me
dressed in the plumage of birds—
orange and red—like birds they nest
among twigs and sing songs,
strut, flap their arms in the cold.

They would sooner bare their souls
than their flesh, so they come to me
swathed in fur, down and leather

they strip from lesser beasts,
and walk through my crystal orchards
quilted in tight posses of life—
needing the world's full bestiary to face
my staggering chasms, my cascading glare.

They come to me during the longest night
they can find, a night elaborate and deep,
with none of the pastel preambles of twilight,
to lie long in my flesh and fill me with fire.
Bringing their starry eyes, their cunning,
their hot blood, their beautiful fever,
they pour like lava through my limbs,
pour slowly, from one shore to the other,
and leave me shaking with unearthly calm.

They are coming now—I feel their pulse
rapid as wings beating at my fingertips,
taste their salty skin, as they sweat hard
under layers of goose down and silk.
Lusty as waterfalls, tough as granite,
they have come to seize me, chaste and sparkling,
with their small arms and huge hearts,
these madmen who yearn like the sun,
torrid, molten, who mood like chameleons,
these fierce dreamers, these bright blades.

To A Woman Caving

Linda Rose Parkes

Backbone to rockbone; the
pitch of commitment, the
total cave;

relief tempered with
fear.

The unmoving contours of
rockface, the
grip and
flex of limbs; and
everywhere the
water echo into limestone
caverns;

stalagmites and
stalactites, the flower-glass of
stems,
embedded in this
cove, this close dark,

your own exhilarated
blood and
taliswoman limbs,
primal, new

Biking at Dusk along the Charles

Jean Monahan

> At this hour, this late in summer,
> night air sweats with a pulpy chill.
> The sky hews open like a ripe-bellied melon,
> tender, juiceslick seeds overrunning
> the teablack edges of the eastern half.
> Above the glinting pedals, my knees
> paddle the air's whitewater: every muscle
> hunched to a quiver, my quick breath
> spiced with the new-mown grass. The river
> shifts its mood toward sleep, collects
> under bridges and curls against banks,
> wanly indulgent of the loose-knit boats
> that slap and moan into its mossy shanks.
> I gather speed with the dying light,
> warming to my own heat as I turn and leave
> the river. Cattails sough
> with wading wind. The moon unknots
> her silk bedgown and softly slips
> down amongst men.

Runner at Twilight

Grace Butcher

> I move, shining, over dim hills.
> The grass unwinds a blur of rivers
>   on the bottom of the night;
> I cross with no bridges.

My hair is heavy with fog,
and my breathing is the force
   that spins the universe.
There is more to the spectrum
   than was supposed:
beyond violet are endless miles
of impossible colors.

Swimmers

Ruth Harriet Jacobs

We are sweatless
and weightless
purity personified
our rhythmic motion
comforting as we
unite with fluids
of our individual
and species birth.

Runners on roads
skiers on slopes
chasers of balls
we are grateful
you leave oceans
lakes and pools
for those knowing
how body merges
intimately with
perfect medium
so even those
unlucky or clumsy

everywhere else
glide and hide
gracefully into
crystal refuge . . .

The Nude Swim

Anne Sexton

On the southwest side of Capri
we found a little unknown grotto
where no people were and we
entered it completely
and let our bodies lose all
their loneliness.

All the fish in us
had escaped for a minute.
The real fish did not mind.
We did not disturb their personal life.
We calmly trailed over them
and under them, shedding
air bubbles, little white
balloons that drifted up
into the sun by the boat
where the Italian boatman slept
with his hat over his face.

Water so clear you could
read a book through it.
Water so buoyant you could
float on your elbow.

I lay on it as on a divan.
I lay on it just like
Matisse's *Red Odalisque.*
Water was my strange flower.
One must picture a woman
without a toga or a scarf
on a couch as deep as a tomb.

The walls of that grotto
were everycolor blue and
you said, "Look! Your eyes
are seacolor. Look! Your eyes
are skycolor." And my eyes
shut down as if they were
suddenly ashamed.

Swimming the Body's Water

Lucia Cordell Getsi

In the beginning, chill
I can never anticipate seeps
through bone, and more alone
than I could ever imagine, my unschooled
arms stroke the water, cold
that swells the heart, distends the tight
arteries, teases heat from opened
pores as water and skin begin
a mating

and only when I fill
with cold so natural the arms flinch

against the rasp of air, when time
measures in laps and the counting
stops, does my mouth work open
and shut with water, narrow dam
of teeth and tongue protect lungs that ache
for more than vapor, for water that slides
across my throat in search of gills

then this body drilled by water
remembers the sea that spilled
like blood toward a lifting sun
how the legs opened and closed
on brine so soft they barely sensed
the inward flow, how it emptied,
surged again, so that the legs forget
the land, the loosened hips grow wide with sea,
the body swims the sea inside

The Swimmer

Angela Gatteschi
Translated by Ruth Griffiths

When from the forest,
Sprayed with a fine sweat
The sweet maid returns to her fine chorus,
There stirs in her a vague desire
To refresh her limbs—oh sweet balm,
In the clear cool wave.
With her soft hand
She gathers up her golden hair
And from her tired and weary flank

Draws the shift and the finer veil,
Appearing quite naked
A new Aphrodite amidst the Sea.

At such sweet intrusion
The waters laugh and vie
To rush and kiss her breast,
And she with the fine arc
Of her arms scatters the clear
And foaming wave: in pure delight
At such fair apparition,
The mute inhabitants of the
Crystalline humours
Feel their hearts stir;
And rapt once more, deeply entranced,
The Winds stay their wings, and,
Enamoured, hover and gaze.

Part III

Woman and Nature: The Bond With the Hunted

Dip me from the water.
Kiss the gash. Say *fish*.
Say *woman*.

Song of the Fisherman's Lover
Roseann Lloyd

Pam Houston argues in her book *On Hunting* that women view hunting in circular and spatial terms, like the hunt itself, moving around it while viewing it from all sides. Perhaps because women have been at once objective in their role as outsiders and subjective in their ability to empathize with hunted creatures, their views on hunting, fishing, bullfighting, and falconry are unique, far different from the traditional approaches which pit hunter against hunted in a struggle for domination. It is evident that females are never indifferent to killing, even when they are the hunters themselves, and rarely is killing a cause for joyful celebration.

In many of these works, females connect with the animal world by identifying or sympathizing with the hunted and chased, understanding that woman is, as Anna Wickham called her, "the contemplative quarry," accustomed to being the prize of the contest, the hunted, and the captured. Because women align themselves with animals, many writers passionately and vehemently react to the brutality of hunting, chasing, and killing by rejecting it completely. Others, however, come to understand the complexity of its appeal, its dualities, even accepting, at times, its cruelty.

As we have seen before, the earliest British works on hunting in the 15th and 17th centuries are again written by female outsiders who were at the time chronicling the sporting pastimes of the male nobility. In some of the later works, authors continue the earlier tradition of observing men in sport, and some, like Mrs. J. B. Worley, cannot ignore the humor involved. In her mock epic poem, "The Mighty Hunter," she parodies the bravado of her husband who, after a completely unsuccessful hunting expedition, brags to his friends, "Boys, I got the limit." Others, such as Elizabeth Jennings, are intrigued by the patience and longing of the fisherman, the metaphorical possibilities for "a whole way of living" that spring from their "secret desires" and "sense / Of order outwardly," their ability to be "satisfied with little" yet "not surprised" by bounty.

In much of this literature women explore their own intimate bond with hunted creatures. Nancy Boutilier knows that she and her captive fish "are caught / in the same / net," and Kay Ryan feels the odd hook that "stays in the flesh." May Sarton's falconer is "hooded" like her falcon, and Edna St. Vincent Millay wonders what the huntsman's quarry will be—a deer, a fox, or she?[1] It is no wonder that in her now-famous poem, "The Fish,"[2] Elizabeth Bishop "let the fish go," or that Olive Senior's little girls in, "Birdshooting Season," whisper "Fly Birds Fly."

Animals in women's literature—such as Sylvia Plath's raging bull in "The Goring," and Joyce Carol Oates's injured deer in "The Buck"—are often hunted and vulnerable males. Gabriela Melinescu mourns the loss of one intriguing fish who risked death and skirted "poles," only to finally make his way to "the world of fishes." In Simonne Jacquemard's "The Falconers," we cannot help but identify with the "timeless cooing" of the captured wood pigeons that are stalked by the hooded and bound falcon. May Swenson's tragic bull is a gory mess, a pitiful spectacle, slipping in his own blood, his tongue "like a gray horn, dripping / blood." Most troubling of all is Sylvia Plath's "The Goring," in which the "botched," ritualistic slaughter of the four bulls does nothing to appease the crowd's "truculence." Instead, it is the man's blood, "faultlessly broached" by the horn of the fifth bull, that becomes a redemptive sacrifice.

Because women identify with the hunted, the killing often becomes personal and inhumane. In Susan Griffin's terrifying prose poem, "His Power: He Tames What Is Wild," both obsessive love and brutal killing, both desired woman and hunted animal, are inextricably linked. Nature is "she"; woman is "she." The hunter "must conquer her wildness, he says, he must tame her before she drives him wild." The hunter in Joyce Carol Oates's short story, "The Buck," is similarly obsessed with tracking and conquering his prey. But this time, like the matriarchal elephants who surround the young mothers in "His Power: He Tames What Is Wild," the elderly woman in "The Buck" is obsessed with protecting that prey. The wild creatures in Louise Erdrich's "Jacklight" are given human voices and perceptions; they are "we." They see the light, and they smell and fear the hunters whose "minds like silver hammers" feel no kinship with anyone or anything.

In other works the passive bystander enables us to experience the savagery of the hunt. In Sharon Old's "Fishing Off Nova Scotia" we are startled by the cruel innocence of her children's admonishments—"Lie still, fishy . . . Shut up, fishy," as the hooks jerk "like upholstery needles through the gills."

Other authors recognize the complexities of hunting—the "answerless / dilemma" and the appeal of hunting—the "abstract hunger." Margaret Atwood acknowledges this feral side, this need "to trap and smash":

I can understand
the guilt they feel because
they are not animals
the guilt they feel
because they are

When the aggressor is nature itself, however, writers such as Jane Hirshfield relinquish their judgment, offering an acceptance of brutality, a forgiveness and an acknowledgment of the giving that is required of all creatures in relationship with one another, eland and lion, woman and man. She writes in "The Weighing,"

> As the drought-starved
>
> eland forgives
>
> the drought-starved lion
>
> who finally takes her, . . .

It is a world that ". . . asks of us / only the strength we have and we give it. / Then it asks more, and we give it." Hirshfield's poems explore the bond of the human and animal worlds and the shared need to escape the "invisible pen," to feel the "richness" of the "wild" earth.

---

[1] Edna St.Vincent Millay's poem, "Huntsman, What Quarry," has been widely anthologized and is not included in this collection. It can be found in Chapin, Henry B. *Sports in Literature*. New York: David McKay and Company, 1976, 156-158. It was originally published in *Huntsman, What Quarry? Poems by Edna St. Vincent Millay*, Edna St. Vincent Millay, New York, Harper & Brothers, 1939.

[2] Elizabeth Bishop's poem "The Fish," also widely anthologized, is not included in this colection. It can be found in Henry B. Chapin's *Sports in Literature*. New York: David McKay and Company, 1976, pp. 154-156.

The Mighty Hunter

Mrs. J. B. Worley

He riseth up early in the morning
And disturbeth the whole household.
    He stampeth down the hall in his heavy boots
    And shouteth, "Where are my shells?"
He consumeth much toast and hot coffee
And partaketh of eggs and of bacon.
    He goeth forth with great expectations
    And boasteth loud of his marksmanship.
He knoweth the flight of the mallard,
The widgeon, the sprig, and the red head,
    The spoonie, the "can," the green-winged teel;
    The call of the brant and the honker.
He baggeth the quail, dove, and pigeon,
The rabbit, the grouse, and the pheasant.
    He knoweth the haunts of the grizzly,
    The caribou, moose, and the mountain sheep;
The wild boar, the wolf, and the cougar,
And the range where the furtive deer feedeth.
    He promiseth his friends much venison
    And inviteth his lodge to a barbecue.
He packeth a heavy knap-sack, a shell-vest,
A rifle, a shot-gun, a kodak, tobacco,
    A canteen, skinning knife, and field glasses,
    Rubber boots, rations, first aid kit.
He trampeth miles in the mountains
And wadeth in streams to his waist-line.
    He chaseth the fleet-footed deer,
    The wolf, and the nimble mountain goat.

From *Poems That Live Forever*, 1965, edited by Hazel Felleman (New York: Doubleday).

He hunteth the fierce grizzly bear.
He waiteth patiently for the elusive snipe
    He returneth home late in the evening,
    Sore of foot, of back, and of temper.
He bringeth no game on his shoulders
Nor game hath he in his knap-sack.
    He devoureth much food from the ice-box
    And the spirit of truth is not in him,
For he braggeth thus to his comrades,
"Boys, I got the limit."

Men Fishing in the Arno

Elizabeth Jennings

I do not know what they are catching,
I only know that they stand there, leaning
A little like lovers, eager but not demanding,
Waiting and hoping for a catch, money,
A meal tomorrow but today, still there, steady.

And the river also moves as calmly
From the waterfall slipping to a place
A mind could match its thought with
And above, the cypresses with cool gestures
Command the city, give it formality.

It is like this every day but more especially
On Sundays; every few yards you see a fisherman,
Each independent, none
Working with others and yet accepting
Others. From this one might, I think,

Reprinted, by permission, from Elizabeth Jennings, 1986, *Collected Poems* (Carcarnet).

Build a whole way of living—men in their mazes
Of secret desires yet keeping a sense
Of order outwardly, hoping
Not too flamboyantly, satisfied with little
Yet not surprised should the river suddenly
Yield a hundredfold, every hunger appeased.

Hooked

Nancy Boutilier

a day between autumn color
and winter stillness
we go fishing.
attention turned
to baiting hooks and casting lines
no one mentions the breezy chill.
I watch you wrestle
a brook trout
teasing tugging finally hooking.
you reel in
send out slack
reel in again.
you rise from the granite shore
rod arched forward
body arched back,
but what I see
is you
torn in half
as you land the trout
my sympathies
are with the fish.

hard lines of concentration
melt into smile
as you triumphantly puppeteer
the dangling captive.
you delight in the iridescent scales
the final slap of fish tail
and the last flash of resistance.
you scoop the exhausted fish
up and out of the water
and pose with your prey
who hangs like a heavy half-moon
a crescent that will shrink away
a fallen leaf decaying in an abandoned well.
our eyes meet—
mine and the lidless fish eyes—
locked in unblinking exchange.
pinched grey fish mouth motioning soundless cries
serrated gills gasping in silent suffocation
unable to shut out vision
the eye bulges through the webbing
to tell me we are caught
in the same
net.

Fishing

Kay Ryan

You can taste it in fish
caught one by one and
brought home from the pond
or river or whatever corner
of water offers. The deep
fanned meander, the silver
well and dimple that nets
would plunder. An
almost drowning patience,
a wish so subtle,
so much a thing of flesh
that change and choice mesh—
the bright barbed hook as strange
to fisherman as fish. How odd
to be caught or to catch; something
of this stays in the flesh.

Lady with a Falcon

May Sarton

> *Flemish Tapestry, Fifteenth Century*
> Gentleness and starvation tame
> The falcon to this lady's wrist,
> Natural flight hooded from blame
> By what ironic fate or twist?

"Fishing" from *Strangely Marked Metal*, © 1985 by Kay Ryan. Used by permission of Cooper Beech Press.

"Lady with a Falcon," from SELECTED POEMS OF MAY SARTON by Serena Sue Hilsinger and Lois Brynes, editors. Copyright © 1978 by May Sarton. Reprinted by permission of W. W. Norton & Company, Inc.

For now the hunched bird's contained flight
Pounces upon her inward air,
To plunder that mysterious night
Of poems blooded as the hare.

Heavy becomes the lady's hand,
And heavy bends the gentle head
Over her hunched and brooding bird
Until it is she who seems hooded.

Lady, your falcon is a peril,
Is starved, is mastered, but not kind.
The bird who sits your hand so gentle,
The captured hunter hunts your mind.

Better to starve the senseless wind
Than wrist a falcon's stop and start:
The bolt of flight you thought to bend
Plummets into your inmost heart.

Song of the Fisherman's Lover

Roseann Lloyd

You stump your way through the tangled
brush, the rocky shore. Listen,
the light in the water
shimmies rainbows across my skin,
the amber sand, my belly
full of roe.

I know the streams
freeze veins blue as ice,
rocks cut swifter than knives. The chill
you love so well turns gray, turns
glitter. Follow the smell. See
my speckles burn.

I'll be glassy-eyed
and quick, teasing feathers, the silver
spinners. Nosing every inlet
I'll dance up over the hills and ridges
where waters rush deeper canyons
through white spray to thinner air.

Hurry. The last arch
to the highest waters. Wait madly
for this split suspension
in air. Then head and tail at once
the headfirst dive slaps
thousands of eggs
quivering down.

Matted and drunk
with honey, you lumber from the brush.
Splash and growl. Say
slime and fur and waters draw
you into me. Dip me from the water.
Kiss the gash. Say *fish*.
Say *woman*.

Birdshooting Season

Olive Senior

Birdshooting season the men
make marriages with their guns
My father's house turns macho
as from far the hunters gather

All night long contentless women
stir their brews: hot coffee
chocolata, cerassie
wrap pone and tie-leaf
for tomorrow's sport. Tonight
the men drink white rum neat.

In darkness shouldering
their packs, their guns, they leave

We stand quietly on the
doorstep shivering. Little boys
longing to grow up birdhunters too
Little girls whispering:
Fly Birds Fly.

The Goring

Sylvia Plath

Arena dust rusted by four bulls' blood to a dull redness,
The afternoon at a bad end under the crowd's truculence,
The ritual death each time botched among dropped capes, ill-
   judged stabs,
The strongest will seemed a will toward ceremony. Obese, dark-
Faced in his rich yellows, tassels, pompons, braid, the picador

Rode out against the fifth bull to brace his pike and slowly bear
Down deep into the bent bull-neck. Cumbrous routine, not art-
   work.
Instinct for art began with the bull's horn lofting in the mob's
Hush a lumped man-shape. The whole act formal, fluent as a
   dance.
Blood faultlessly broached redeemed the sullied air, the earth's
   grossness.

The Buck

Joyce Carol Oates

This is such a terrible story. It's a story I have told a dozen times, never knowing *why*.

Why I can't forget it, I mean. Why it's lodged so deep in me . . . like an arrow through the neck.

Like that arrow I never saw—fifteen-inch, steel-tipped, razor-sharp— that penetrated the deer's neck and killed him, though not immediately. How many hours, I wonder, till he bled to death, till his body turned cold and grew heavier—they say the weight of Death is always heavier than that of life—how many hours, terrible hours, I don't know.

I was not a witness. The sole witness did not survive.

Each time I tell this story of the wounded buck, the hunter who pursued him, and the elderly woman who rescued him, or tried to rescue him, I think that maybe *this* telling will make a difference. *This* time a secret meaning will be revealed, as if without my volition, and I will be released.

But each telling is a subtle repudiation of a previous telling. So each telling is a new telling. Each telling a forgetting.

That arrow lodged ever more firmly, cruelly. In living flesh.

* * *

I'd take comfort in saying all this happened years ago, in some remote part of the country. *Once upon a time*, I'd begin, but in fact it happened within the past year, and no more than eight miles from where I live, in a small town called Bethany, New Jersey.

Which is in Saugatuck County, in the northwestern corner of the state, bordering the Delaware River.

A region that's mainly rural: farmland, hills, some of the hills large enough to be called mountains. There aren't many roads in this part of New Jersey, and the big interstate highways just slice through, gouge through the countryside, north and south, east and west. Strangers in a rush to get somewhere else.

The incident happened on the Snyder farm. A lonely place, no neighbors close by.

The name "Snyder" was always known in Saugatuck County even though, when I was growing up, the Snyders had sold off most of their land. In the family's prime, in the 1930s, they'd owned three hundred twenty acres, most of it rich farmland; in the 1950s they'd begun to sell, piecemeal, as if grudgingly, maybe with the idea of one day buying their land back. But they never did; they died out instead. Three brothers, all unmarried; and Melanie Snyder, the last of the family. Eighty-two years old when she was found dead in a room of the old farmhouse, last January.

In deer-hunting season. The season that had always frightened and outraged her.

She'd been vigilant for years. She'd acquired a local reputation. Her six acres of land—all that remained of the property—was scrupulously posted against hunters ("with gun, bow and arrow, dog") and trespassers. Before hunting with firearms was banned in Saugatuck County, Melanie Snyder patrolled her property in hunting season, on foot, fearless about moving in the direction of gunfire. "You! What are you doing here?" she would call out to hunters. "Don't you know this land is posted?" She was a lanky woman with a strong-boned face, skin that looked permanently wind-burnt, close-cropped starkly white hair. Her eyes were unusually dark and prominent; everyone commented on Melanie Snyder's eyes; she wasn't a woman any man, no matter his age, felt comfortable confronting, especially out in the woods.

She sent trespassers home, threatened to call the sheriff if they didn't leave. She'd stride through the woods clapping her hands to frighten off deer, pheasants, small game, send them panicked to safety.

White-tailed deer, or, as older generations called them, Virginia deer, were her favorites, "the most beautiful animals in creation." She hated it that state conservationists argued in favor of controlled hunting for the "good" of the deer themselves, to reduce their alarmingly fertile numbers.

She hated the idea of hunting with bow and arrow—as if it made any difference to a deer, how it died.

She hated the stealth and silence of the bow. With guns, you can at least hear the enemy.

*   *   *

His name was Wayne Kunz, "Woody" Kunz, part owner of a small auto parts store in Delaware Gap, New Jersey, known to his circle of male friends as a good guy. A good sport. You might say, a "character."

The way he dressed: his hunting gear, for instance.

A black simulated-leather jumpsuit, over it the regulation fluorescent-orange vest. A bright red cap, with earflaps. Boots to the knee, like a Nazi storm trooper's; mirror sunglasses hiding his pale lashless eyes. He had a large, round, singed-looking face, a small damp mouth: this big-bellied, quick-grinning fellow, the kind who keeps up a constant chatting murmur with himself, as if terrified of silence, of being finally *alone*.

He hadn't been able to talk any of his friends into coming with him, deer hunting with bow and arrow.

Even showing them his new Atlas bow, forty-eight inches, sleek blond fiberglass "wood," showing them the quill of arrows, synthetic-feathered, lightweight steel and steel-tipped and razor-sharp like no Indian's arrows had ever been—he'd been disappointed, disgusted with them, none of his friends wanting to come along, waking in the predawn dark, driving out in Saugatuck County to kill a few deer.

Woody Kunz. Forty years old, five feet ten inches, two hundred pounds. He'd been married, years ago, but the marriage hadn't worked out, and there were no children.

Crashing clumsily through the underbrush, in pursuit of deer.

Not wanting to think he was lost—*was* he lost?

Talking to himself, cursing and begging himself—"C'mon, Woody, for Christ's sake, Woody, move your fat *ass*"—half sobbing as, another time, a herd of deer broke and scattered before he could get into shooting range. Running and leaping through the woods, taunting him with their uplifted white tails, erect snowy-white tails like targets so he couldn't help but fire off an arrow—to fly into space, disappear.

"Fuck it, Woody! Fuck you, asshole!"

Later. He's tired. Even with the sunglasses his eyes are seared from the bright winter sun reflecting on the snow. Knowing he deserves better.

Another time the deer are too quick and smart for him, must be they scented him downwind, breaking to run before he even saw them, only heard them, silent except for the sound of their crashing hooves. This time, he fires a shot knowing it won't strike any target, no warm living flesh. Must be he does it to make himself feel bad.

Playing the fool in the eyes of anybody watching and he can't help but think uneasily that somebody *is* watching—if only the unblinking eye of God.

And then: he sees the buck.

His buck, yes, suddenly. Oh, Jesus. His heart clenches, he *knows*.

He has surprised the beautiful dun-colored animal drinking from a fast-running stream; the stream is frozen except for a channel of black water at its center, the buck with its antlered head lowered. Woody Kunz stares, hardly able to believe his good luck, rapidly counting the points of the antlers—eight? ten?—as he fits an arrow into place with trembling fingers, lifts the bow, and sights along the arrow aiming for that point of the anatomy where neck and chest converge—it's a heart shot he hopes for—drawing back the arrow, feeling the power of the bow, releasing it; and seemingly in the same instant the buck leaps, the arrow has struck him in the neck, there's a shriek of animal terror and pain, and Woody Kunz shouts in ecstatic triumph.

But the buck isn't killed outright. To Woody's astonishment, and something like hurt, the buck turns and runs—flees.

* * *

Later he'd say he hadn't seen the NO TRESPASSING signs in the woods, he hadn't come by way of the road so he hadn't seen them there, the usual state-issued signs forbidding hunting, trapping, trespassing on private land, but Woody Kunz would claim he hadn't known it was private land exactly; he'd have to confess he might have been lost, tracking deer for hours moving more or less in a circle, not able to gauge where the center of the circle might be; and yes, he was excited, adrenaline rushing in his veins as he hadn't felt it in God knows how long, half a lifetime maybe, so he hadn't seen the signs posting the Snyder property or if he'd seen them they had not registered upon his consciousness or if they'd registered upon his consciousness he hadn't known what they were, so tattered and weatherworn.

That was Woody Kunz's defense, against a charge, if there was to be a charge, of unlawful trespassing and hunting on posted property.

* * *

Jesus is the most important person in all our lives!
Jesus abides in our hearts, no need to see Him!
These joyful pronouncements, or are they commandments, Melanie Snyder sometimes hears, rising out of the silence of the old house. The wind in the eaves, a shrieking of crows in the orchard, and this disembodied voice, the voice of her long-dead fiancé—waking her suddenly from one of her reveries, so she doesn't remember where she is, what year this is, what has happened to her, to have aged her so.

* * *

She'd fallen in love with her brothers, one by one. Her tall strong indifferent brothers.

Much later, to everyone's surprise and certainly to her own, she'd fallen in love with a young Lutheran preacher, just her age.

Standing just her height. Smiling at her shyly, his wire-rimmed glasses winking as if shyly too. Shaking her gloved hand. Hello, Miss Snyder. Like a brother who would at last see *her*.

Twenty-eight years old! She'd been fated to be a spinster, of course. That plain, stubborn, sharp-tongued girl, eyes too large and stark and intelligent in her face to be "feminine," her body flat as a board.

In this place in which girls married as young as sixteen, began having their babies at seventeen, were valued and praised and loved for such qualities as they shared with brood mares and milking cows, you cultivated irony to save your soul—and your pride.

Except: she fell in love with the visiting preacher, introduced to him by family friends, the two "young people" urged together to speak stumblingly, clumsily to each other of—what? Decades later Melanie Snyder won't remember a syllable, but she remembers the young man's preaching voice, *Jesus! Jesus is our only salvation!* He'd gripped the edges of the pulpit of the Bethany church, God love shining in his face, white teeth bared like piano keys.

How it happened, how they became officially engaged—whether by their own decision or others'—they might not have been able to say. But it was time to marry, for both.

Plain, earnest, upright young people. Firm-believing Christians, of that there could be no doubt.

Did Melanie doubt? No, never!

She was prepared to be a Christian wife and to have her babies one by one. As God ordained.

There were passionate-seeming squeezes of her hand, there were chaste kisses, fluttery and insubstantial as a butterfly's wings. There were Sunday walks, in the afternoon. Jesus is the most important person in my life, I feel Him close beside us—don't you, Melanie?

The emptiness of the country lane, the silence of the sky, except for the crows' raucous jeering cries. Slow-spiraling hawks high overhead.

Oh, yes, certainly! Oh, yes.

Melanie Snyder's fiancé. The young just-graduated seminary student, with his hope to be a missionary. He was an energetic softball player, a pitcher of above-average ability; he led the Sunday school children on hikes, canoe trips. But he was most himself there in the pulpit of the Bethany church, elevated a few inches above the rapt congregation, where even his shy stammering rose to passion, a kind of sensual power. How strong the bones of his earnest, homely face, the fair-brown wings of hair brushed back neatly from his forehead! *Jesus, our redeemer. Jesus, our only salvation.* As if the God love shining in the young man's face were a beacon, a lighthouse beacon, flung out into the night, giving light yet unseeing, blind, in itself.

The engagement was never officially terminated. Always, there were sound reasons for postponing the wedding. Their families were disappointed but eager, on both sides, to comply. His letters came to her like clockwork, every two weeks, from North Carolina, where he was stationed as a chaplain in the U.S. Army. Dutiful letters, buoyant letters about his work, his "mission," his conviction that he was at last where God meant him to be.

Then the letters ceased. And they told Melanie he'd had an "accident" of some kind; there'd been a "misunderstanding" of some kind. He was discharged from his army post and reassigned to a Lutheran church in St. Louis, where he was to assist an older minister. But why? Melanie asked. Why, what has happened? Melanie demanded to know, but never was she told, never would a young woman be told such a thing, not for her ears, not for an ignorant virgin's ears; she'd wept and protested and mourned and lapsed finally into shame, not knowing what had happened to ruin her happiness but knowing it must constitute a rejection of her, a repudiation of the womanliness she'd tried so hard—ah, so shamefully hard!—to take on.

That feeling, that sense of unworthiness, she would retain for years. Studying her face in a mirror, plain, frank, unyielding, those eyes alit with irony, she realized she'd known all along—she was fated to be a spinster, never to be any man's wife.

And didn't that realization bring with it, in truth, relief?

Now, fifty years later, if those words *Jesus! Jesus abides in our hearts, no need to see Him!* ring out faintly in the silence of the old house, she turns aside, unhearing. For she's an old woman who has outlived such lies. Such subterfuge. She has taken revenge on Jesus Christ by ceasing to believe in Him—or in God, or in the Lutheran faith, or in such pieties as meekness, charity, love of one's enemies. Casting off her long-dead fiancé (who had not the courage even to write Melanie Snyder, finally, to release her from their engagement), she'd cast off his religion, as, drifting off from a friend, we lose the friends with whom he or she connected us, there being no deeper bond.

*   *   *

What is it?

She sees, in the lower pasture, almost out of the range of her vision, a movement of some kind: a swaying dun-colored shape, blurred by the frost on the aged glass. Standing in her kitchen, alert, aroused.

An animal of some kind? A large dog? A deer?

A wounded deer?

Melanie hurries to pull her sheepskin jacket from a peg; she's jamming her feet into boots, already angry, half knowing what she'll see.

Guns you could at least hear; now the slaughter is with bow and arrow. Grown men playing at Indians. Playing at killing.

The excuse is, the "excess" deer population in the county has to be kept down. White-tailed deer overbreeding, causing crop damage, auto accidents.

As if men, the species of men who prowl the woods seeking innocent creatures to kill, need any excuse.

Melanie Snyder, who has known hunters all her life, including her own brothers, understands: to the hunter, killing an animal is just a substitute for killing another human being. Male, female. That's the forbidden fantasy.

She has never been frightened of accosting them, though, and she isn't now. Running outside into the gusty January air. A scowling wild-eyed old woman, sexless leathery face, white hair rising from her head in stiff tufts. She is wearing a soiled sheepskin jacket several sizes too large for her, a relic once belonging to one of her brothers; her boots are rubberized fishing boots, the castoffs of another, long-deceased brother.

Melanie is prepared for an ugly sight but this sight stuns her at first; she hears herself cry out, "Oh. Oh, God!"

A buck, full grown, beautiful, with handsome pointed antlers, is staggering in her direction, thrashing his head from side to side, desperate to dislodge an arrow that has penetrated his neck. His eyes roll in his head, his mouth is opening and closing spasmodically, blood flows bright and glistening from the wound; in fact it is two wounds, in the lower part of his neck near his left shoulder. Behind him, in the lower pasture, running clumsily after him, is the hunter, bow uplifted: a bizarre sight in black jumpsuit, bright orange vest, comical red hat. Like a robot or a spaceman, Melanie thinks, staring. She has never seen any hunter so costumed. Is this a man she should know? a face? a name? He's a hefty man with pale flushed skin, damp mouth, eyes hidden behind sunglasses with opaque mirrored lenses. His breath is steaming in the cold; he's clearly excited, agitated—dangerous. Fitting an arrow crookedly in his bow as if preparing, at this range, to shoot.

Melanie cries, "You! Get out of here!"

The hunter yells, "Lady, stand aside!"

"This land is posted! I'll call the sheriff!"

"Lady, you better gimme a clear shot!"

The buck is snorting, stamping his sharp-hooved feet in the snow. Deranged by terror and panic, he thrashes his antlered head from side to side, bleeding freely, bright-glistening blood underfoot, splattered onto Melanie Snyder's clothes as, instinctively, recklessly, she positions herself between the wounded animal and the hunter. She's pleading, angry. "Get off my land! Haven't you done enough evil? This poor creature! Let him alone!"

The hunter, panting, gaping at her, can't seem to believe what he sees: a white-haired woman in men's clothes, must be eighty years old, trying to shield a buck with an arrow through his neck. He advances to within a few yards of her, tries to circle around her. Saying incredulously, "That's my arrow, for Christ's sake, lady! That buck's a goner and he's *mine*!"

"Brute! Murderer! I'm telling you to get off my land or I'll call the sheriff and have you arrested!"

"Lady, that buck is goddamned dangerous—you better stand aside."

"*You* stand aside. Get off my property!"

"Lady, for Christ's sake—"

"You heard me: *get off my property*!"

So, for some minutes, there's an impasse.

Forever afterward Woody Kunz will remember, to his chagrin and shame: the beautiful white-tailed full-grown buck with the most amazing spread of antlers he'd ever seen—*his* buck, *his* kill, *his* arrow sticking through the animals neck—the wounded buck snorting, thrashing his head, stamping the ground, blood everywhere, blood-tinged saliva hanging from his mouth in threads, and the crazy old woman shielding the buck with her body, refusing to surrender him to his rightful owner. And Woody Kunz is certain *he* is the rightful owner; he's shouting in the old woman's face, he's pleading with her, practically begging, finally; the fucking deer is *his*, he's earned it, he's been out tramping in the cold since seven this morning, God damn it if he's going to give up! Face blotched and hot, tears of rage and impotence stinging his eyes: oh, Jesus, he'd grab the old hag by the shoulders, lift her clear, and fire another arrow this time into the heart so there'd be no doubt—except, somehow, he doesn't do it, doesn't dare.

Instead, he backs off. Still with his bow upraised, his handsome brand-new Atlas bow from Sears, but the arrow droops useless in his fingers.

In a voice heavy with disgust, sarcasm, he says, "OK. OK, lady, you win."

The last glimpse Woody Kunz has of this spectacle, the old woman is trying clumsily to pull the arrow out of the buck's neck, and the buck is naturally putting up a struggle, swiping at her with his antlers, but weakly, sinking to his knees in the snow, then scrambling to his feet again; still the old woman persists; sure, she *is* crazy and deserves whatever happens to her, the front of her sheepskin jacket soaked in blood by now, blood even on her face, in her hair.

* * *

It isn't until late afternoon, hours later, that Woody Kunz returns home.

Having gotten lost in the countryside, wandered in circles in the woods, couldn't locate the road he'd parked his goddamned car on, muttering to himself, sick and furious and shamed, in a state of such agitation his head feels close to bursting, guts like a nest of tangled snakes. Never, *never*, is Woody Kunz going to live down this humiliation in his own eyes.

So he's decided not to tell anyone. Not even to fashion it into an anecdote to entertain his friends. Woody Kunz being cheated out of a twelve-point buck by an old lady? Shit, he'd rather die than have it known.

Sure, it crosses his mind he should maybe report the incident to the sheriff. Not to reiterate his claim of the deer—though the deer *is* his—but to report the old woman in case she's really in danger. Out there, seemingly alone, so old, in the middle of nowhere. A mortally wounded full-grown whitetail buck, crazed with pain and terror, like a visitation of God, in her care.

*   *   *

She's begging, desperate: "*Let* me help you, oh, please! Oh, please! Let me—"

Tugging at the terrible arrow, tugging forward, tugging back, her fingers slippery with blood. Woman and beast struggling, the one disdainful, even reckless, of her safety; the other dazed by trauma or loss of blood, not lashing out as ordinarily he would, to attack an enemy, with bared teeth, antlers, sharp hooves.

"Oh, please, you must not die, please—"

It's probable that Melanie Snyder has herself become deranged. All of the world having shrunk to the task at hand, to the forcible removal of this steel bar that has penetrated the buck's neck, fifteen-inch steel-glinting sharp-tipped arrow with white, synthetic quills—nothing matters but that *the arrow must be removed.*

The bulging eyes roll upward, there's bloody froth at the shuddering nostrils, she smells, tastes, the hot rank breath—then the antlers strike her in the chest, she's falling, crying out in surprise.

And the buck has pushed past her, fleeing on skidding hooves, on legs near buckling at the knees, so strangely—were she fully conscious she would realize, *so* strangely—into her father's house.

*   *   *

It won't be until three days later, at about this hour of the morning, that they'll discover her—or the body she has become. Melanie Snyder and the buck with the arrow through his neck.

But Melanie Snyder has no sense of what's coming, no cautionary fear. As if, this damp-gusty January morning, such a visitation, such urgency pressed upon her, has blotted out all anticipation of the future, let alone of danger.

In blind panic, voiding his bowels, the buck has run crashing into the old farmhouse, into the kitchen, through to the parlor; as Melanie Snyder sits dazed on the frozen ground beneath her rear stoop he turns, furious, charges into a corner of the room, collides with an upright piano, making a brief discordant startled music, an explosion of muted notes; turns again, crashing into a table laden with family photographs, a lamp of stippled milk glass with a fluted shade. A renewed rush of adrenaline empowers him; turning again, half rearing, hooves skidding on the thin loose-lying Oriental carpet faded to near transparency, he charges his reflection in a mirror as, out back, Melanie Snyder sits trying to summon her strength, trying to comprehend what has happened and what she must do.

She doesn't remember the buck having knocked her down, thus can't believe he *has* attacked her.

She thinks, Without me, he is doomed.

She hears one of her brothers speaking harshly, scolding: What is she doing there sitting on the ground?—*For the Lord's sake, Melanie!*—but she ignores him, testing her right ankle, the joint is livid with pain but not broken—she can shift her weight to her other foot—a high-pitched ringing in her head as of church bells, and where there should be terror there's determination, for Melanie Snyder is an independent woman, a woman far too proud to accept, let alone solicit, her neighbors' proffered aid since the death of the last of her brothers: she wills herself not to succumb to weakness now, in this hour of her trial.

Managing to get to her feet, moving with calculating slowness. As if her bones are made of glass.

Overhead, an opaque January sky, yet beautiful. Like slightly tarnished mother-of-pearl.

Except for the crows in their gathering place beyond the barns, and the hoarse *uh-uh-uh* of her breathing: silence.

She enters the house. By painful inches, yet eagerly. Leaning heavily against the door frame.

She sees the fresh blood trail, sees and smells the moist animal droppings, so shocking, there on the kitchen floor she keeps clean with a pointless yet self-satisfying fanaticism, the aged linoleum worn nearly colorless, yes, but Melanie has a house owner's pride, and pride is all. The buck in his frenzy to escape the very confines he has plunged into is turning, rearing, snorting, crashing in the other room. Melanie calls, "I'm here! I will help you!"—blindly too entering the parlor with its etiolated light, tasseled shades drawn to cover three-quarters of the windows as, decades ago, Melanie Snyder's mother had so drawn them, to protect the furnishings against the sun. Surely she's a bizarre sight herself, drunk-swaying, staggering, her wrinkled face, hands glistening with blood, white hair in tufts as if she hasn't taken a brush to it in weeks, Melanie Snyder in the oversized sheepskin jacket she wears in town, driving a rusted Plymouth pickup truck with a useless muffler—everybody in Bethany knows Melanie Snyder though she doesn't know them, carelessly confuses sons with fathers, granddaughters with mothers, her own remote blood relations with total strangers—she's awkward in these rubberized boots many sizes too large for her shrunken feet, yet reaching out—unhesitantly, boldly—to the maddened buck who crouches in a corner facing her, his breath frothing in blood, in erratic shuddering waves, she is speaking softly, half begging, "I want to help you! Oh—"as the heavy head dips, the antlers rush at her—how astonishing the elegance of such male beauty, and the burden of it, God's design both playful and deadly shrewd, the strangeness of bone growing out of flesh, bone calcified and many-branched as a young apple tree—clumsily he charges this woman who is his enemy even as, with a look of startled concern, she opens her arms to him, the sharp antlers now striking her a second time in the chest and this time breaking her fragile collarbone as easily as one might break a chicken wishbone set to dry on a windowsill for days, and the momentum of his charge carries him helplessly forward, he falls, the arrow's quill brushing against Melanie Snyder's face; as he scrambles in a frenzy to upright himself his sharp hooves catch her in the chest, belly, pelvis; he has fallen heavily, as if from a great height, as if flung down upon her, breath in wheezing shudders and the blood froth bubbling around his mouth, and Melanie Snyder lies pinned beneath the animal body, legs gone, lower part of her body gone, a void of numbness, not even pain, distant from her as something seen through the wrong end of a telescope, rapidly retreating.

*   *   *

How did it happen, how strange; they were of the same height now, or nearly: Melanie Snyder and her tall strong indifferent brothers: Never married, none of them, d'you know why? No woman was ever quite good enough for the Snyder boys, and the girl, Melanie—well, one look at her and you know: a born spinster.

It's more than thirty years after they informed her, guardedly, without much sympathy—for perhaps sympathy would have invited tears, and they were not a family comfortable with tears—that her fiancé had been discharged from the army, that Melanie dares to ask, shyly, without her customary aggressiveness, what had really happened, what the mysterious "accident," or was it a "misunderstanding," had been. And her brother, her elder by six years, an aged slope-shouldered man with a deeply creased face, sighs and passes his hand over his chin and says, in a tone of mild but unmistakable contempt, "Don't ask."

She lies there beneath the dying animal, then beneath the lifeless stiffening body, face no more than four inches from the great head, the empty eyes—how many hours she's conscious, she can't gauge.

At first calling, into the silence, "Help—help me! Help—"

There *is* a telephone in the kitchen; rarely does it ring, and when it rings Melanie Snyder frequently ignores it, doesn't want people inquiring after her, well-intentioned neighbors, good Lutherans from the church she hasn't set foot in, except for funerals, in twenty-odd years.

The dying animal, beautiful even in dying, bleeding to death, soaking Melanie Snyder's clothes with his blood, and isn't she bleeding too, from wounds in her throat and face, her hands?

And he's dead, she feels the life pass from him—"Oh, no, oh, *no*," sobbing and pushing at the body, warm sticky blood by degrees cooling and congealing—the wood-fire stove in the kitchen has gone out and cold eases in from out-of-doors; in fact the kitchen door must be open, creaking and banging in the wind. A void rises from the loose-fitting floorboards as from the lower part of Melanie's body; she's sobbing as if her heart is broken, she's furious, trying to lift the heavy body from her, clawing at the body, raking her torn nails and bleeding fingers against the buck's thick winter coat, a coarse-haired furry coat, but the buck's body will not budge.

The weight of Death, so much more powerful than life.

Later. She wakes moaning and delirious, a din as of sleet pellets against the windows, and the cold has congealed the buck's blood and her own, the numbness has moved higher, obliterating much of what she has known as "body" these eighty-odd years; she understands that she is dying—consciousness like a fragile bubble, or a skein of bubbles—yet she is able still to wish to summon her old strength, the bitter joy of her stubborn strength, pushing at the heavy animal body, dead furry weight, eyes sightless as glass and the arrow, the terrible arrow, the obscene arrow: "Let me *go*. Let me *free*."

Fainting and waking. Drifting in and out of consciousness.

Hearing that faint ringing voice in the eaves, as always subtly chiding, in righteous reproach of Melanie Snyder, mixed with the wind and that profound agelessness of wind as if blowing to us from the farthest reaches of time as well as space—*Jesus! Jesus is our only salvation! Jesus abides in our hearts!*—but in pride she turns aside unhearing; never has she begged, nor will she beg now. Oh, never.

And does she regret her gesture, trying to save an innocent beast? She does not.

And would she consent, even now, to having made a mistake, acted improvidently? She would not.

* * *

When after nearly seventy-two hours Woody Kunz overcomes his manly embarrassment and notifies the Saugatuck County sheriff's office of the "incident" on the Snyder farm and they go out to investigate, they find eighty-two-year-old Melanie Snyder dead, pinned beneath the dead white-tail buck, in the parlor of the old farmhouse in which no one outside the Snyder family had stepped for many years. An astonishing sight: human and animal bodies virtually locked together in the rigor of death, their mingled blood so soaked into Melanie Snyder's clothes, so frozen, it is possible to separate them only by force.

time of fish dying

Gabriela Melinescu
Translated by Stavros Deligiorgis

> colors shifting
> silver to yellow and
> > I could say that much only
> he has not been seen since
> > not once

> risking death
> skirting poles and corners
> hung with the yellow magnetic strip

> but the fish had left
> for the world of fishes
> > and I can but say
> he has not been seen since
> > not once

Reprinted, by permission, from Gabriela Melinescu, 1980, published by Barnstone and Barnstone. Permission for use of the translation from the Romanian by Stavros Deligiorgis.

The Falconers

Simonne Jacquemard
Translated by Patricia Nolan

Sheltered from the tearing wind
that bends and unbends the exalted space,
the falconers girded in white wool,
their fists encircled in leather
stand motionless like priests in front
of their lookout, a bush with stiff plumed leaves
dried by the salt air.
An island,
the form of a broken vessel, an abandoned fort
on whose summit once the horizon
was haughtily surveyed, its stone borders
lie in ruins where unseen beings watch
and wait

Suddenly the air erupts
scattering the wood pigeons
who wheel back and forth together
like an elusive thought entering a ghostly body
explodes in cries of flapping wings,
into a thousand facets where the downy triangle
beats the air in terrified movements.

They land, glistening like a star
from the Milky Way by the side
of a forked rivulet flowing to the sea
and ripple like the unnamed wave,
suddenly from their numbers they are reborn
in a leap like dull thunder, being both the gong

of alarm and the alarmed. Together they unfold
the dazzling and terrified flower
of their flight.

They, the gazing standard bearers, admire the signs
flashed on high, falconers
of silent supplication, the bird
of their passion released, they watch
the point where the collision
terrifying the skies will be enacted,
exposing the futility of circling and pursuit,
the harrying forces that lurk
in the very shadow of each man.

Immense, arched, flaunting his persuasive arrogance,
the predator circles among these spent small fry
whose ragged lines reveal the chasm
over which the assailant struggles in his headlong dive.

Futile dancing lines, dull circles of silence
where the provocative scene takes place,
the transgression, gods pitted against gods
beyond the touch of the bright sands, the ecstatic sea,
the exhausted sun, in full negation of being,
in full madness of eruptions and abruptness

Behind the leafy ridge camouflaging their whiteness,
do the falconers admit their ruthlessness,
mirrors directed at tenuous images that ebb and flow.
Tragic, a falcon his eyes obscured by the hood
pecks away at the night that obsesses him.
Talons bound, he grips the woven straw net from which
flows the timeless cooing of the captured wood pigeons.

Death Invited

May Swenson

Death invited to break his horns
on the spread
cloth. To drop his head
on the dragged flag on the sand.
Death's hooves slipping
in blood, and a band
of blood down the black side.
Death's tongue, curved in the open mouth
like a gray horn, dripping
blood. And
six colored agonies decking the summit
of his muscled pride.
Death invited to die.

The head
of death, with bewildered raging eye,
flagged down,
dragged down to the red
cloth on the sand.
Death invited to stand,
legs spread,
on the spot of the cape.
To buckle stubborn knees and lie
down in blood on the silken shape.

The sword, sunk at the top of the shoulder's pride—
its hilt a silver cross—drawn forth now lets
hot radiant blood slide

from bubbling nostrils
through cloth to thirsty ground.

Yearning horns found
fleeing cloth and bloodless pillow,
substance none. Arrogant thighs,
that swiped and turned death by,
now, close as love, above lean lunging,
filling the pain-hot eye.
That stares till it turns to blood.
With the short knife dug
quick!
to the nape.
And the thick
neck drops on the spot of the cape.

Chains are drawn
round the horns, whose points are clean.
Trumpets shout.
New sand is thrown
where death's blood streamed.
Four stout,
jingling horses with gilded hooves
tug death out.

Life is awarded ears and flowers.
Pelted with hats and shoes, and praise,
glittering life, in tight pink thighs,
swaggers around a rotunda of screams and *Oles*

Death is dragged from the ring,
a clumsy hide,
a finished thing—

back to his pen.
The gate swings shut.

The gate swings wide.
Here comes trotting, snorting death
let loose again.

His Power: He Tames What Is Wild

Susan Griffin

Is it by its indefiniteness it shadows forth the heartless voids and immensities of the universe, and thus stabs us from behind with the thought of annihilation when beholding the milky way?

—Herman Melville
Moby-Dick

And at last she could bear the burden of herself no more. She was to be had for the taking. To be had for the taking.

—D. H. Lawrence
Lady Chatterley's Lover

The Hunt

She has captured his heart. She has overcome him. He cannot tear his eyes away. He is burning with passion. He cannot live without her. He pursues her. She makes him pursue her. The faster she runs, the stronger his desire. He will overtake her. He will make her his own. He will have her. (The boy chases the doe and her yearling for nearly two hours. She keeps running despite her wounds. He pursues her through pastures, over fences, groves of trees, crossing the road, up hills, volleys of rifle shots sounding, until perhaps twenty bullets are embedded in her body.) She has no mercy. She has dressed to excite his desire. She has no scruples. She has painted herself for him. She makes supple movements to entice him. She is without a soul. Beneath her painted face is flesh, are bones. She reveals only part of herself to him. She is wild. She flees whenever he approaches. She is teasing him. (Finally, she is defeated and falls and he sees that half of her head has been blown off, that one leg is gone, her abdomen split from her tail to her head, and her organs hang outside her body. Then four men encircle the fawn and harvest her too.) He is an easy target, he says. He says he is pierced. Love has shot him through, he says. He is a familiar mark. Riddled. Stripped to the bone. He is conquered, he says. (The boys, fond of hunting hare, search in particular for pregnant females.) He is fighting for his life. He faces annihilation in her, he says. He is losing himself to her, he says. Now, he must conquer her wildness, he says, he must tame her before she drives him wild, he says. (Once catching their prey, they step on her back, breaking it, and they call this "dancing on the hare.") Thus he goes on his knees to her. Thus he wins her over, he tells her he wants her. He makes her his own. He encloses her. He encircles her. He puts her under lock and key. He protects her. (Approaching the great mammals, the hunters make little sounds which they know will make the elephants form a defensive circle.) And once she is his, he prizes his delight. He feasts his eyes on her. He adorns her luxuriantly. He gives her ivory. He gives her perfume. (The older matriarchs stand to the outside of the circle to protect the calves and younger mothers.) He covers her with the skins of mink, beaver, muskrat, seal, raccoon, otter, ermine, fox, the feathers of ostriches, osprey, egret, ibis (The hunters then encircle that circle and fire first into the bodies of the matriarchs. When these older elephants fall, the younger panic, yet unwilling to leave the bodies of their dead mothers, they make easy targets.) And thus he makes her soft. He makes her calm. He makes her grateful to him. He has tamed her, he says. She is content to be his, he says. (In the winter, if a single wolf has leaped over the walls of the city and terrorized the streets, the hunters go out in a band to rid the forest of the whole pack.) Her voice is now soothing to him. Her eyes no longer blaze, but look on him serenely. When he calls to her, she gives herself to him. Her ferocity lies under him. (The body of the great whale is strapped with explosives.) Now nothing of the old beast remains in her. (Eastern Bison, extinct 1825; Spectacled Cormorant, extinct 1852; Cape Lion, extinct 1865; Bonin Night Heron, extinct 1889; Barbary Lion, extinct 1922; Great Auk, extinct 1944.) And he can trust her wholly with himself. So he is blazing when he enters her, and she is consumed. (Florida Key Deer, vanishing; Wild Indian Buffalo, vanishing; Great Sable Antelope, vanishing.) Because she is his, she offers no resistance. She is a place of rest for him. A place of his making. And when his flesh begins to yield and his skin melts into her, he becomes soft, and he is without fear; he does not lose himself; though something in him gives way, he is not lost in her, because she is his now: he has captured her.

Jacklight

Louise Erdrich

The same Chippewa word is used both for flirting and hunting game, while another Chippewa word connotes both using force in intercourse and also killing a bear with one's bare hands.

—R. W. Dunning
(1959) *Social and Economic Change Among the Northern Ojibwa*

We have come to the edge of the woods,
out of brown grass where we slept, unseen,
out of knotted twigs, out of leaves creaked shut,
out of hiding.

At first the light wavered, glancing over us.
Then it clenched to a fist of light that pointed,
searched out, divided us.
Each took the beams like direct blows the heart answers.
Each of us moved forward alone.

We have come to the edge of the woods,
drawn out of ourselves by this night sun,
this battery of polarized acids,
that outshines the moon.

We smell them behind it
but they are faceless, invisible.
We smell the raw steel of their gun barrels,
mink oil on leather, their tongues of sour barley.
We smell their mothers buried chin-deep in wet dirt.
We smell their fathers with scoured knuckles,
teeth cracked from hot marrow.
We smell their sisters of crushed dogwood, bruised apples,
of fractured cups and concussions of burnt hooks.

We smell their breath steaming lightly behind the jacklight.
We smell the itch underneath the caked guts on their clothes.
We smell their minds like silver hammers

Fishing Off Nova Scotia

Sharon Olds

Visiting their father's childhood home,
a blood culture, the children that week
were raised on blood. They let the line out
and let it out and let it out,
the sea was so deep.

We were floating in a small dory on top of those
tons of water. They yanked the line
up from the bottom, over and over,
jigging for fish: the hooks jerking
like upholstery needles through the gills.

It made a sound like plastic being broken
to get the barb out. In a wooden box
in the bottom of the boat, the supple metal
bodies would slap and twist, silver
gods dug up. *Lie still, fishy,*
the kids would say, *Shut up, fishy,*
with scales on their hands and traces of gut on their shoes.

I was playing the mother in this,
the wife from the States, so I did not speak,
the steel cracking those clenched jaws,
the bright glaze of blood on the children.

The Trappers

Margaret Atwood

The trappers, trapped
between the steel jaws of their answerless
dilemma, their location,
follow, stop, stare down
at dead eyes
                    caught in fur

Each time there is a repetition
of red on white, the footprints, the inevitable
blood. The dead thing, the
almost-dead that must be
bludgeoned, the few they leave
alive to breed for next year's
traps. The chain, the
steel circles

The snow snaps in their faces;
the forest closes
behind them like a throat.
The branches have
cold blood

            Their following, the abstract hunger
            to trap and smash
            the creature, to crush
            the red sun at the centre

also the wish
to mark the snow with feral
knowledge, to enter the narrow
resonant skull, to make each
tree and season an owned
territory

      but then the recurring fear
      of warm fur, the puritan
      shunning of all summer

I can understand

the guilt they feel because
they are not animals
the guilt they feel
because they are

The Weighing

Jane Hirshfield

The heart's reasons
seen clearly,
even the hardest
will carry
its whip-marks and sadness
and must be forgiven.

As the drought-starved
eland forgives
the drought-starved lion
who finally takes her,
enters willingly then
the life she cannot refuse,
and is lion, is fed,
and does not remember the other.

So few grains of happiness
measured against all the dark
and still the scales balance.

The world asks of us
only the strength we have and we give it.
Then it asks more, and we give it.

"The Weighing" from THE OCTOBER PALACE by JANE HIRSHFIELD.

In Yellow Grass

Jane Hirshfield

In the yellow grass
each gathers with its own kind—
and the lion-beauty cuts that invisible pen,
the bright wires trampled or leapt.

So, love, it will be with us, both
lion and prey—our mouths so deep in richness
only the wild scent of earth will be left
to tremble, after.

"In Yellow Grass" from THE OCTOBER PALACE by JANE HIRSHFIELD.

Part IV

The Contact Imperative

We know now we have always been in danger
down in our separateness ·
and now up here together   but till now
we had not touched our strength

Phantasia for Elvira Shatayev
Adrienne Rich

Just as the literature concerning the body and the natural world reflects a yearning for mutuality, continuity, and connection, so too does the literature regarding human relationships in sport. Whether the connection is between spectator and athlete, daughter and father, mother and child, friends or acquaintances or lovers, sport is the connective force. In some of this literature the woman remains a spectator, but now she is observing other women, female athletes whose achievements create a vicarious sense of freedom for the spectator who is too often, as Hyacinthe Hill describes her in her poem *To the Olympians*,[1] left as a spectator of a game she'd rather be playing herself. In this poem, Hill insists that it is the athletes who "have saved me . . . I sit and watch you leap and spin / flexing my muscles, winning when you win." In her poem *Basket-Ball at Bryn Mawr*, Ethel le Roy de Koven calls these athletes "lithe young figures, with their striving, joyous strength," and Nancy Carter thanks them in her poem "Wings"[2] for taking her beyond vicarious enjoyment to a celebration of personal freedom.

Although much of the literature pays homage to the female athlete as liberator, sometimes it paints her as the source of entangled fascination and pride, comparison and envy. In Adrienne Rich's "Transit," Diane Wakoski's "Red Runner," and Theresa W. Miller's "Running With Helena," the observer sees herself as the "cripple" or the "slow / sea creature, / crawling along the bottom of the ocean" in the shadow of the athlete, who is described as a "bird," a "flame," or as one who "without let or hindrance / . . . travels in her body." Movement is posited against stasis, superior athlete contrasted with inferior nonathlete. But in these poems the need to connect remains strong, as does the need to answer the question: Where do our "minds converge"?

Frequently it is through sport that females seek to know their fathers and grandfathers, whose communication with them is often confined to the language of sports, the vernacular of the game. Carole Oles in "The Interpretation of Baseball" tries to listen to memory, to understand her father's attempt—even though he saved the Babe Ruth baseball for his son—to connect with *her* through the game. In "City Ball" by Roberta Israeloff, a young girl comes to understand the egotism of childhood through her gruff, immigrant grandfather whose only way of connecting with her is through their mutual love of baseball. And in "The Pain Business," Linda France remembers her grandfather, a man she never met, a fighter whom she now wishes her sons, "limbering up to be men," could know.

Sport is a place where women find their own heritage and their own strength through their relationships with fathers and brothers. In "The Cyclist" Cherry Clayton recognizes that the race connects her to her father, who was connected in the same way to his own father, the one who held "him poised / for the starter's gun." In Mary Anne Waters's "Ping-Pong Doubles Match," a girl, observing her father and brother compete, realizes that she is ready "to play [her] brother's game." Jean Rhys also seeks connections with her brothers in "On Not Shooting Sitting Birds," but she was never interested in playing their game.

In more and more literature females are the participants and athletes, and their relationships with their grandmothers, mothers, and daughters, in and through sport, are often replacing the standard model of female observer–male participant, which has for so long imbued the literature on and influenced the images of sport. In Jewelle L. Gomez's prose memoir, "A Swimming Lesson," a young black girl's grandmother, unable to swim herself, teaches the girl not only how to hold up her head in water but also, as she says, how "to stand on any beach anywhere and be proud of my large body, my African hair."

The water also freed Patricia Goedicke and provided a respite for her, a place—away from her sneering, critical, and lame father—where she, her mother, and sister could be "safe / In the oval of each other's arms / . . . weightless, / As guiltless, utterly free." In Margaret Atwood's "Woman Skating," the mother is the hero, the miracle worker who can balance on "steel / needles / . . . on time / sustained, above / time circling."

In other works the mothers connect with their daughters, sometimes by observing their diving and golf lessons, sometimes by teaching them to play chess. For those mothers who are the participants themselves, sport becomes a metaphorical universe, a place to explore the changing relationships with their children. Barbara Smith and Lucia Cordell Getsi create a simultaneous sense of union and separation in their poems. For Smith, the rope that holds her to her son as they mountain-climb a thousand feet in the air is like an umbilical cord, but she knows that her son's breathing now is "far beyond" her own. Likewise, Getsi's mother and daughter seem to "have the same heart, one organ" until the daughter "surges / ahead." Sometimes the intensity of these connections between mother and child makes Linda Pastan envy those who have no such ties, those "who are attached / to earth only by / silver blades moving / at high speed."

Most often, however, sport seems to provide an atmosphere for connections, a place where friendships are solidified, as in Marge Piercy's "Morning Athletes," and a place where bonds are forged, often among women who have little else in common, as in Anita Skeen's "Soccer by Moonlight." In Skeen's poem, women who are doctors, lawyers, teachers, and accountants come together to share one abiding passion—soccer. For Susan Richards Shreve, "The Locker Room" is a place where women who are really strangers, who have no contact with one another outside those walls, can share a certain intimacy.

Among competitive athletes, who must by the very nature of competition differentiate and separate themselves from others, this need to connect remains strong. Competition, in women's sport literature, has a different feel, a more relational rather than an all-conquering attitude. Mariah Burton Nelson's "Competition" and Maxine Kumin's "Prothalamion" reflect this alternative view of competition by recognizing the need not to destroy a competitor, but rather to seek union with her. Nelson's swimmer needs the other to be her best, and Kumin's tennis players "improve each other."

Indeed, the natural connection that athletes have with their teammates is heightened among female athletes. In Janice Bultmann's "Pair Partner," a certain intimacy is felt between one rower who watches the other's back "for direction" as they match "blade for blade." For Lucy Jane Bledsoe's gay, 15-year-old softball player, who falls "seriously in love for the first time during a double play," the need to connect with others in sport through sex results in the painful realization that "softball and sex [are] two separate things."

Adrienne Rich's "Phantasia for Elvira Shatayev," which concludes this section, is a eulogy written on behalf of Shatayev—leader of a doomed women's climbing team, all of whom perished in a snowstorm—to her husband who later found and buried the bodies. In this poem there is no room for regret, no place for fear, even in the face of an impending, icy death. Because of the deep and abiding love the women have for each other, the terrible reality of their fate—"burning together in the snow"—becomes not their nightmare but the dream they have shared all of their lives.

[1]Hyacinthe Hill's *To the Olympians* can be found in *Atalanta*, edited by Sandra Martz. Los Angeles: Papier-Mache Press, 1984, p.12.

[2]Nancy Carter's *Wings* can be found in *Atalanta*, edited by Sandra Martz. Los Angeles: Papier-Mache Press, 1984, p.2.

Basket-Ball at Bryn Mawr

Ethel le Roy de Koven

An amphitheatre built when Nature wrought her will,
Curve upon curve—a glinting, grass-grown citadel;
A tawny hollow worn by many a well-fought rout,
And there a vivid, changing maze wreathes in and out.

The lithe young figures, with their striving, joyous strength,
Entwined, rock to and fro in all their supple length;
Bright in October scarlet, gay in forest green,
They run like scurrying leaves, wind-blown
    through Autumn's scene.

Here, first, a struggling knot will waver, swerve, and form;
There, then, it breaks, like scattering clouds before a storm;
Wrenched bravely out with strength of straight
    young arms, the ball
An instant hovers buoyant, high above them all.

Transit

Adrienne Rich

When I meet the skier she is always
walking, skis and poles shouldered, toward the mountain
free-swinging in worn boots
over the path new-sifted with fresh snow
her greying dark hair almost hidden by

From *The Athlete's Garland: A Collection of Verse in Sport and Pastime*, 1905, compiled by Wallace Rice (Chicago: A. C. McClurg & Co.), 32-33.

"Transit," from THE FACT OF A DOORFRAME: Poems Selected and New, 1950-1984 by Adrienne Rich. Copyright © 1984 by Adrienne Rich. Copyright © 1975, 1978 by W. W. Norton & Company, Inc. Copyright © 1981 by Adrienne Rich. Reprinted by permission of the author and W. W. Norton & Company, Inc.

a cap of many colors
her fifty-year-old, strong, impatient body
dressed for cold and speed
her eyes level with mine

And when we pass each other I look into her face
wondering what we have in common
where our minds converge
for we do not pass each other, she passes me
as I halt beside the fence tangled in snow,
she passes me as I shall never pass her
in this life

Yet I remember us together
climbing Chocorua, summer nineteen-forty-five
details of vegetation beyond the timberline
lichens, wildflowers, birds,
amazement when the trail broke out onto the granite ledge
sloped over blue lakes, green pines, giddy air
like dreams of flying

When sisters separate they haunt each other
as she, who I might once have been, haunts me
or is it I who do the haunting
halting and watching on the path
how she appears again through lightly-blowing
crystals, how her strong knees carry her,
how unaware she is, how simple
this is for her, how without let or hindrance
she travels in her body
until the point of passing, where the skier
and the cripple must decide
to recognize each other?

Red Runner

Diane Wakoski

She comes at me in red tights
showing satin skin underneath,
and red shorts,
a red runner's jacket,

like a bird I don't expect to see
in the rain.

Thinking of fires I have built
and how flames are not
gratuitous,
how hard it is to get even
combustible material
>> to burn,

I wonder
how
she burns
through the continuous rain

(of Juneau),
this runner, young woman,
product of the 20th century.

When I passed her,
we exchanged a rather frank
brutal
glance.

She saw
a middle-aged woman,
bundled in a coat,
walking fast on her short legs.
Probably, to this red runner,
I appeared to be some slow
sea creature,
crawling along the bottom
of the ocean.

She ran past me,
like firecrackers
(Which frightened me in my youth)
or sequins glittering on a dancer's costume,
a bottle of Tabasco which had put on Adidas,
and, irrelevantly, I think of
a Carmen Miranda movie.

But this rain has come to mean
that things don't change.
When you reach a certain age, even the flame of a
red satin-shorted runner,
coming like a can-can girl
out of the silver twilight
was not so much a change, as a proof of
sameness.
Red runner,
reminder that I live
if not
in another time,
another world,
one where a flame is not easy
to coax into life,
one where I am outdated,

or extinguished,
or under water;
certainly no location for a flame.

Tonight
with a blue sweater
her red jacket tied around her waist
red shorts again,
this time legs naked and
white as sea scallops.
She frowned
as she passed me again.
Scorpion fish,
sea slug,
slow mover in the silvery twilight.

Running With Helena

Theresa W. Miller

It's like being her shadow,
shorter and thicker
then disappearing
altogether behind her.

Like her name, she slips past
easily, sure of her direction.
Running is a business move—
she quotes the rates,
knows stocks and percentages,

wears high-tech shoes,
has a positive attitude.

I fall behind,
learning the merger
of the neighborhood:
bacon, flowers and coffee,
voices and dogs,
my own feet and the pavement,
wet, a window slammed,
the pitch of an argument.

The Interpretation of Baseball

Carole Oles

It took time to study who was missing
from the dream ball club that paraded
through the dark in uniforms and numbers
holding up posters of the lost teammate
as if campaigning for their man.

I had to walk the dream railroad track again
where my son followed me at first, then took
the lead, balanced, leaped forward over the ties,
poof—gone.
And to sit with the inquisitor who wore
my dachshund around his neck like a precious
fur with lacquered eyes.

I had to listen then to memory,
your fastball, your grand slams out of the park.

Reprinted, by permission, from Carole Oles, 1988, "The Interpretation of Baseball" *Poetry* 152 (3): 133.

And go back to the bleachers at Yankee Stadium
where you took me at 7 though I was not the son
whose heart, that sly courser, unseated him.
He was the one you saved your prize for,
the baseball Babe Ruth signed.
At the game you tried to show me what you saw
but I was gabbing about something else:
another hot dog, how many more minutes.

It took time, Father, to see
you swinging, connecting.

City Ball

Roberta Israeloff

Moony, who's named for all the obvious reasons—his belly's roughly spherical, as if he'd once swallowed a barrel of baseballs—usually sits right there, in his vinyl recliner to the left of the TV, hands clasped behind his head. Each year, as he shrinks a fraction of an inch, his feet rise slightly off the floor, but it's like the continental drift—you can't see it. He calls everyone on my favorite team a bum and advises managers against any pitching change whatsoever at any time. And this Saturday, which should be no different than any other and hasn't been up to this very minute—in the car we had the same conversations; around exit three of the Cross Bronx Expressway, Webster Avenue, my mother said, That's where Neila Thorpman used to live, and two exits later, as we swung off the highway onto the Grand Concourse she said, I won't even park, we'll just stay a minute, and I said, We'll park, and she does, but first she lets me off and I run upstairs (the door is always open) and into the living room, and there's Moony sitting in his chair—is suddenly special, Moony isn't there.

"What do you mean, not here?" I asked my grandmother, Cassie, who sits with her knees spread as wide apart as the Lincoln Memorial, her skirt and apron making a lap the size of many tables. In it rest her crocheting, two handkerchiefs, three hair combs, an apple, a nougat candy and her change purse. "Where is he?" Where could he possibly be? I tried to remember if I'd seen him walk anywhere recently, especially on a weekend. We used to go out to dinner once a month to City Island, but around the second course he'd say he had to go to the toilet and end up in the kitchen catching the game with the waiters, his food getting cold and Cassie getting mad.

Cassie indicated the window, which looks out over the Armory. I crossed the jungle, her tangle of plants with dust-free leaves, and peered out. There he was, I saw him, Moony and "the kid from downstairs," the Russian kid, the dark-haired, serious Ivan who's three years older than me and wears old clothes. He and Moony were looking toward Kingsbridge Road. Moony had his arm on the boy's shoulder. I knew what he was saying, too: Signals. Signals are the heart of baseball. No one else knows that, except for me and every major league manager, that's all. And then Moony told him some signals. Lick your middle finger and touch the side of your nose, hitch up your pants. And if you don't believe him he'll ask you what you think the manager is doing standing there on the dugout steps anyway? Why do you think he takes long drinks of water and spits three, clean times? It's all

From "Pig Iron," 1982. Also appeared in DIAMONDS ARE A GIRL'S BEST FRIEND, edited by Elinor Nauen. Copyright © by Roberta Israeloff. Reprinted by permission of the author.

signals. Baseball is a game in code, a game of signs between manager, coach, catcher, pitcher, batter. It's not a lonely game. Unwritten letters, entire encyclopedias of baseball knowledge flutter across the field every minute.

That's not how Moony would say it, that was me. Some fans are more poetic than others.

"I can't believe it," I said, and I couldn't.

"Did you ever ask Moony to teach you to play?" Cassie asked. She was looking into thin air, not at me or the television or what she was doing. If she stopped patrolling for as much as a second, who knew what could happen? A particle of dust could fall, a leaf could drop, a smell could come out of nowhere and embarrass her. No, she was always working.

I had never asked him, but that wasn't the point. I never cared about the physical aspect of the game. Not that I wasn't athletic. I made sure I learned how to throw like a boy when I was young, before any of the boys on my block learned. But baseball's subtler side is what hooked me, and for all the years I can remember sprawled on the floor next to the vinyl recliner, listening to Moony digest baseball, I had been hounding him to take me to a game at Yankee Stadium. Cassie and my mother would tell me to lay off, that he was tired, old, fat, too newly into retirement to want to stir. Leave him alone, give him a break, they said. And now he's downstairs with a strange kid.

"I thought we had nothing to do with those Russians," I said. Only last week we were treated to a half hour's harangue on how only poor people cook smelly like the Russians do—this from a woman who doesn't like to use salt—how the husband works two shifts, how their windows face the street, with no shades, how the children are hooligans, murder incorporated, big trouble.

"The girl is wild. His sister, Lana. But the boy is very nice. He comes to visit us some afternoons."

"Oh really." I felt like crying but didn't. It seemed ridiculous to be jealous of my grandfather. When I looked again, I saw Lana, the wild sister, ride her bike toward the field. She jerked the handlebars so it bucked the curb, then gave it a last pedal and levitated off it, abandoned it in midair. The bike, a rusty, clanging racer, ran for a few seconds without her, upright, before crashing into a tree. She ran to the pathetic pile of baseball equipment her brother managed to collect over the months—a broom stick, two tennis balls, two of their father's gloves stuffed one inside the other, fingers sewn together. Then they huddled, all three of them, a conference on the mound. She turned and took 45 paces, turned and threw a pitch. Too high. Not so high, I heard Moony saying. She tried again. Too low. Moony tossed the ball back to her. His arm looked like a tree branch. She scooped the ball out of the dirt. Tried again. This time it came in waist level. Ivan, who'd been waiting with the stick, made a sudden, spastic movement at the last possible second.

He twisted his body, his toes came through his sneakers and his shoulder blades sliced through his tee shirt. He smashed the ball, busted its seams, so that as it sailed over the Armory tower it looked like an exploded bird.

Moony wouldn't be saying anything now. He doesn't believe in undue praise.

That's when my mother came up, puffing faintly; she needed to lose some weight. "Where's Moony?" she asked too, first thing.

Cassie indicated the window. "And what's with you," my mother asked, as I moved out of the jungle, steaming, so she could move in and catch a glimpse of her father acting a quarter of his age. I walked to the vinyl chair, looked at it, studied the huge indentation made by Moony, and fell into it. No one expected this. I put my hands behind my head, and moved the seat back so my feet were slightly off the floor. It was the third inning. It always was when we got there. During the commercials I turned to my mother and said, "How's business?"

"Don't be fresh," said Cassie. My mother didn't know whether to laugh or cry. Sometimes she blamed the breakup of her marriage on this one question, asked every week of a surgeon, her husband, who never understood why he should have to apologize to his wife's parents for not having the kind of business Moony meant when he asked, every Saturday at this time, How's business? Business, to Moony, meant sitting on a crate on 8th Avenue and 18th Street, watching lumber supply trucks jockey into driveways, watching Lillie's hands grow arthritic as she works the cash register, watching plumbing hardware go up and down the open elevator, watching couriers with mob connections, watching the cops. The kind of business that gets into the folds of the skin of your hands and under your fingernails. The kind you have to change clothes for. Well, my father used to change clothes too, but into cleaner ones than he stepped out of.

Now it's the bottom of the third, that all important inning, says Moony, when the wild pitcher settles down, when the tired pitcher falters. Moony claims you can predict which games will be no hitters in the third. He did just that with Larsen's game, 1956. So he says.

"You shouldn't make fun of your grandfather," said Cassie, out of nowhere.

"How come you're nicer to Moony when he's not here than when he is?" I asked.

"Someday you'll understand." She sat up suddenly, as if she said something impossibly funny, and reached for her daughter's hand. Cassie's always making jokes no one else gets. Mom, meanwhile, dug around in her pockets for the surprise of the afternoon—these big orange, plastic ears she got at the five and ten which have earplugs inside. When she put them on she looked like something from outer space. "What's the idea?" asked Cassie.

"I can't stand the baseball announcers, Mother," she said. "You know that."

"So turn off the sound, I don't care."

"Don't touch it," I roared, just like Moony, and they turned around to stare at me. I could imitate him to a tee. When Cassie asked if I wanted fruit, I brushed her away with the back of my hand. When she asked How's school, I said "Oke." No one should get in the habit of talking when the baseball game's on.

Only then we heard crazy footsteps out in the hall and a wild knocking, then a slower, heavier step that had to be Moony. Lana burst in—that girl always looked as if centrifugal force tore her apart each night and she had to shake herself down like a cat to get her limbs on straight—yelling, "I didn't mean it. Please. We were practicing curves."

Moony stumbled in next, a purple bruise over his right eye. Ivan was right behind him, as if the boy would have been of any use had Moony fallen backward. Cassie got up in a flutter but remembered to hold her apron out so that her things wouldn't fall. She looked like those statues in rich people's fountains, and she started making those noises which mean I'm not as concerned as I sound.

"Out of my way, Lady," he said. "I'm fine, just fine. Got brushed back, that's all." He sank into his chair which I'd kept warm for him. The cushions gave their familiar whistle at this weight, and the wood creaked too. "I'm fine," he said again. "What's the matter with you? See a crowd?"

Lana ran out, but Ivan stayed, trying to explain exactly what happened. He had his mitt with him. Cassie didn't waste a moment. "You had no business playing ball at all," she scolded her husband. "No business at all."

He gave her the brush. "What's the score here, Donna?"

So that's what I was good for. The score. "Fourth, Top. Two out."

"Yeah? Who's up? Who's ahead?"

"Kaline." Couldn't he tell? I thought that was the point—study the shadows on the field, the way the umpire makes his calls, who's hanging around near the water fountain in the dugout, who's on deck—that's your job, as a fan. Wasn't that what he'd been training me to do? Wasn't that why he never answered me, completely?

"Yanks ahead by one. Three and two on Kaline."

"Thank you," he said. "What's eating her?"

"Think about it," I said. "You'll figure it out."

"I'm calling the doctor, Moony. You hear me?" That was Cassie, who else.

He ignored her. She put down the receiver without dialing, and noticed Ivan standing in the foyer, near the cedar chest, which houses Moony's woolen navy jerseys. The boy was still apologizing. In a moment Cassie would ask him if he needed any nice, warm clothing. Then she'd remove all eight objects from the top of the chest, including the dust cover, explaining how she made it herself with fabric from Russia, how lovely it is to have a cedar chest, ask if his mother has one. Then she'd shake out a jersey, make Ivan slip it on, and cluck sorrowfully when it's way too big, too moth-ball smelly.

When that was over, she brought out a folding chair from the bedroom for Ivan to sit on. "Would anyone like some nice fruit?" she asked.

"Quiet, please," Moony said. "The bum is up."

"Lovely language," Cassie sang. She muttered something in Yiddish and got up to get the apples no one wanted, the same ones she brought out last week. I leaned over and said to Moony, "Do you understand her when she speaks Yiddish?" He brushed me away with the back of his hand—no.

"He's lying," Cassie shouted. Her voice was scratchy when she yelled, but she had the best pair of seventy-five-year-old ears I'd ever seen.

"Now here's an interesting situation," Moony said. I wasn't sure if he was talking to me or Ivan. We both moved closer, dutifully. "Two men aboard, one and two, one out. Good bunter up. Would you have him sacrifice? Or take?"

"Swing away," said Ivan.

"Sharp kid," said Moony.

"Let him take," said Cassie. The man swings and misses. Moony shrugs.

Now there's a conference on the mound. The one question I always wanted to ask Moony was this: what do they really say during these meetings. I didn't think anyone bothered to mention the pitcher's stuff. Whether the pitcher has his stuff is obvious, anyone can see that, even my mother could. No, I thought they call these conferences because first of all the manager wants to take a stroll, he's getting chilly, and the catcher needs to get up, stretch, flip that mask up over his head, you can go crazy looking through bars all day. And the pitcher wants attention. He's been out there struggling all alone. So the other guys come on out and they have a little conversation that goes like this. How's the wife, kids? Fine, fine, couldn't be better. They here today? Nah, kids had a dentist appointment. Too bad. Yeah. Hey, you about ready for that cold beer? You bet! Then the pitcher steps back, rubs his eyes with his fists like a baby, and spits.

"Do that again," Mom said. "I love it when they spit."

"No, not me, I don't like that part," said Cassie. "I like when they give each other love pats on their behinds."

"Lady, we're trying to watch a baseball game here," Moony said.

I had plenty of questions. Like suppose this next guy strikes out. Will the other players talk to him in the clubhouse? Say you go four for four, five RBIs, but your team loses. Are you allowed to be happy later, in the clubhouse? If your team is behind, bases loaded, two out in the bottom of the ninth and you're on deck, do you pray that the guy ahead of you will end it, any way he can, just so you won't have to deal with the pressure? That's how I'd be. That's why you're not a ballplayer, Moony would say. But those are the kinds of questions I'd like to ask, if I weren't in the habit of only asking those questions I already know the answers to.

"You know, Ivan," Cassie said, crocheting again, "my family originally came from a town near Odessa. That's where you're from?"

"Yep," he said. "It is."

"I used to remember a lot about the village," she went on. "When I was a young girl and couldn't sleep, my grandmother knew it was because I had a big memory. And when my parents decided that we'd go to America, the elders of the village walked me around for days. They'd point to things, and I'd remember them. We walked everywhere, they'd point and say, 'That. And that.' And I put everything into my head, each in its own compartment, until I had to cry, 'Enough! I can't fit any more in.'"

Moony got up, reached the set in a single stride, leaned over like a seesaw, and raised the volume.

"You don't need the sound," Cassie said, "you know all the answers. Anyway my mother and I left soon after that, on a boat for America. It was for twenty days. And I had to keep my head tilted so, because I didn't want anything to slip out. I was afraid to yawn, or sneeze, afraid that something would fly out, like where was Mitya's chicken coop, or the color of the school. I kept my eyes closed until America, when we settled in with cousins on the Lower East Side. And then, no paper, no pencil, no peace and quiet."

She stopped. From my mother's expression I knew she had never heard this story before either. Mickey Mantle was at bat. He had a full count, three and two. No one would ask Cassie what happened next so I did.

"I stole a paper bag from the butcher," she said, "and I found a pencil in the gutter and I sharpened it with my teeth. I tore the bag in half and wrote in the tiniest script you can imagine. I wrote for days, two days and two nights straight, in the little corner next to the kitchen."

Mickey Mantle struck out. Roger Maris was at bat. He was the cleanup hitter. Once I thought the term cleanup referred only to Mick. He was the cleanest looking player I'd ever seen. It looked as if he scrubbed his hair with scouring brushes. His Oklahoman blondness was as exotic as anything from Odessa.

"You wrote it all down?" asked Ivan. "You wrote about your entire village?"

"Yes, I did, and then I had no place to put the pages for safekeeping, so I rolled them into a tube and wrapped my hair around them and fastened them with a hair clip. And when I finished, the second night, I went for a walk to the East River, alone, and that's where I first met Moony."

Moony was squirming in his chair. Maris hit a home run and the Yankees went ahead by five. Moony said, "I told you he'd hit one out of here."

But no one was listening to him. "I walked along the river," Cassie said, "feeling as if a fever had lifted. And there, on a field under a streetlight, a field littered with glass, I saw some boys playing a game that reminded me of a game we played at home, called brennball.

"Brennball, I play that game," Ivan said. He was tremendously excited. "I was brennball champion in my town."

"Only this wasn't brennball," Cassie said, "it was American baseball. And I watched a skinny, red-haired man in the field, who used an old leather glove and scrambled to his left, his right. I watched them play the whole night. When it got light and the streetlights went off, the others left. The red head walked toward his bicycle; that's where I was standing. He gave me a ride home on the handlebars."

"Shortstop?" I asked. "You played shortstop?"

"I don't know what she's talking about," Moony said. His hands were gripping the arm rests of the recliner.

"What happened next," Cassie said, "is that I took very sick, very ill, and my mother blamed it on my being out all night. But it wasn't. It was from going into that trance to write out everything that I remembered. She took me to the doctor, who didn't believe me, and they pulled my hair out and all my teeth out, that's what they did in those days, and I came home crying that no one would want to marry me, ever. But Moony did. We called him Moony, then, you know, because his eyes had a far away look, like he was looking for the moon."

"Are you finished?" Moony asked. His eyes didn't look far away now, they looked close, tiny, narrow. He started to get up. He'd never left a game before it was all over. Usually he kept the set on till the game was long over, past the presentation of the Schick player of the day and the Old Spice player of the week, he outlasted all the announcers, the scoreboard, the wrap-up, the theme song—Moony had an affair with televised baseball, usually. He never even got up to go to the bathroom. But now he was on his feet.

"Where're you going, Dad?" My mother sounded concerned. She kept her eyes on him as Cassie started talking again.

"You know how funny it is to think about when we were young. He used to be skinny then. Skinnier than me. Until he got sick and had to stop smoking. That's when he put on all the weight. You know this story, don't you? Oh god, he was so skinny and his hands were always so dirty I never wanted him to come near me. I was afraid I'd hurt him, you see, and I wanted his hands to be clean. Not for years after we were married could I stand him touching me. It sounds funny to say but it's true."

"You talk too much, lady," Moony said, reappearing with his hat, his jacket.

"Where are you going, Moony?" she cried, "Moony, wait."

He slammed the door shut. "I'm his biggest fan," Cassie said.

"Go after him," my mother said. "Go, follow him."

"He doesn't want me," I said.

"Go," said Cassie, standing up. This time everything rolled out of her lap onto the floor. "Go, of course he wants you. What are you waiting for, a silver invitation with your name engraved? He doesn't want anyone else to go after him but you. Go."

So I went. I ran after him. I wouldn't have been surprised if Cassie had engineered the whole afternoon so she could throw me and Moony together like this. She knew that was what I wanted more than anything.

I was a good half a block behind him, walking toward the bus stop, but he walked slowly and we got on the same bus. I ended up sitting behind him. We didn't acknowledge each other. I wasn't sure where we were going but I had a good idea. We rode under the el tracks. And after about ten minutes I saw it, the beige and blue towers of Yankee Stadium, the giant heart, arising out of nowhere like a modern day castle.

Moony took a few minutes to get his bearings once we were on the street. Then he took off for the ticket windows, all closed now. In fact, people were leaving. I'd lost track of the game, forgot who was winning, couldn't calculate the inning. We kept walking and walking, nearly all around the stadium, until we came to a door marked No Admittance. There Moony stopped and knocked. A man in a cap, with a big stomach, same vintage as Moony, answered, saw Moony, hugged him. They spoke for a few moments, laughed—the man opened the door for Moony and Moony called me. "This is where the players' wives go in," Moony said. "Jake's an old friend of mine."

We walked through a narrow concrete corridor. We passed arrows pointing to the clubhouse, one to the tunnel. "That's it," Moony said. "Want to go?" It was the tunnel I'd always wanted to explore, the one through which pitchers walked from dugout to bullpen and back. It was the best place to get autographs.

"Nope," I said. "I'll go with you." He kept walking in what seemed like circles, but then just ahead I saw some light, and heard noise, and smelled an acrid smell. We passed vendors counting their money, and I turned around to watch them, they winked at me—now there's a job I hadn't thought of; why not, maybe next summer—and when I turned around to find Moony, we were already out there, under a ledge, out, near the field. The baseball diamond, the players, the bloody dirt basepaths, the grass, everything scrubbed and shorn and raked as clean and perfect as Mickey Mantle's crewcut. Everything trim as pinstripes, oh it was so lovely. I got dizzy, walked into Moony, who had stopped to get his bearings again. Seats and tiers rose everywhere, people were standing, it must have been the middle of a rally. I heard the crowd roar, and didn't know if I was screaming too, or not.

"I used to like the third base side," Moony said. "That OK with you?"

It sure was. We walked toward left field, along the aisle just above the reserved box seats. We walked until we were at the foul pole, to a pretty deserted section. Moony picked out two seats from which we could see right into the Yankee dugout. Couldn't be better. I had a perfect view of that water cooler.

Next surprise—when the vendor came by Moony ordered two beers. "Don't tell your grandmother," he said. "Go ahead, drink up." I took a sip. Moony just sat there, holding his, as if he wanted to simply feel the heft of the brew, the spongy wet plastic.

"How'd you get us in here?"

"I used to know all those guys. We came here nearly every afternoon, after work, in the summer. With Mike Acre and Johnny Sparrow. This is between you and me, you understand."

I nodded. "It's so quiet here." I couldn't put my finger on what was missing.

"The Voice of the Yankees, that's what's missing," he said. "No one announces here. You have to keep your own score."

"What inning is it? What's going on?"

"I don't know," Moony said. "It never matters as much, once you get here. That's the beauty of the thing."

"Well the Yankees are behind by three," said the man sitting in front of us. "Where have you birds been?" Moony and he, Conklin, chewed over the game—Moony was interested after all, I knew it—and I sat back in my seat, looking around. Mickey Mantle's in center field. If I yelled to him he would probably hear me. His neck and thighs were really tremendous, just like they said. But for some reason, everything looked distant, almost more distant than things did on TV. I mean, there I was, in concrete stands, full of city filth and grime—beer and mustard, the seats were sticky, my feet were sticky. And there on the field, on the grass and the most manicured dirt I'd ever seen, stood men dressed like boys, in clean uniforms which were probably dry cleaned in between innings, who never spoke to each other, or heard us. They were in the country and we were in the city, and what a country game it was. And in that country you talk to each other by spitting, by patting each other's tails, by taking long drinks from the water cooler, kicking it sometimes, by taking skinny spits, where you always say less than you mean and count on your body to say the rest.

"What's the matter?" Moony asked. "Aren't you having fun? Didn't you hear, this guy Conklin's son is up there, hitting. He was just called up from the farm team yesterday. This here's an exciting game."

The kid looked mighty nervous to me, up there at home plate. Even with his coaches and manager signalling to him, he looked alone and sweaty.

"Don't hit it to Mick," Conklin yelled.

"He's a bum," Moony said.

The kid ran the count to three and two. The runners, on first and second, would be going with the pitch. The kid took a deep breath, you could hear it throughout the stadium, and leaned into the pitch. It took off, rising steadily for enough seconds to lose track of how many. And he broke into a run. If the ball stayed fair he'd have a homer. If it went foul, he'd have another crack. The ball hung in the air for impossible seconds, and then took a turn in our direction. It's coming, I started to say, but never finished. Conklin's eyes widened. Moony stayed in his seat, and the ball came toward us, a gorgeous curve, and landed right in Moony's stomach. Right against his beer, which exploded like a bomb. Moony started gasping, I couldn't tell if he was choking or laughing. He turned blue, the wind knocked out of him, and I was afraid that he would die. On camera. We were on camera, they always turn the cameras to the guy who gets the ball. "Hey," I started yelling, "Hey there, hi." And I waved. And I pointed to Moony, and said, "He's all right," to Cassie and my mother, who I knew were watching. And soon Moony stopped choking, but he didn't stop smiling, and he clutched the ball to his stomach as if it was a baby.

Still, it was a foul ball, and the rookie went on to strike out and the Yankees couldn't get a thing across in the bottom of the ninth and lost. It didn't much matter, they'd already clinched the pennant. One of the things you have to get used to as a Yankee fan is that most of the normal excitement is gone from the game by about July. And here it was August, but I didn't mind. It was the best afternoon I could remember having.

When the game was over, we all stood up and shook hands with the kid's uncle, who stood around, expecting Moony to give him the ball, I think. But Moony was holding on to it, moving it from one hand to the other, clasping his hands around the seams and releasing them, rubbing it up as if he were going to throw a spitter. Finally, Conklin left, to see if he could get into the dugout. "Go with him, if you want," Moony said, "I'll wait for you right here." But I didn't want to go underground. I wanted to stand where I was and watch the stadium empty like a giant drain. I wanted to think about how it would be when we went home and Moony gave me the ball.

Maybe he would give it to Ivan. What then? I would be too jealous to speak. But Moony wouldn't do that. He was saving it for me. He was biding his time. Like at home, when we waited for the game to be completely, totally over. We watched the batboy, the last one in the dugout, disappear down the tube to the clubhouse. We watched the grounds crew pull the tarp over the bases, and the shadows grow longer in the outfield.

One of Moony's friends, in a cap, came and told us to move on. We started slowly down the ramp, up the aisle, back through the cavern to the street. We had a long, silent wait for the bus. People all around us were full of tips on how the Yankees could have won. Moony never liked to second guess. His only advice: don't change pitchers. It's a man's game to win or lose.

But something happened to Moony on the bus, he got a seat in the back, near the window, and started talking. "There was one night I came here, after work, a Thursday in 1954, 55. Me and Johnny and Mike, we had the bleachers to ourselves. It was late in the game. Maybe it was 56. Anyway DiMaggio was up. He hit a long ball, I mean a long ball, dead away center field, practically right to me. Watch out, they yelled, those guys, what a bunch of clowns, and they hid under their seats. Me, I wasn't afraid of the ball. As I watched it sailing to me, I thought that everything is about right, just as it is, now. I had a job, my family, a roof over my head, it was a late summer evening, I had half a pack of smokes left, and enough money for a beer and the bus home. I thought, That ball is gonna sail on outta here and we'll never have to worry again.

"The ball was caught," he said, "up against the center field wall. And for some dopey reason, nothing was the same after that."

"Really?" We were walking home now, from the bus stop. I could see the light on in Cassie's living room. I had just learned about his bad illness, that he had lost fifty pounds, then put on three times as much, that he had lost his own parents within a year—I knew events, I wondered if these were what he meant. I realized how little I knew him, how insignificantly I figured in his life, how I hadn't put in an appearance until he was two thirds of the way out. Suddenly he looked like a dinosaur trudging up the Kingsbridge hill. He was still holding the baseball.

"You should give that ball to Ivan," I said.

"No, I don't think so," Moony said. And then I knew he'd be giving it to me. We climbed the stairs, I went as slowly as he did, and Cassie and my mother met us at the door, telling us how they saw us, how great we looked.

Moony brushed them away, sank into the recliner. It whistled and moaned to welcome him home. He put the ball in his lap. Then he put it in a drawer of the table next to his chair. And I never saw him take it out.

The Pain Business

Linda France

The fight game's like prostitution: you do it for love first; and then you do it for a few friends; then you do it for money.

—Bill Barich

If a man is going to fight, he is going to fight. The question of morality doesn't arise.

—Henry Cooper

1. *Apocryphal*

Somewhere there's a photo I've never seen
of my grandfather, valiant, thin

in woolly vest and baggy shorts, fists cocked
at Jimmy Wilde, flyweight champion, circa 1910.

My grandfather didn't win. The fight
and the photo were good enough for him,

my father, me. He hit and got hit
to fill out a pitman's wage, rising

from dark tunnels, a mole with restless paws,
coming up to scratch. He'd give my sisters

a penny each, big as their palms.
We never met.

I wouldn't even know him if I saw him
in black and white, hanging from a wall

Linda France, *Red*, (Bloodaxe Books, 1992).

of the Men Only bar in Blackett Street.

2. *Significant Other*

A ring that's square; canvas vast, clean
as a god's eye; three thick ropes, holding them in.

A couple of strangers, bodies shimmering
like cadillacs, fists flexed with half a pound

of cowhide, shotgun stares. Dream the way
their sweat smells—creased leather;

a week's work in each armpit: layered
with bathroom disguise, elbowed and punched.

Recall a child covering her face
with her hands at some curdling sight—

a beast with teeth, a tonguing snake—unable
to resist peeping through the cracks, not

wishing to miss what she didn't want to see.
She's here again, sitting at the ringside,

inching in some place she's not meant to be.

3. *Slinging Leather*

He hits the streets, a kid never much nimble
with words, dealing in punches and insults.

Some sharp white guy, steamrolling a cigar
between his teeth, teaches him how to box,

not fight—chess with muscles—dancing
on canvas, playing pat-a-cake, eating eggs,

steak. Better fed than a cotton-picking slave,
he looks tough, keeps his trap shut.

His super-hero's chest's mahogany,
polished so high you might see your face in it.

He wants to be the best, world champ;
will risk killing for it, being killed.

Knocked out in the gutter like an empty can
or crimsoning a bouquet of soft white towels—

he reckons the odds are even.

4. *Natural Selection*

A white carnation—*Dianthus
caryophyllus*—shares a black boxer's name,

the thin petals whorled
like a cauliflower ear.

Pain is a seed sown every season,
vital as bread, tobacco, booze;

its dangerous blooms—*Dementia
pugilistica*—commonplace as cabbage.

Everything in the garden's punch-drunk, reeling.
A rose might be a rose might be a rose

but considering the game, the rules,
is it true that everything is so dangerous,

nothing is really frightening?
Pour another drink. Listen

to your hand shaking.

5. *The Queensberry Rules*
Paris 1900

His cognac's running out. No one
left to stand another round. He sits

like a king whom gold has made a fool, mocked
by amber dregs. A man on one knee

is considered down. To hit's against the rules.
And hugging. When the bell rang to begin

and end the match, Bosie feinted the moves
Oscar desired; couldn't decide which

of his father's rules to follow.
The judges sat in his corner. He caught

him off his guard; fought below the belt.
Melmoth drains his glass; a prize-fighter

put out to grass, waiting for the long count.

6. Southpaw

Time was when rules were there to be broken;
now it's us who're tamed like horses, broken

in; mouths so full of tackle there's no room
for tongues, the articulate anarchy of kisses.

The danger's high as the stakes,
the fistful of cards close to the chest,

ducking under the left hook—impulse,
strategy, sweat. I watch my sons

limbering up to be men, can not put them through
their paces for an audience baying for blood.

They choke on tears if they think they've lost
and I wish my grandfather were there,

an impresario, mining pockets to press winking coins,
a white handkerchief into small steady hands

that can give or take a second skin.

The Cyclist

Cherry Clayton

A child in the thicket of legs on the stand
I watched my father race between
the sweating crowd of smooth-suited riders,
crash-helmeted, often crashing down
but up to ride again, oiled with wintergreen.

From the glittering bunch on the track
one would break—sometimes it was him—
the crowd would roar for the single rider
with gritted teeth, glancing back.

His father, white-headed, holding him poised
for the starter's gun, the 'old man'
with the same smooth head.
'I was handsome there', he said.

The road races, orange quarters to pass
to the hero's hand to refresh,
bikes in a steel heap in the van,
silver-spoked reels of wheels.

All the albums, medals, cuttings
yellowed with age. 'The Games of 36'.
The men who were kind or great,
the 'skaaps' who knew from nothing.

There's a small silver bike on the mantelpiece.
But he still goes out to ride.
Last seen, he threw his hands in the air

like a winner over the line
as he rode into the sun.

My father's race is almost run.

Ping-Pong Doubles Match

Mary Ann Waters

> The score was eighteen-all, and the look
> on my father's face severe enough
> to inspire my little brother
>
> who knew the next serve would come at him
> low and fast. He nodded to us,
> winked at my mother, then threw back
>
> his head, waved his left hand like a wand,
> shook himself all over, howled,
> and vanished in a cloud of chartreuse smoke.
>
> Or so it seemed. We stopped, blinked,
> not yet stone, the child of Oz was back,
> cracked his paddle on the table,
>
> wiggled his fingers into donkey ears,
> stuck out his tongue. *Nyaahhh,*
> *I'm gonna get this one,* he hissed,
>
> and when it came, slammed that eggshell
> back so hard it struck the table's edge
> and glanced off to the side, impossible

to return. That's when I understood it: that
crazy luck he got from acting crazy.
The sun went down and I went out

into the dark, faced the west, scowled,
and raised my arms like a conductor or a god.
Sure enough, the sleepy birds began to sing

funny little backwards songs, the sky
turned pale, then blushed,
and up that fireball rose again

like an enormous balloon, wobbling
as if I'd jerked the string but climbing
just the same, and I was brilliant,

ready now to play my brother's game.

On Not Shooting Sitting Birds

Jean Rhys

There is no control over memory. Quite soon you find yourself being vague about an event which seemed so important at the time that you thought you'd never forget it. Or unable to recall the face of someone whom you could have sworn was there for ever. On the other hand, trivial and mean-ingless memories may stay with you for life. I can still shut my eyes and see Victoria grinding coffee on the pantry steps, the glass bookcase and the books in it, my father's pipe-rack, the leaves of the sandbox tree, the wallpaper of the bedroom in some shabby hotel, the hairdresser in Antibes. It's in this way that I remember buying the pink milanese silk underclothes, the assistant who sold them to me and coming into the street holding the parcel.

I had started out in life trusting everyone and now I trusted no one. So I had few acquaintances and no close friends. It was perhaps in reaction against the inevitable loneliness of my life that I'd find myself doing bold, risky, even outrageous things without hesitation or surprise. I was usually disappointed in these adventures and they didn't have much effect on me, good or bad, but I never quite lost the hope of something better or different.

One day, I've forgotten now where, I met this young man who smiled at me and when we had talked a bit I agreed to have dinner with him in a couple of days' time. I went home excited, for I'd liked him very much, and began to plan what I should wear. I had a dress I quite liked, an evening cloak, shoes, stockings, but my underclothes weren't good enough for the occasion, I decided. Next day I went out and bought the milanese silk chemise and drawers.

So there we were seated at a table having dinner with a bedroom very obvious in the background. He was younger than I'd thought and stiffer and I didn't like him much after all. He kept eyeing me in such a wary, puzzled way. When we had finished our soup and the waiter had taken the plates away, he said: "But you're really a lady, aren't you?" exactly as he might have said, "But you're really a snake or a crocodile, aren't you?"

"Oh no, not that you'd notice," I said, but this didn't work. We looked glumly at each other across the gulf that had yawned between us.

Before I came to England I'd read many English novels and I imagined I knew all about the thoughts and tastes of various sorts of English people. I quickly decided that to distract or interest this man I must talk about shooting.

I asked him if he knew the West Indies at all. He said no, he didn't and I told him a long story of having been lost in the Dominican forest when I

| 183 |

was a child. This wasn't true. I'd often been in the woods but never alone. "There are no parrots now," I said, "or very few. There used to be. There's a Dominican parrot in the zoo—have you ever seen it?—a sulky bird, very old I think. However, there are plenty of other birds and we do have shooting parties. Perdrix are very good to eat, but ramiers are rather bitter."

Then I began describing a fictitious West Indian shooting party and all the time I talked I was remembering the real thing. An old shotgun leaning up in one corner of the room, the round table in the middle where we would sit to make cartridges, putting the shot in, ramming it down with a wad of paper. Gunpowder? There was that too, for I remember the smell. I suppose the boys were trusted to be careful.

The genuine shooting party consisted of my two brothers, who shared the shotgun, some hangers-on and me at the end of the procession, for then I couldn't bear to be left out of anything. As soon as the shooting was about to start I would stroll away casually and when I was out of sight run as hard as I could, crouch down behind a bush and put my fingers in my ears. It wasn't that I was sorry for the birds, but I hated and feared the noise of the gun. When it was all over I'd quietly join the others. I must have done this unobtrusively or probably my brothers thought me too insignificant to worry about, for no one ever remarked on my odd behaviour or teased me about it.

On and on I went, almost believing what I was saying, when he interrupted me. "Do you mean to say that your brothers shot sitting birds?" His voice was cold and shocked.

I stared at him. How could I convince this man that I hadn't the faintest idea whether my brothers shot sitting birds or not? How could I explain now what really happened? If I did he'd think me a liar. Also a coward and there he'd be right, for I was afraid of many things, not only the sound of gunfire. But by this time I wasn't sure that I liked him at all so I was silent and felt my face growing as stiff and unsmiling as his.

It was a most uncomfortable dinner. We both avoided looking at the bedroom and when the last mouthful was swallowed he announced that he was going to take me home. The way he said this rather puzzled me. Then I told myself that probably he was curious to see where I lived. Neither of us spoke in the taxi except to say, "Well, goodnight." "Goodnight."

I felt regretful when it came to taking off my lovely pink chemise, but I could still think: Some other night perhaps, another sort of man. I slept at once.

A Swimming Lesson

Jewelle L. Gomez

At nine years old I didn't realize my grandmother, Lydia, and I were doing an extraordinary thing by packing a picnic lunch and riding the elevated train from Roxbury to Revere Beach. It seemed part of the natural rhythm of summer to me. I didn't notice how the subway cars slowly emptied of most of their Black passengers as the train left Boston's urban center and made its way into the Italian and Irish suburban neighborhoods to the north. It didn't seem odd that all of the Black families stayed in one section of the beach and never ventured onto the boardwalk to the concession stands or the rides except in groups.

I do remember Black women perched cautiously on their blankets, tugging desperately at bathing suits rising too high in the rear and complaining about their hair "going back." Not my grandmother, though. She glowed with unashamed athleticism as she waded out, just inside the reach of the waves, and moved along the riptide parallel to the shore. Once submerged, she would load me onto her back and begin her long, tireless strokes. With the waves partially covering us, I followed her rhythm with my short, chubby arms, taking my cues from the powerful movement of her back muscles. We did this again and again until I'd fall off, and she'd catch me and set me upright in the strong New England surf. I was thrilled by the wildness of the ocean and my grandmother's fearless relationship to it. I loved the way she never consulted her mirror after her swim but always looked as if she had been born to the sea, a kind of aquatic heiress.

None of the social issues of 1957 had a chance of catching my attention that year. All that existed for me was my grandmother, rising from the surf like a Dahomean queen, shaking her head free of her torturous rubber cap, beaming down at me when I finally took the first strokes on my own. She towered above me in the sun with a benevolence that made simply dwelling in her presence a reward in itself. Under her gaze I felt part of a long line of royalty. I was certain that everyone around us—Black and white—saw and respected her magnificence.

Although I sensed her power, I didn't know the real significance of our summers together as Black females in a white part of town. Unlike winter, when we were protected by the cover of coats, boots and hats, summer left us vulnerable and at odds with the expectations for women's bodies—the narrow hips, straight hair, flat stomachs, small feet—handed down from the mainstream culture and media. But Lydia never noticed. Her long chorus-girl legs ended in size-nine shoes, and she dared to make herself even bigger as she stretched her broad back and became a woman with a purpose: teaching her granddaughter to swim.

My swimming may have seemed a superfluous skill to those who watched our lessons. After all, it was obvious that I wouldn't be doing the backstroke on the Riviera or in the pool of a penthouse spa. Certainly nothing in the popular media at that time made the "great outdoors" seem a hospitable place for Black people. It was a place in which we were meant to feel comfortable at best and hunted at worst. But my prospects for utilizing my skill were irrelevant to me, and when I finally got it right I felt as if I had learned some invaluable life secret.

When I reached college and learned the specifics of slavery and the Middle Passage, the magnitude of that "peculiar institution" was almost beyond my comprehension; it was like nothing I'd learned before about the history of my people. It was difficult making a connection with those Africans who had been set adrift from their own land. My initial reaction was "Why didn't the slaves simply jump from the ships while they were still close to shore, and swim home?" The child in me who had learned to survive in water was crushed to find that my ancestors had not necessarily shared this skill. Years later when I visited West Africa and learned of the poisonous, spiny fish that inhabit most of the coastal waters, I understood why swimming was not the local sport there that it was in New England. And now when I take to the surf, I think of those ancestors and of Lydia.

The sea has been a fearful place for us. It swallowed us whole when there was no escape from the holds of slave ships. For me, to whom the dark fathoms of a tenement hallway were the most unknowable thing so far encountered in my nine years, the ocean was a mystery of terrifying proportions. In teaching me to swim, my grandmother took away my fear. I began to understand something outside myself—the sea—and consequently something about myself as well. I was no longer simply a fat little girl: My body had become a sea vessel—sturdy, enduring, graceful. I had the means to be safe.

Before she died last summer I learned that Lydia herself couldn't really swim that well. As I was splashing, desperately trying to learn the right rhythm—face down, eyes closed, air out, reach, face up, eyes open, air in, reach—Lydia was brushing the ocean's floor with her feet, keeping us both afloat. When she told me, I was stunned. I reached into my memory trying to combine this new information with the Olympic vision I'd always kept of her. At first I'd felt disappointed, tricked, the way I used to feel when I'd learn that a favorite movie star was only five feet tall. But then I quickly realized what an incredible act of bravery it was for her to pass on to me a skill she herself had not quite mastered—a skill that she knew would always bring me a sense of accomplishment. And it was more than just the swimming. It was the ability to stand on any beach anywhere and be proud of my large body, my African hair. It was *not* fearing the strong muscles in my own back; it was gaining control over my own life.

Now when the weather turns cold and I don the layers of wool and down that protect me from the eastern winters, from those who think a Black woman can't do her job, from those who think I'm simply sexual prey, I remember the power of my grandmother's broad back and I imagine I'm wearing my swimsuit. Face up, eyes open, air in, reach.

In the Ocean

Patricia Goedicke

> At first my mother would be shy
> Leaving my lame father behind
>
> But then she would tuck up her bathing cap
> And fly into the water like a dolphin,
>
> Slippery as bamboo she would bend
> Everywhere, everywhere I remember
>
> For though he was always criticizing her,
> Blaming her, finding fault
>
> Behind her back he would sneer at her
> All through our childhood, to me and my sister,
>
> She never spoke against him
>
> Except to take us by the hand
> In the ocean we would laugh together

Reprinted, by permission, from Patricia Goedicke, 1989, *The Tongues We Speak (New and Selected Poems)*, Milkweed Editions.

As we never did, on land

Because he was an invalid
Usually she was silent

But this once, on her deathbed

Hearing me tell it she remembered
Almost before I did, and she smiled

One last time to think of it:
How, with the waves crashing at our feet

Having thrown ourselves upon her, for dear life
Bubbling and splashing for breath,

Slithering all over her wet skin

We would rub against her like minnows
We would flow between her legs, in the surf

Smooth as spaghetti she would hold us
Close against her like small polliwogs climbing

All over her as if she were a hill,
A hill that moved, our element

But hers also, safe
In the oval of each other's arms

This once she would be weightless
As guiltless, utterly free

Of all but what she loved
Smoothly, with no hard edges,

My long beautiful mother
In her white bathing cap, crowned

Like an enormous lily

Over the brown arrow of her body
The limber poles of her legs,

The sad slanted eyes,
The strong cheekbones, and the shadows

Like fluid lavender, everywhere

Looping and sliding through the waves
We would swim together as one

In a rainbow of breaking foam

Mother and sea calves gliding,
Floating as if all three of us were flying.

Woman Skating

Margaret Atwood

A lake sunken among
cedar and black spruce hills;
late afternoon.

On the ice a woman skating,
jacket sudden
red against the white,

concentrating on moving
in perfect circles.

> (actually she is my mother, she is over at the outdoor
> skating rink near the cemetery. On three sides of her
> there are streets of brown brick houses; cars go by; on
> the fourth side is the park building. The snow banked
> around the rink is grey with soot. She never skates here.
> She's wearing a sweater and faded maroon earmuffs, she
> has taken off her gloves)

Now near the horizon
the enlarged pink sun swings down.
Soon it will be zero.

With arms wide the skater
turns, leaving her breath like a diver's
trail of bubbles.

Seeing the ice
as what it is, water:
seeing the months
as they are, the years
in sequence occurring
underfoot, watching
the miniature human
figure balanced on steel
needles (those compasses
floated in saucers) on time
sustained, above
time circling: miracle

Over all I place
a glass bell

Daughter, Diving

Paulette Roeske

The game is grace
for the gangly teen-ager
balanced like a sleepwalker
on the end of the board.
More than a spectator,
I follow her thoughts
through a stop/start
review of the stages
of a backward somersault,
as if two minds rehearsing
the *Jump Tuck Reach*
could charm her limbs

into the image.
When she jumps
the gift is twins
imprinted on the air.
Round as a wheel
she catches up with herself,
holds the classic pose
isolated, midair.

Golf Lesson

for Polly
Susan Ioannou

The pro's firm hands
lay a driver across her palm,
and wrap thin fingers around.
Thumbs hug inverted Vs toward ground.
   Head down. . . .

Slow motion unfolds her.
   Swing. . . .
   Again now,
   again. . . .

Arms slide back the club,
testing new faith in its arc
until wrists cock
and silver parallels earth.

   Breathe!

Reprinted, by permission, from Susan Ioannou, 1996, *Where the Light Waits*, (Victoria, BC: Ekstasis Editions).

And the arms sweep down.
— PLOCK —
A white dot climbs
its long graceful parabola
toward faint trees, the sky,

while freed by the swing's force
my daughter's whole body flows after,
opened toward flight and future.
Wrists loosen, then fall.

The circle perfected,
a first, small moon has soared
far into the next moment.

Closer—
it must be closer—
to the cup.

Teaching Chess to a Daughter

Jo Casullo

The pieces line up so: pawns out front,
benign, the most expendable.
They may be left in dangerous positions
but should never be forgotten.

If any pawn survives, reaches
the enemy's back line alive,
he may become a Queen. One calls this
"queening a pawn," a promotion, the Queen

being most versatile, moving in any
direction as far as she chooses.

Like all other pieces, her purpose
is to protect the King, who likewise
moves in all directions but
only one step at a time.

Lines

Barbara Smith

Anchoring, I watched him climb,
His legs still smooth, his ringless hands
Grasping, inching at the cliff,
His eyes turned upward toward my own,
My own smiling downward at my son.
Trying not to look beyond
At what lay a thousand feet below
We climbed, he climbed, his hair blown wild,
His fear clenched tight between his teeth,
Our courage on raw fingertips.

And then a piton went. He fell
Into the space that welcomed him
And toward the rocks that waited. . . .
My hand, not knowing, reached far out,
Reached empty into empty air.
The mountain turned him upside down.
And then the falling stopped.

He dangled there —

A diver diving half a sky
His body limp,
Suspended on a nylon line
Drawn taut, mere twisting from his waist
To mine, from which that life,
Now saved, now caught,
Now breathing far beyond my own,
Had come.

Outswimming

Lucia Cordell Getsi

She has shaped, so long, this body
that scythes the water alongside
mine. We both ride our muscles

deep, but I sense she talks to each
one privately in a language like prayer,
a cellular utterance, a physical
song. I admire
her grace, turn my head
more to watch
                    than to take in air
the supplication of her swimming,
the power of her arms like windmills
signaling, her once paralyzed legs
that rudder the dark lanes
of direction painted below.
Some shared rhythm holds us

together. I know she thinks, *last month*
I could not keep up, she pulled me
in her draft.
                    I believe we must
have the same heart, one organ,
like a thought divided, but also
like a thought, thinking us

together. Lap after lap we match
longer, stronger strokes. Then she surges
ahead, beyond my reach, her red cap

an aurora of water, like her birth.

Sometimes in Winter

Linda Pastan

> when I look into
> the fragile faces
> of those I love,
>
> I long to be
> one of those people who skate
> over the surface
>
> of their lives, scoring
> the ice with patterns
> of their own making,
>
> people who have
> no children.
> who are attached

to earth only by
silver blades moving
at high speed,

who have learned to use
the medium of the cold
to dance in.

Morning Athletes
for Gloria Nardin Watts
Marge Piercy

Most mornings we go running side by side
two women in mid-lives jogging, awkward
in our baggy improvisations, two
bundles of rejects from the thrift shop.
Men in their zippy outfits run in packs
on the road where we park, meet
like lovers on the wood's edge and walk
sedately around the corner out of sight
to our own hardened clay road, High Toss.

Slowly we shuffle, serious, panting
but talking as we trot, our old honorable
wounds in knee and back and ankle paining
us, short, fleshy, dark haired, Italian
and Jew, with our full breasts carefully
confined. We are rich earthy cooks
both of us and the flesh we are working
off was put on with grave pleasure. We
appreciate each other's cooking, each

other's art, photographer and poet, jogging
in the chill and wet and green, in the blaze
of young sun, talking over our work,
our plans, our men, our ideas, watching
each other like a pot that might boil dry
for that sign of too harsh fatigue.

It is not the running I love, thump
thump with my leaden feet that only
infrequently are winged and prancing,
but the light that glints off the cattails
as the wind furrows them, the rum cherries
reddening leaf and fruit, the way the pines
blacken the sunlight on their bristles,
the hawk flapping three times, then floating
low over beige grasses,
                      and your company
as we trot, two friendly dogs leaving
tracks in the sand. The geese call
on the river wandering lost in sedges
and we talk and pant, pant and talk
in the morning early and busy together.

Soccer by Moonlight

for S. Massoth and the Sizzlers

Anita Skeen

They come to this schoolyard after work forgetting
patients, clients, students, and columns
of figures dead on the page. It is evening,

mid-November. Trees still argue
with stubborn leaves. Grass creeps back
into the earth for warmth.

On the bloodshot horizon, the curious eye
of the moon surfaces from sleep.
The blue team kicks off the ball.

In this strange light their feet
skate the silver pond of the ground.
The ball loops in the air.

To the east legs tangle,
to the west, voices in shadow.
The ball scurries across the field, trailed

by two in blue, scoots just outside the posts
toward the ready shoe of the player whose leg leans
in to it, a hammer swinging. The ball skids

through the goalie's outstretched arms, vanishes
into the net. The moon, buoyant overhead, lights
the night as the women embrace.

The Locker Room

Susan Richards Shreve

In the morning early, I swim in the Olympic-size pool underneath the basketball court of a boys' Episcopal school. Back and forth in the turquoise dawn, keeping to the left of the black line, careful not to crash into the wall. Half a mile, predictably, and then the locker room. This morning is no different.

The locker room is like a men's locker room without privacy—a tile room with showers lined up against one wall. You will rub against the flesh of the woman next to you unless you are centered neatly under the spray from your own nozzle. That's how familial and democratic this locker room is, with women I have seen every day for ten years first off in the morning before coffee and the newspaper, more regular than my husband or my mother.

I don't know their names. I probably wouldn't recognize them on the street. Many of them are older than I am and have been swimming much longer than this sport has been popular. They swim for survival because they have lost a breast or have had back surgery or arthritis. One has a pin in her hip and walks with a walker. Another has had heart attacks.

What is striking about older women, I have noticed, is that the flesh on the torso remains supple in spite of the assaults of age on the face, the slackening of the skin on the arms and legs. I did not know this about women until I started to swim here. In fact I knew very little about nakedness.

When I was a girl, especially in junior high school, I never dressed in the locker room. I stood on the toilet behind the locked cubicle door and only exposed my breasts to the empty space for half a minute between changing from school clothes to gym clothes and back.

So this locker room has been a liberation for me. To stand naked, one in a line of naked women, to know them intimately without knowing their names, has made me feel a kind of membership I never knew before.

This morning, the very tall woman with white hair to her waist is back. "Rapunzel," I call her to my husband. She is fair and freckled, with one small breast, a long incision crosswise on her belly, and high hips. She comes into the shower just after me, takes off her suit slow motion, lets her hair fall out of the white old-fashioned rubber cap. Everyone is glad to see her.

"Hello," I say. "We missed you."

"Thank you," she says. She has a certain dignity that commands a room in spite of the lopsided oddness of her figure.

"Were you on holiday?" the sweet-faced round woman who keeps her walker just in front of her while she showers asks.

"No," the Rapunzel woman says. "There was of course no way for you to know." She turns the shower to hot and stands facing out, underneath the nozzle, her eyes closed, her head tilted back. "My younger child died."

We are stunned. The soft round woman takes hold of her walker, forgetting to rinse the shampoo out of her hair. Weak-kneed, as though this news is personal, I sit on the wooden bench next to Abigail, the one woman whose name we all know because she is southern and gregarious and insists we know her name.

"Oh, my God," Abigail says. "How awful. This is such terrible news." She seems to be the only one among us to whom language comes as easily as living.

"She was ill for a very long time," the Rapunzel woman says. "I didn't tell you because I didn't want to believe it was true."

She pours Flex shampoo into the palm of her hand, lathers it quickly, washing and rinsing her hair simultaneously so her whole body is sudsy.

"I don't know what to say, dear," the woman with the walker says. "I am so sorry."

"Thank you," Rapunzel says. She turns off the shower and steps out.

I embrace her wet and slippery body. I am weeping. The woman with the walker takes her hand and kisses the fingers. Abigail steps into the room where the lockers are and tells the other women, half dressed, drying their hair, putting on stockings, tying their shoes.

"Thank you," Rapunzel says as she embraces one after another of the women. "It was only bad in the last weeks." She combs out her long white hair, puts on gray wool slacks and a turtleneck. I notice that she doesn't once look in the mirror at herself.

"Suddenly she got much worse." She puts on a wool cap over her wet hair and a down ski jacket.

"Thank you all very much." Shyly, she blows a kiss toward the rest of us dressing. Just as she is about to leave, she says, as if in answer to a question, "Her name was Caroline Marie."

After the door closes, the woman with the walker, bundled for winter, shakes her head.

"I would send her flowers if I knew where." She touches my cheek. "Goodbye, dear."

"Goodbye," I say.

"Goodbye," she says to the others.

I put my hood up, tie the laces of my heavy boots.

"Goodbye," I call, opening the door to the cold. "See you tomorrow," I say, flooded unaccountably with gratitude. "See you tomorrow."

Outside, it has begun to snow—a thin gray city snow, falling in sheets at an angle to the earth, obscuring the people on the sidewalk hurrying to work. But I am suddenly lifted out of the darkness of a winter dawn.

Competition

Mariah Burton Nelson

> I like to swim naked
> I like to swim fast
> swimming next to you I swim
> faster
> shed more layers of skin
> learn your rhythms
> as well as my own
>
> Each time I breathe I see you
> breathe
> stroke
> breathe
> stroke
> and see you again
>
> You can tell by my stroke
> that I need you
> you can tell by my stroke
> by the way that I breathe
> that I need your stroke
> your breath
> that to be my best I need you
> swimming beside me

Prothalamion

Maxine Kumin

The far court opens for us all July.
Your arm, flung up like an easy sail bellying,
comes down on the serve in a blue piece of sky
barely within reach, and you, following,
tip forward on the smash. The sun sits still
on the hard white canvas lip of the net. Five-love.
Salt runs behind my ears at thirty-all.
At game, I see the sweat that you're made of.
We improve each other, quickening so by noon
that the white game moves itself, the universe
contracted to the edge of the dividing line
you toe against—limbering for your service,
arm up, swiping the sun time after time—
and the square I live in, measured out with lime.

Pair Partner

Janice Bultmann

My pair partner
Waits in the dark,

In Frankfurt, in her
Underwear. Her husband

Is in Saudi, she waits a lot these days.
Ruth, remember we shovelled the docks

In the dark, cursed the geese before dawn,
Shattered the lake's edge of light.

We savored the smack of the shell on that surface.
I watched your back for direction, we matched

Blade for blade. Sound was a flaw in execution.
Champagne bubbled under the hull.

Taking the boat in we swung
It above our heads and stopped,

Waiting for the water
To run down our arms.

State of Grace

Lucy Jane Bledsoe

When I was fifteen I believed that sex was nearly the same thing as softball. The feelings were the same anyway. I fell seriously in love for the first time during a double play. Charlene played shortstop and I played third base. We led by one run and it was the bottom of the ninth, bases loaded, one out. We had to win this game to go on to the State Championships, so when the best hitter in the league, probably in all of New Mexico, stepped up to home plate I got scared. On the first pitch she belted a one-bouncer right between Charlene and me. Charlene called for the play and snagged the ball while she dove through the air horizontal to the ground. Even before her body thudded into the dust she scooped the ball to me at third. I tagged up and fired it to first base for a flawless double play. We'd won the game. I looked at Charlene and fell instantly in love, deep in love, and could tell by the fervor in her eyes that she had too. In the exact same moment.

The next thing I did, after falling in love, was look for Michael in the stands. He was my best friend and primary coach. He also happened to have been living with my mom for the past seven years. Scanning the bleachers I found him sitting alone, far from Mom, and remembered that they had broken up last week. A fireball of anger and sadness tore through my stomach, but I discharged it by thinking of Charlene and the double play. It was as if Charlene rolled like a boulder right into the spot where Michael had been. All in about five seconds.

After the game the rest of the team went straight to Galluchio's for pizza. Charlene and I lingered in the locker room, said we'd be right along, but didn't hurry. First I couldn't pull myself out from under the shower nozzle where the water slid down my body in dozens of hot rivulets. Then I wanted to take my time with the lotion, getting each toe and between my shoulder blades. Finally dressed, Charlene and I walked slowly back to the softball diamond, just talking, not planning to go there but that's where we wound up. We walked deep into left field where the grass became patchy under the pine needles of the piñon forest. Twice Charlene had slugged homers into these woods. I liked to think about those two softballs that no one bothered to chase down, and wondered where they were now. Coyotes might have carried them off or they could be sinking into the forest floor, slowly decomposing, the earth sucking them in.

Charlene dropped down next to the first tree in left field, placed her hands behind her and threw back her head. I knew just how she felt. A hot dusk swelled up around us, and as I took deep breaths the smell of fresh cut grass raked through my chest. I laid my hand on Charlene's thigh to feel her shortstop muscles. Charlene picked up my hand and examined my calluses, touching them with the tips of her fingers. She said, "Here is the hand that can stop any hard-driven ball in the league. And you're only a sophomore." She lifted my hand to her mouth and ran her tongue along each callous, then licked the center of my palm, swirling her tongue in slow circles.

I waited a long time, as long as it took the full moon to rise over the top of the backstop, expecting Charlene, being a senior, to kiss me. When she didn't I kissed her.

Charlene was a loud, sturdy girl. She was tall, big-boned and had long dark hair which she usually wore in a ponytail or long braid. Her mouth and eyebrows seemed to jump off her face they were so aggressive, bold. She was team captain that year, gregarious and so brassy that some people couldn't quite take her. I could take all of her.

The funny thing about Charlene, though, was that when she wasn't cracking jokes and taking charge, she had a raw shyness. Hardly anyone knew that about her, but once you looked closely it was obvious. Her brown eyes, for example, even as she shouted some obscene remark across the shower room, always had a tentative glint. As long as we all kept laughing, Charlene kept performing, but she was ready, at any given moment, to back off. I was just the opposite. I was quiet most of the time, and people usually thought I was shy. Actually, I'm not shy at all. I have a way of going for what I want. That night, out in left field, when I pulled Charlene's face to mine and kissed her, she folded right into me. The moon climbed higher and higher as we lay on the borders of the softball field and the piñon forest, its light sanctifying every touch. Still, even then, it was all softball to me.

From then on, every day after practice we walked home together. She wasn't allowed over to my house, on account of the lack of supervision there, so we usually went to hers. Charlene's mother didn't like me. My mother let me do whatever I wanted, and I guess it showed. I wasn't wild or anything, just free. My hair looked like straw, bleached and dry and nearly the same color. I didn't comb it enough. My nose was usually sunburned and peeling. Besides the way I looked, I made Charlene laugh too much and we rarely did any homework. Also, when we walked home together we were often late because we liked to take the long woods route. The way we went there wasn't even a trail, just dry pine trees and thick, sweet air. One of us always found a reason to start wrestling even though Charlene established early on that she could whoop me. I liked lying on my back, afterwards, watching the clouds in the sky. I imagined they were giant beds on which Charlene and I floated. I didn't want to talk much at these times because I wanted to savor her salty softball taste in my mouth. Neither of us could wait until the middle of June when school let out.

The last thing I wanted to think about that spring was Mom and Michael's breakup. At home it was always in my face. In the mornings Mom didn't just leave toast crumbs all over the kitchen counter, she didn't even bother to brush them off her shirt anymore. She gained ten pounds, which was a lot of extra on Mom who was already big, and let her hair grow lank and long. She even cancelled a class she was teaching at the junior college. Suddenly we weren't even saying hello and goodbye, just coming and going in the house like two stray cats. Michael had moved out, or was thrown out, and was sleeping in the back room of his auto parts shop.

I didn't need to tell Mom anything about me and Charlene for her to get the picture. She had to know by the music I played, by my face every evening when I came home, by the fact that I *lost* ten pounds. Besides, I had an attitude a mile high. I believed I had surpassed Mom in the realm of Knowing About Love. Mom had left Michael because she'd discovered he was having his second affair (actually, it was his third but she didn't know this) in their seven years together. I pitied Mom for allowing herself to be abused like that. I knew that Charlene would never be unfaithful to me. I *knew* that. I knew it like I knew how to belt a ball into left field with the full force of my body. For the first time Mom's and my lives seemed to be forking off in different directions. I felt sorry to be leaving her behind.

On a clear Saturday morning in early June Charlene's mother opened the door to Charlene's bedroom and found me on top of her daughter, buck naked the both of us. I had been deep in softball at the moment, the smell of blue sky lying against the back of my throat, the dampness of spring soil between my legs, the strength of the best shortstop in the league beneath me. When I heard the door bust open I flipped off of Charlene and looked her mother dead in the eye. In that moment I learned that this wasn't softball at all. This was sex. I felt not fear but an overwhelming sadness that I would never again be able to confuse the two. Sex was fucking and I was doing it with another girl.

In softball there is one perfect moment. You are standing at home plate, the bat cocked over your shoulder, waiting for a pitch. You watch the pitcher's feet, the scuffle of dust, the strength in her calves as she winds up then lets fly. As the pitch comes your way you feel a surge through your groin, a racing of blood down your arms and into your wrists. You lead with your left arm, pulling the bat even and hard until that one perfect moment, exact contact with the ball, the *crack* of a well-hit pitch.

Ever since I was eight and Michael began teaching me baseball, that crack of the bat against a ball has been my mantra, a sound I hear when I want something very badly but can't express what it is. When Charlene's mom opened the door that Saturday morning and found me lying on top of her daughter, buck naked the both of us, my mind filled with the sound of bat-driven balls, one after another in quick succession, as if I were at some marathon batting practice. Perfectly hit balls flew from my mind and slammed across the dusty floor into the astonished gut of Mrs. Duffy.

Charlene's parents pulled her out of school that Monday. I heard the news from our coach, Mr. Kaufman. He looked miserable. "Charlene won't be with us anymore. She's taking her finals early and going on a trip with her parents. She won't play in the State Championships. Of course, we'll still go to the tournament. And," he added, not at all convincingly, "we'll still win."

I couldn't quite believe what I'd just heard.

When I called Charlene that night, her mother answered. "You are not to call here anymore, Kathy." She hung up. I called back.

"You'd better listen to me carefully." This time it was Charlene's father. He worked as a missionary on the Navaho Reservation. The family used to live on the reservation until their home had been vandalized too many times and they moved to town. Mom thought trying to be a Christian missionary among Native Americans was as sick as making nuclear bombs or raping women, but she tried to keep her opinions to herself when Charlene became my best friend. Of course I agreed with Mom. But I knew Charlene was different. Not many people got to see the authentic Charlene, she was buried so deeply under that loud voice and coarse language. The authentic Charlene knew remarkable things, but she carried her genius in her muscles. I could see it all when she played ball. I liked to think that one day Charlene would let the authentic Charlene take over. With a father like hers, though, I understood why she kept herself a secret. He said to me on the phone, "One more call to our household and there will be serious repercussions. We've decided, for Charlene's sake, not to talk to your mother or the school officials, but that will become necessary if you don't understand that—"

"You can talk to whomever you fucking want to talk to," I interrupted. I knew the difference between whom and who because Mom was a writer. "Put Charlene on the phone."

He hung up on me.

I wished he *would* call Mom. I needed her. Until this spring we had always talked about everything. She treated me like another adult, not only because I was all she had until we met Michael, but also because she believed children should be treated as full people. Mom does just about everything by principle. Or at least she tries incredibly hard to. She'll do anything to avoid making a mistake. I always figured that was because of the couple of big ones she made early on. First she hooked up with my father and then she had me. She hates it when I remind her that I was a mistake, because she says I'm the best thing in her life. I believe that, because she says so, but that doesn't mean I wasn't a mistake. "There can be good mistakes," I used to tell her.

Mom was in the next room and must have heard me shouting on the phone, but if she did, she ignored me, which never would have happened before Michael moved out. I kicked the wall a couple of times and still got no response from her. It struck me just then that Michael was gone, Charlene was gone, and now even Mom was gone. I felt too alone to even cry.

I met Michael when I was eight. He was driving a truck for Van Lines at the time and dating Sandra, another waitress at the truck stop where Mom worked. Sandra looked like those chrome decals on the mud flaps of trucks, big head of hair, size three waist, and huge pointy tits. She had about as many brains as those chrome babes have too. Though Michael was dating Sandra, he always sat in Mom's station at the cafe because he liked talking to her. The first thing I ever heard Mom say about Michael was, "He's so typical. Likes to talk to women with brains but have sex with airheads."

When Michael learned that Mom had childcare problems with me on Saturdays, he started taking me to ball games. Mom wouldn't have ever given Michael the time of day if I hadn't adored him so much, but we started going out for barbecue on Saturday nights after Mom's shifts and Michael's and my ball games, and before long they were sleeping together. I had never seen Mom so happy. It was as if Michael had reached in and turned her inside out. He was pretty ecstatic too. He'd never been with a serious woman and Roberta—my mom—is definitely a serious woman. He said it was the first time, since he was sixteen, that he'd been really in love.

Then Mom found out he'd never quit sleeping with Sandra. She canceled out her relationship with Michael like a check she hadn't meant to write. She could be that methodical and thorough. After that Mom managed to take a couple of Saturdays off and tried taking me to ball games, but they were no fun without Michael. Mom had no idea how to keep statistics and I hadn't yet learned enough from Michael to do it on my own. "We'll look for a class, Kathy," she had said. As if there were a class on baseball statistics out here in the New Mexican desert.

That was just the beginning. We ran into Michael in the grocery store a month after they broke up and I blurted out that I'd like to go to the ball game. At that age I didn't understand faithlessness and I pretty much blamed my deprivation of Michael and baseball on Mom. He instantly agreed to take me to a ball game and Mom fired him a vicious look. I thought she was being a bad sport.

I began to realize the extent of my power over my mother's life when, after Michael and I had gone to several ball games, she began seeing him again too.

Mom's first novel got published the following year. She began a second one right away. When that got published, her publisher sent her off on a reading tour. That's when Michael had his next affair, the one that Mom never knew about, though everyone else in town did. I was eleven. Michael was living with us by then. He'd quit driving the big rig and had opened his own auto parts shop. The whole time Mom was out of town he moped, at least around me. I think he wanted me to know how hurt he was that she'd left him for so many weeks. As if that would justify his affair. I was torn. I didn't think it was justified, but I loved Michael. I pretended I didn't know.

This third time (second to Mom's knowledge), there was no pretending. When Mom found out in the early spring she remained calm. She announced that Michael's problem was maintaining intimate relationships.

"Seems like he maintains too many of them if you ask me," I commented.

"Kathy, when a person is afraid of his own depth of feeling, he'll try to spread out his feelings so that he doesn't have to feel so deeply."

Mom repeated her diagnosis every day for a week, then she abandoned reason altogether and blew up. At first I was relieved. All that psychology talk made me nervous. Then I was frightened. Her rage hurled her into some kind of twilight zone that I thought she would never come out of.

When Charlene's parents censored Charlene from my life I joined Mom, attaching myself like a caboose to her rage at Michael. From what I could tell it was all his fault. If he hadn't cheated on Mom I'd still have a family. It was his bad luck that he chose the Monday following the Saturday in June that Charlene's mother discovered us in bed to come beg forgiveness of Mom. I heard it all because it took place in Mom's bedroom which is next to mine. Michael was so quiet through Mom's reasoned speech (she could pull off a show of rationality even at the heights of her fury) that I wondered if she'd killed him first. She finished in a low steady voice. Michael had to know that that voice meant now and forever dead to Roberta. She said, "I've loved you more than anyone in the world and I've given you every break I can think of. Now I don't want to ever see you again. This is a small town, Michael, so I'm going to ask you to do one last thing for me: respect my feelings. Please don't try to see me or call me. It's over and this time it's so final you could be a lead weight dropped in the sea's abyss as far as I'm concerned."

Leave it to Mom to be dramatic and literary even while ending the love relationship of her life.

I snuck out of my bedroom to watch Michael leave. His face was gray and slack. I'd never seen him cry, but I could tell he was going to now. "Michael," I said as he opened the front door. Michael is over six feet tall and he nearly cracked his head on the top of the door I'd startled him so. A tiny burst of hope skidded across his face. How many times had I saved him from Mom's fury? Well he had the wrong idea this time. I told him, "You deserve it, every single word. You're a slime bucket and the whole fucking town knows it." Then I just stared at him until he got up the courage to continue out the door and leave. I watched out the window and saw him drop his head down on the steering wheel. His back started heaving. I have to admit a very big part of me wanted to run out there and throw my arms around him. I loved Michael, but he had hurt Mom so badly I didn't know if I'd ever see her throw her hands on her hips and die laughing again. Even a smile seemed damn near impossible at this juncture. And me, I had no one. Not Michael, not Mom, and now not even Charlene. So I let Michael cry. I wanted him to feel the full extent of the damage he'd done.

The next day I stopped by his auto parts shop on my way home from school. When I walked in he looked so pleased to see me that I almost couldn't do what I'd come for. "Kathy! Here, sit down, want some coffee?"

Even then I knew my hatred was for Charlene's parents, not Michael, but that didn't stop me. I snarled, "Since when do I drink coffee?"

"Well, it's all I have."

I said, "Michael, you are not invited to any more of my games, including the State Championships. I want nothing more to do with you." I waited to see the agony register on his face.

"Sugar." He'd always called me sugar. "This is between your mother and me. It doesn't have to have anything to do with you and me. We've always had a separate relationship." Since being with my mother, Michael had learned all kinds of relationship-talk.

"It has everything to do with me," I said. "Roberta's my mother. You've cheated on her three times. You think I never knew about that second time, but I did. Everyone in town knew except Mom. If you can't control where you stick your dick then forget it. I don't want to see you at *any*, and I repeat, *any* of my games. Got it?"

Michael looked devastated. I was his only link to Mom and I knew he counted on somehow working his way back to her through me. He always had. Sometimes I thought Michael and I had been closer than he and Mom. We were definitely more alike. He claimed he got involved with Mom, back when I was eight years old, because of me. He said, "Any woman who could raise a daughter like Kathy, I wanted to know." Besides being his link to Roberta, Michael had taught me everything I knew about softball. He'd bought my first glove, showed me how to tie a softball in it and oil it for shape, and taught me how to keep statistics at games. He'd coached me for hours and hours and hours over the past years. I knew that my going to the State Championships was one of the proudest moments of his life. I intended to deprive him of it. For hurting Roberta. For hurting me. And because I missed Charlene so much that even my toes ached.

"What can I do?" he asked. "For god's sake, Kathy, what can I do?"

"There's nothing you can do. You've fucked up royally."

If I had known everything about love in April and May, I began to know a lot about loss by late June. A week before the State Championships I broke down. I called Michael at the shop. When he answered, "Main Automotive. Can I help you?" I just said, "Okay, you can come."

"Kathy!"

"Yeah."

"Hold on a minute." He must have put his hand over the receiver because I could only hear his muffled voice say, "I've got to take this call. I'll be with you in a minute." Then he was back. "To the games next weekend, you mean?"

"Yeah."

"Well, uh, great." Like, what else could he say? Then he thought of something. "Does Roberta know?"

"Know what?"

"That you said I could come."

"I didn't mention it."

"Oh."

"She doesn't own the ball park."

I could hear him smile. It was like I was dangling a bit of bait. My power to grease his way back to Roberta, if I chose to. "Right," he said. "You know I'll be there."

"Right," I answered, still all business. I wouldn't cut him much slack. I needed to have the feeling he was wrapped around my little finger.

"Kathy," Mom said the morning of the State Championship finals. We'd already breezed through the quarter- and semi-finals. "You're in some kind of trouble. I've been a bad mother. I'm sorry, but I'm just cracking up right now."

"Then crack." Why was she laying all this on me now? On the morning of the most important game of my life?

"You're in trouble, aren't you?"

"No more trouble than you're in." For the last two nights Mom had sat with Michael in the bleachers watching the quarter- and semi-finals. Both nights she came home, went to bed and cried. I'd never seen her so broken, nor so stripped of pride. Mom has pride even in private, even alone in her bedroom. I got the feeling she suddenly wanted to talk about my trouble now because hers had become so acute.

"What happened to Charlene? Why isn't she in the games?"

"Fine time for you to be asking," I answered.

"I'm sorry I haven't been there for you."

What could I say? In a way, Mom and I were going through the same thing. Only Michael had been a shit to her. Charlene had no control over what happened to us. I felt superior to Mom, for having sense in whom I chose to fall in love with. So I sighed and said, "You got your own problems, Mom. Deal with them. I have a game to play tonight."

Mom looked bad, sallow and puffy. I sort of hated myself for not caring, for needing Michael for my own reasons.

"Well," she said. "It's only right of course that Michael should come to the games." She said this as if it were a conclusion to the discussion we'd just had about her and me.

"It's the principle of the thing," I said, sarcastically tossing her one of her own favorite expressions.

Everyone turned out that night for the State Championship finals, which by luck were held in our town. The Lions sold hot dogs, popcorn and sodas. The fans in the bleachers began rhythmic stomping even before we started warming up. The local radio station prepared to broadcast the game for those who couldn't be there. I wondered if Charlene, who was back from her trip with her parents, would be able to listen.

Michael had painted an enormous purple and red (our school colors) banner that read, "Wildcats Shred the Trojans," which he hung off the railing of the upper bleachers. He sat beside Mom in the lower bleachers right next to third base. Mom had that brown and orange Navaho blanket, the one she brought to all my games, wrapped around her shoulders. During warm-ups, as I fielded grounders and tossed them to first, I could read the tension between them. Michael sat with his hands folded and dangling between his knees which he held humbly close together. He slouched a little as if to diminish himself. Roberta held the blanket around her like some kind of armor and wore her best "I don't give a shit" expression which was way too obvious to be effective. Both of them, I could tell, were trying very hard to let the game be the focus of the night, not each other. I also tried to let the game be the focus, not them and not Charlene's absence.

We won, of course. Not that it was an easy game, but I never questioned our winning. I felt as if everything rode on our victory. If we won that game, I had reasoned with myself, everything else would fall into place.

The fans swarmed onto the field. They picked up every last one of us on the team and passed us over their heads, shouting and singing the school song. Very corny. I didn't usually go in for the school spirit stuff, but it was fun for a few minutes.

I had plans, though, and needed to get out of there before the crowd thinned too much. I didn't want anyone to notice me leaving.

"Listen, Kathy," Mom yelled into my ear to be heard over the screaming fans. "Michael and I are going somewhere for coffee. I don't think we'll go over to Galluchio's. That okay with you?"

"Sure," I said, thinking *perfect.* "I'll see you later." I hardly had time to think about the significance of their going for coffee together I was so glad to have them leave. My knapsack was already packed. I'd go right now, straight from the game.

Though ten at night, it was hot, around seventy degrees, and I was still sweating from the game. I wore my uniform and walked as fast as I could. Mom and Michael running off together after the game made my getaway a cinch. Even so, I felt funny about them not going to Galluchio's with the rest of the team to celebrate. I mean, couldn't their stale old romance wait one more evening to get glued back together? After all we'd just won the State Championship! Yet, it *was* perfect because I wasn't going to go to Galluchio's myself, at least not for long, and would have had to come up with some fantastic excuse to get away, which I hadn't thought of yet. So I had no right to be so hurt. Still, I was.

Soon though, as I drew closer to the Desert View Motel, I forgot all about Mom and Michael. The anticipation of having Charlene in my hands, under my thighs, made me sweat more. She was supposed to arrive first because she looked an easy eighteen, and I barely looked the fifteen I was. We chose the Desert View Motel, the last one on the highway out of town, about four miles from my house, two from hers. The place was a complete dump. We'd always wanted to go away together, to Alaska or Hawaii. A motel room, I thought, is a motel room. Tonight we could be near the Arctic Circle or at the base of a volcanic cone for all we'd know. I cared only that I would have Charlene to myself.

A car slowed and its driver asked if I wanted a ride. I almost took it, to get there faster, but I knew she wouldn't be there yet. I wasn't supposed to arrive first.

A few minutes later, there I was, standing in the small weedy courtyard of the Desert View Motel. I didn't know whether I should hang around and wait or try to check in. If I tried to check in and they didn't let me, we'd be stuck. If I hung around someone might see me, even call the police. A breeze scuttled across the courtyard. I felt exposed, spotlit, so I walked into the office. A middle-aged woman shuffled out of a doily- and afghan-draped living room adjacent to the office. She rubbed her hip as she walked, making sure that I knew I'd caused a woman with a bad hip to rise from the couch.

She didn't speak and I saw that she considered asking for a room to be some sort of affront.

"Has a Cassandra Ogilvy checked in?" I asked. As I spoke, I caught the nauseous smell of hot wool, a mixture of the woman's dinner and the afghans. If I wasn't tasting Charlene's mouth on mine, smelling her lotion in my face, I'd have left in a second. Nothing short of Charlene could have kept me there.

The woman looked me over before checking her book. I felt conspicuous in my uniform. "No."

I pulled out thirty dollars and laid it on the counter. "I'd like a room."

She shook her head, as if I'd done something disgusting, and gripping her hip, bent to open a drawer where she kept cash. She took my money and handed me the key to number six.

The rug was gritty with dirt and the green walls smudged. The only light bulb that worked was in the bathroom. I pulled off the bedspread and wadded it up in the corner on the floor. It was made of that polyester material that gets lots of little balls on it. The sheets were not much better, full of cigarette burns, but at least they looked clean. I sat down and bounced on the springs, then closed my eyes and imagined the Pacific Ocean crashing against a beach outside the window. Possible, but Charlene would never buy it. I tried alpine slopes, a sharp slanting roof overhead, icicles pointing off the rafters right out the window. The sweat baking under my arms, running down the back of my neck, canceled out that one. I didn't mind that we were going to be right outside of town in a creepy motel, but I thought Charlene would.

I decided to clean up. The shower head was a good one and the cold water felt great. I let it leach the salt out of my hair first and then run down my front and back. I couldn't help touching myself, thinking about Charlene walking toward me now. She said she knew a back woods way to get here and would only have to come into sight of the main road when she ducked into the motel. She'd like it, I thought, if I watched for her out the window so she didn't have to go into the office and ask for me. We'd said midnight and it was eleven-thirty. So there was time to wait. And to shower. I thought of Charlene striding through the night heat, her big legs filling her jeans, her arms swinging wide the way they did. And I moved my fingers through the hair between my legs, let the water stream down my breasts. I thought of Charlene not wanting to be late, of her jogging a little, a light wetness forming on the back of her neck as I eased a finger up myself and then let it slide out and across my clit. I wanted her to taste like salt when she got here, I wanted Charlene to be flushed with anticipation. As I came, I saw Charlene's tongue, instead of my finger, sliding across me, easing into me. I fell back against the metal shower stall and moaned her name.

I heard a knock on the door. She was early! I quickly toweled myself dry and shouted, "Hold on one minute!" Suddenly I was shy and didn't want to open the door naked. I pulled on my jeans without underpants and found the clean white sweatshirt I'd brought in my knapsack. My hair a wet tangle, I pulled open the door, unable to control my enormous grin.

The proprietor of the motel stood at the door. She wore pea green stretch pants and her hair in curlers under a plastic cap. "Your change, you forgot it."

I took the money. She and I both knew the price of a room was twenty-eight dollars, there were signs everywhere, but when she hadn't offered me the two dollars back I figured she was accepting some kind of bribe. I wasn't sure what I would have bribed her for, silence maybe, but I'd let her keep it. Why had she changed her mind?

"You say you have a friend coming?"

I nodded. What was it to her?

"I'll send him along when he gets here."

"*Her* and *she*. Cassandra, remember?"

The woman looked me over once again.

"I'm renting a motel room, okay? Is it that big a deal?"

"I don't tolerate no drug dealing." Her eyes were keen, a metallic hazel. She could be as young as twenty-five, I realized, but she desperately wanted to be much older.

"I'll deal my drugs somewhere else then." I shut the door. I had to before I killed her for not being Charlene.

While I combed my hair I heard someone turning a key into the room next door. A bag was thrown against the wall, the TV clicked on.

I waited.

Being late was not unusual for Charlene. Who knew what she had to do to get away from her parents? Our plan was that she would go to bed at ten as usual, then slip out after they fell asleep. What if her father had to stay up late writing a sermon? She might not be able to even leave the house before midnight in which case she wouldn't get here for at least forty-five minutes.

The heat pushed in on my head. I couldn't get the window open so I opened the door. Between my room and number seven were two metal chairs and a man sat in one. "Who are you?"

"Ronald Sweisinger. You?"

"Laura Smith."

Ronald put out his hand. "Too hot for sleep, no?"

I fell into the chair next to him. I couldn't tolerate another second in that fetid motel room. This way Charlene could see me.

Ronald Sweisinger had a huge mouth with the largest and whitest teeth I'd ever seen. His hands were also very large and he combed them through his hair, over and over again, to keep the few long strands over his bald head.

"I used to be a carpet cleaner," he said. "Yourself?"

"I'm a high school student."

"I'm unemployed now. Out of work and out of a family. Wife left me."

I looked at him carefully, wondering if my room would be better.

"But I'm living it up tonight. A motel room. A bottle of rum. A six-pack of coke. Join me?"

"No thank you."

"Good girl. I didn't really want to be corrupting youth anyway. You hardly look old enough for high school. What are you doing in a dump like this? She your mother?" He pointed to the face pressed against the window of the room next to the office.

"No." I didn't want to talk about mothers. "I'm meeting a friend here."

Ronald leaned back and suddenly looked melancholy. "Savor it," he sighed. "Just savor it."

I tried to ignore him, but finally couldn't help asking, "Savor what?"

"Your sweetheart. Laura, you'll never again feel how you do now. Oh, god, do I remember my high school romance. Carla Remington. Homeliest little gal you ever laid eyes on, but what could I expect?" Ronald smiled apologetically and checked the hair covering his bald head.

"You're not bad looking," I said, surprising myself. I hated it when people didn't like the way they looked. Charlene always talked about looking horsey or being too fat.

"You're kind," Ronald said. He dropped a few pieces of ice from a bucket at his feet into a styrofoam cup, poured rum into the cup and then pulled open a coke and added it. "Carla had a head full of curly hair. Ever notice that all Carlas have curly hair?"

I knew one and she did.

"Carla and I were madly in love. We eloped, but her parents found us hitchhiking to Michigan and had the marriage annulled. I'd hoped that she'd gotten pregnant in our two days together, but she hadn't. So we were separated forever. I like to play a game with myself. I think of a certain juncture in my life and try to guess as accurately as possible how my life would have been different if I had done the thing I didn't do. There's a theory, you know, that every time you try to order something in the universe you simply set loose randomness somewhere else. For all I know, by keeping us apart Carla's parents might have started a civil war on another planet or caused the beginning of the greenhouse effect."

I smiled. I liked Ronald.

"Who's your young man, or do you mind my asking?"

"She's a young woman."

Ronald was quiet for a minute. Then he said, "Is it, well, a romantic relationship?"

"I guess so." I was not one for analyzing. Mom did enough of that for both of us.

"I never much understood that. You know, two gals or even two guys. That sort of thing is big out here, in the West I mean, isn't it?"

"Ronald, I don't know." I felt like a child just then and wanted him to treat me like one.

"I'm sorry," he said as if he understood.

Charlene was supposed to have been here an hour and a half ago. I worried. I knew she would want me to be inside hiding now. After all, it could be anything. Her father could be on his way with the sheriff. But what did I care? I had absolutely nothing to lose. Every last thing I wanted would meet me in this motel room—or would not.

Sometimes Ronald and I talked, sometimes we didn't. The minutes passed like the growth of a plant. If I watched, which I did most of the time, nothing changed. But now and then my mind broke loose and rose out over the desert like the moon, ethereal, light, and free. Then time grew and the hours passed.

At three in the morning, Ronald offered me some rum and coke again and I took it. The night was cool now, the moon had set, and the stars were dim. We sat silently for an hour, Ronald having caught me up on his entire life since Carla. I had told him the play-by-play account of the championship game that I had been preparing for Charlene. At four in the morning the phone in my room rang.

"Kathy. It's me."

My relief to hear her voice lasted only a second, then I was furious. "Charlene, where *are* you?"

"I can't get out," she whispered, her voice barely audible. "Tomorrow night. I'll try again."

"Charlene!"

She hung up.

I awoke the next day at noon and opened the door. A couple of cokes and a half a bag of sour cream and onion potato chips sat next to our chairs from the night before. Ronald had left. I popped open a warm coke and slouched in one of the chairs. As I finished off the chips, I began to doubt everything that had happened between me and Charlene. Who was she, anyway? Maybe I'd made it all up so I didn't have to deal with Mom and Michael's breakup.

I knew that wasn't true. If nothing else, there had been that one moment at practice about a week before her mother found us in bed. I'd walked out to my position, paced off a few steps from third base. An afternoon breeze came up, and I was a little hungry—I always liked to play ball slightly hungry—and this peace came over me. It was like complete happiness, steadiness, all the squiggles in my head lying down and relaxed. It was a clean and spacious euphoria. I smiled at Charlene at shortstop and she knew exactly what I was feeling.

"State of grace," she said.

"What?" I asked.

"It's a state of grace."

At six in the morning, after my second night in the Desert View Motel, I walked home. Charlene hadn't even called the second night. I felt like a dog. That loyal. That stupid.

The day was dusty and hazy. I scuffled along slowly wondering if Mom had sent out the police. I wondered if Michael would be there at the house. My eyes felt gritty and there was coke spilled on my sweatshirt. I wanted a shower, a good sleep, and then I wanted to toss the softball around a little.

The screen door to our place scraped the porch, as it always did, when I pulled it open. Mom and Michael jumped off the couch. Mom's eyes looked red and swollen. They both cried, "Kathy!" and fell all over me. For a few moments, as I clung onto Mom and Michael, I forgot all about Charlene. I finally cried.

That afternoon, after Mom called off the police and I slept, we barbecued some chicken and Michael made his special potato salad. I felt completely drained, both in the good relieved sense and in the bad empty sense. We didn't talk much, just sat on the porch together, the three of us, watching it grow dark and listening to the crickets.

I saw Charlene around town a few times that summer. She had graduated and gotten a job checking at Safeway. She ignored me and I never tried talking to her. I didn't really even want to talk to her anymore. Oh, she was still the same old Charlene, shouting jokes to the other checkers in Safeway, throwing groceries in the bags without caring whether she bruised avocados or squashed strawberries. But I saw that the authentic Charlene had sunk even deeper into her body and that she wasn't going to even try to coax her out.

It's not like I just let it all go easy, presto, I'm over her. I cried and sulked, took long soulful walks out to the ball field and lay on my back in left field for hours at a stretch. But I knew better than to look for the Charlene I loved—the Charlene who knew the meaning of grace—in the Charlene who checked groceries at Safeway and wouldn't speak to me. I'm not stupid. I realized pretty quickly that surviving Charlene was just another way of beginning my life.

Besides, I had learned that softball and sex were two separate things, and understanding that distinction was a far greater loss than losing Charlene. For the rest of my life I would be looking for the kind of sex that was synonymous with pine nuts and spring breezes, hardball and aching muscles. For love that was grass stains under a sky full of stars, the snap of my wrist and a hurtling softball, the taste of hard-won sweat. For the rest of my life, love would be letting go of Charlene.

Phantasia for Elvira Shatayev*

Adrienne Rich

*Leader of a women's climbing team, all of whom died in a storm on Lenin Peak, August 1974. Later, Shatayev's husband found and buried the bodies.

The cold felt cold until our blood
grew colder   then the wind
died down and we slept

If in this sleep I speak
it's with a voice no longer personal
(I want to say   *with voices*)
When the wind tore   our breath from us at last
we had no need of words
For months   for years   each one of us
had felt her own *yes*   growing in her
slowly forming   as she stood at windows   waited
for trains   mended her rucksack   combed her hair
What we were to learn   was simply   what we had
up here   as out of all words   that *yes*   gathered
its forces   fused itself   and only just in time
to meet a *No* of no degrees
the black hole   sucking the world in

I feel you climbing toward me
your cleated bootsoles leaving   their geometric bite
colossally embossed   on microscopic crystals
as when I trailed you in the Caucasus
Now I am further
ahead   than either of us dreamed   anyone would be
I have become
the white snow packed like asphalt by the wind
the women I love   lightly flung   against the mountain
that blue sky
our frozen eyes unribboned   through the storm
we could have stitched that blueness   together   like a quilt

You come (I know this) with your love   your loss
strapped to your body   with your tape-recorder   camera
ice-pick   against advisement
to give us burial in the snow   and in your mind
While my body lies out here
flashing like a prism   into your eyes
how could you sleep   You climbed here for yourself
we climbed for ourselves

When you have buried   us told your story
ours does not end   we stream
into the unfinished   the unbegun
the possible
Every cell's core of heat   pulsed out of us
into the thin air   of the universe
the armature of rock beneath these snows
this mountain   which has taken   the imprint of our minds
through changes elemental and minute
as those we underwent
to bring each other here
choosing ourselves   each other   and this life

whose every breath   and grasp   and further foothold
is somewhere   still enacted   and continuing

In the diary I wrote: *Now we are ready*
and each of us knows it   I have never loved
like this   I have never seen
my own forces so taken up and shared
and given back
After the long training   the early sieges
we are moving almost effortlessly in our love

In the diary as the wind   began to tear
at the tents over us   I wrote:
We know now we have always been in danger
down in our separateness
and now up here together   but till now
we had not touched our strength

In the diary torn from my fingers I had written:
What does love mean
what does it mean   "to survive"
A cable of blue fire ropes our bodies
burning together in the snow   We will not live
to settle for less   We have dreamed of this
all of our lives

Part V

Encounters With Sport: Discovery of Self

the sea is another story
the sea is not a question of power
I have to learn alone
to turn my body without force
in the deep element.

Diving into the Wreck[1]
Adrienne Rich

The works in this part chronicle the story of the participation of women in sport during the last century. For the first time, women tell their own stories about encountering sport. And as their stories begin, we first see that the women engaging in recreational pursuits are fearful of falling off bicycles and dancing in public. In later works, they are diving and swimming, confronting their fears by accepting the risks and dangers in their encounters with sport. In the more recent works competitive athletes face such challenges as completing a marathon, surviving a tidal wave while surfing, climbing a 1,500-foot vertical mountain of snow and ice, and returning to horse racing after rupturing organs and breaking bones. They confront the physical and emotional challenges of sport; they come to understand competition and face loss, failure, even death. And they enjoy the freedom that sport can offer; they run freely at night and in the mountains, embrace fear, and declare themselves "former first-basemen." Ultimately they identify themselves as athletes who suffer defeat, discrimination, and even death as a result of being athletes.

The passionate desire to connect with something outside of themselves seems to have been turned inward in the works in this part, as women seek connections with themselves in sport. They want to know themselves in this world and to create a female identity defined by their own personal experiences in sport. As this literature suggests, and as female athletes have learned, to encounter sport is more than to meet it or even to experience it. It is to take the experience in, unto oneself, and be defined by it. It is to encounter oneself, to confront oneself.

As Adrienne Rich says, it is "to learn alone . . . in the deep element." The sporting experience is such that it requires a deeper reflection, a refracted view back on oneself. Reading the literature in this part, one discovers the gradual emergence of self-confidence and the carving out of a female identity in sport. The tendency to circle around ideas, an approach found earlier in the literature of outsiders, has been abandoned for a fiercely direct and confident movement toward the center, a piercing movement toward a female reality in sport.

Before the turn of the 20th century, the eccentric American poet Amy Lowell wrote "A Winter Ride," a poem about horseback riding. In contrast to the swooning, anemic Victorian maidens in tight corsets, Lowell reveled in her own vitality, expressing a connection with both her horse and with nature. She penned, "Strong with the strength of the horse as we run. . . . With the vigorous earth I am one." At approximately the same time, a number of upperclass women from other cultures were also writing about the exhilaration of participating in such recreational activities as cycling and dancing.[2] In her prose memoir, "I Dance," Valeska Gert becomes "overwhelmed with the sheer joy of dancing," with the feeling she is "floating through the air."

Soon after Lowell and her contemporaries wrote about their encounters, other authors began to write about their own experiences of fear or confidence in more challenging and physically vigorous sports, such as diving, mountain climbing, and surfing. In some of these works, including poems by Florence McNeil and Cornelia Brownell Gould, we find an unfolding of confidence in the young divers who confront their fears. Janet Roddan's mountain climber and Ellen Phethean's surfer, older and more accomplished, seem fascinated by fear; they seek it out, needing it in a way, and confidently embracing it.

An almost inevitable sense of accomplishment and a confident knowledge of competition appears in this literature as girls and women, regardless of age, experience the joys of competitive sport. Again we see a difference between the young girls and the older athletes. The young girl in Merril Mushroom's prose memoir, "The Tournament," has the buoyant, cocky confidence toward competition that is so common in the very young. An older girl, Stephanie Grant's basketball player, however, must first overcome the onslaughts of adolescent self-doubt and learn to "be in [her] body" before she can experience the great joys of competition. And Jenifer Levin's marathoner, a grown woman who has never before experienced sport, learns that competitive running can take her from feeling like a "loser" to feeling that "all the dried-up pieces" of herself had "come to life."

The freedom available through sport seems a paramount theme in much of the literature in this part, a freedom shared by both dancers and athletes. In Louise Erdrich's poem, "Balinda's Dance,"[3] the dancer is freed from the men's staring eyes as she floats away, down "the river" of her hair. The runners in Laurel Starkey's and Ellen E. Moore's poems are also "free spirits" who are unafraid and powerful, made free, it seems, by running.

From this kaleidoscope of experiences women come to understand who they are, and through their encounters as athletes they come to understand the world outside sport. Often sport is a metaphor for life, as it seems to be for the swimmer in Svava Jakobsdóttir's story whose sense of helplessness in the pool parallels her experience at home: "there was nothing to hold on to, nothing . . ." For others, such as Mary Bacon and Gretel Bergmann, whose identities were formed by sports they can no longer play, it would perhaps have been easier, as Bergmann suggests, not to have been an athlete after all.

Most often, the athlete's identity is a source of much pride, confidence, and knowledge. Accused of being a "gossamer poet" who needs some "fresh air," the athlete in Florence Victor's "Contest" defeats her accusers in baseball, hiking, and rock-throwing exercises; then she goes home, her identity as an athlete very much intact. In "The Uni-Gym," by Anne Rouse, the unisex weight room provides an opportunity for a woman to strengthen her heart *and* her resolve. And in "Early Morning Swim," Vicky Darling also comes to new understandings about who she is through swimming, which helps her push away "encumbrances" and learn that "women are different."

[1]"Diving into the Wreck," from THE FACT OF A DOORFRAME: Poems Selected and New, 1950-1984 by Adrienne Rich. Copyright © 1984 by Adrienne Rich. Copyright © 1975, 1978 by W. W. Norton & Company, Inc. Copyright © 1981 by Adrienne Rich. Reprinted by permission of the author and W. W. Norton & Company, Inc.

[2]Among the more notable of these writers and their works are American Frances E. Willard, "How I Learned to Ride the Bicycle," in Stephanie L. Twin, *Out of the Bleachers: Writings on Women and Sport* (Old Westbury, NY: The Feminist Press, 1979); Hungarian Margit Kaffka, "*Diadal*" (Victory) in Tamas Tarjan, *Fakutya* (Budapest: Magyar Konyvklub, 1994, pp. 65-73); and German Marieluise Fleisser, "*Radfahren wider Willen,*" (Biking Against One's Will) in Gertrud Pfister, *Frau und Sport* (Frankfurt: Fischer Taschenbuch Verlag, 1980, pp. 39-44).

[3]"Balinda's Dance" can be found in Rayna Green, *That What She Said: Contemporary Poetry and Fiction by Native American Women*. Bloomington: Indiana University Press, 1984, p. 88).

A Winter Ride

Amy Lowell

Who shall declare the joy of the running?
    Who shall tell of the pleasures of flight?
Springing and spurning the tufts of wild heather,
    Sweeping, wide-winged, through the blue dome of light.
Everything mortal has moments immortal,
    Swift and God-gifted, immeasurably bright.

So with the stretch of the white road before me,
    Shining snow crystals rainbowed by the sun,
Fields that are white, stained with long, cool, blue shadows,
    Strong with the strength of my horse as we run.
Joy in the touch of the wind and the sunlight!
    Joy! With the vigorous earth I am one.

From *Winter Sports Verse*, William Haynes and Joseph LeRoy Haynes, Editors. New York: Duffield and Company, 1919.

I Dance

Valeska Gert

Translated by Kathryn Seris

The dancer Rita Sacchetto wanted to give an evening ballet using young ballerina students. She couldn't find enough students so she borrowed me from Frau Moissi. I never took another dance lesson again. However, I put together a dance routine with my friend, the wife of the painter Erich Heckel.

My dancing was tomboyish, boisterous and rather exotic. Siddy Heckel's dancing was languid and decadent. We both were bizarre. The day before the performance I made a pair of wide, orange plus-fours for myself that stood out stiffly and which came to just above the knee. I squeezed my upper body into a tight fitting bodice. I painted my face chalk white, my eyes bright blue and put a bright blue ribbon around my neck. I also wound bright blue ribbon around my feet as I disliked both bare feet and ballet shoes, the classical wear for ballet dancers. For a time this costume, with variations, was standard attire for dancers who were trying to be funny. Sometime later I became the first to dance in high heels. In those days this was just as outrageous as bare foot dancing, introduced by Duncan some years previously. I was the first to bring strong, primary colors and simple cutout designs to the stage.

To begin with I did not have a dance to go with the costume, but quickly worked out a sequence of steps and then further improvised in front of the audience. These wild improvisations developed into jerky, defensive movements expressing fear. By alternating between graceful and discordant dancing, I introduce expressions and movements which reflected that turbulent period. All later works were influenced by these initial dances.

In the evening I shot out onto the stage. I was so high-spirited and burning with desire to rouse the audience that, into the sweet, genteel atmosphere created by the other dancers, I exploded like a bomb. The audience went wild. Some stamped enthusiastically, others whistled in derision. The dance with Siddy got a similar reception.

Nevertheless, someone must have taken offense because the police descended on us the next day. Indecorous dancing was against the law in those early days. In turns we had to dance in front of the police. Rita Sacchetto was petrified when it came to my turn. But, while the police found some fault with everyone else, they judged me kindly. With every step I took, I counted out loud so that I looked like a sweet school girl only anxious to keep in time! I was saved.

A few days later I was invited to perform both dances twice daily during the intermission at the Nollendorfplatz cinema. I let myself be brow-beaten into accepting very little money but insisted that between performances my friend and I were offered chocolates.

There was a terrific uproar every day. For all the yelling, clapping and whistling, we could hardly hear the music. This was the first break from a classical, bourgeois dance style to the dynamics of a new, harsher era.

My partner could hardly stand the abuse of the audience. While all the commotion was the breath of life to me, she collapsed half-unconscious behind the scenes after each of the first few performances. I threw myself across the stage enthusiastically. I was primed to do battle. I wanted to break all boundaries. My movements became exaggerated, my face contorted into mask-like expressions and my rhythm became frenzied, until I was only a grotesque, stamping automat. The audience screamed. This guest performance, however, was not prolonged beyond the first week. The honorable UFA had no stomach for all the commotion.

In "Sport" I mixed ice-skating, bicycling, fencing, tennis and swimming.

In "The Horserace" I am both rider and horse. I crouch on an imaginary horse like a jockey, whipping it and galloping over the stage. The tempo becomes frantic—now for the finish. Without a real whip I wildly whip the flanks of the horse. I then lie flat on the animal's back, hardly touching it. The audience believes it sees a real race and shouts excitedly. It urges me on and yells "faster, faster." I've got to win the race. I've got to. I race even more furiously and am first past the post.

I was an animal trainer, an athlete with a pulled muscle, a weight-lifter turning to the audience in triumph, a clown tumbling around an arena, a ballerina riding bare-back—letting myself slip off the horse and then jumping back on with a friendly wave to the crowd. This was my "Circus" and, like all my pantomimes, was copied. "Music Hall" includes juggling, magician's tricks and tight-rope dancing. A long-distance runner, a racing cyclist, a film director operating a projector, a vamp, a soldier on parade, a silly, giggling teenager, are all part of the "Weekly Newsreel." The dynamism came from energetic, fast action. I sometimes became overwhelmed with the sheer joy of dancing and during these pantomimes felt as if I was floating through the air.

First Dive

Florence McNeil

Shivering in the hot August sun
   I stand on the lowest diving board
watching above me the giants
fearlessly twist and knife
into their dark waters

I measure distance
in terms of
multiple whales
and weigh my eleven years
against the terrors
circulating quietly and steadily
under the surface
the eyes that stare from green rocks
at my naked feet
the hands weaving seaweed nets
to complete the ambiguity
of my needless capture
a surfeit of teeth and claws gathering
to oversee my fate

Reckless with fear
I become a wavering sigh
   a reluctant bird
lose head and hands and atmosphere
to trespass suddenly
into adult depths
bobbing up   transfigured   victorious
out of an unclaimed ocean.

The Dive

Cornelia Brownell Gould

> One moment, poised above the flashing blue:
> The next I'm slipping, sliding through
> The water that caresses, yields, resists,
> Wrapping my sight in cooling grey-green mists.
> Another moment—and I swirl, I rise,
> Shaking the water from my blinded eyes,
> And strike out strong, glad that I am alive,
> To swing back to the grey old pile from which I dive.

From *The Athlete's Garland: A Collection of Verse of Sport and Pastime*, 1905, compiled by Wallace Rice (Chicago: A. C. McClurg & Co.), 45.

April Fools on Polar Circus

Janet Roddan

Polar Circus is a long, alpine climb, 1,500 feet of vertical gain, involving both snow and ice pitches on Cirrus Mountain in the Athabascan Icefields of the Canadian Rockies. Janet Roddan's story relates a female ascent of this route on April Fool's Day, 1988.

The dance with fear fascinates me. Learning to accept fear, to take it in without letting it take over is one of the challenges of climbing ice. Climbing leads me into myself, through my hidden doors, into corners and attics. The doorway through fear always appears ominous, locked shut, insurmountable, impossible. Fear talks to me, whispers my weakness; it speaks of conditions, of my own mortality—it whispers "hubris." Fear sharpens my senses. It dances through my body. It tunes me. It wraps its fingers around my heart and squeezes gently. I learn to welcome fear and the edge it brings me, the whispered warnings, the adrenaline. The tango with fear makes me wise.

Two fireflies glimmer in the darkness. The tiny puffs of light float slowly upward and burn deeper into a maze of ice, snow and rock. Snatches of our conversation drift up. We are on a quest, in search of ice. A note of opera breaks the white silence. We are singing as we approach the climb.

I learn the language; I articulate the right series of moves, body positions, ice axe and crampon placements to dance with a frozen tongue of ice. To talk with the mountain is strong medicine. Ice climbing allows me the privilege of witnessing the world. The couloir leads us into the mountain, up there to wild, silent places that wait, unconcerned with whether we view them or not.

An initial pitch of ice, steep enough to burn our calves, increases the intensity with which we communicate with this frozen world. This pitch is followed by a long, rambling walk, past the Pencil, a once free-standing pillar of ice that now lies broken and crushed in a heap. Then on up to the knoll, where we look out from the dark, claustrophobic couloir to see sun on the peaks. We continue to snake along a snowfield and arrive at last at the base of the route proper, six long pitches of undulating ice . . . varied, interesting, alpine.

Kafka said, "The words of literature are an ice axe to break the sea frozen inside us." We use our ice axes to shatter our frozen worlds into crystals of ice and fear. One of the strong pulls of ice climbing is the tremendous range of feelings one is forced to endure—tingling, shivering pain . . . bubbling, shining elation. We hold on, struggling to control the fear that pounds through our veins and capillaries. But just as fear begins to steal into the soul, a good axe placement thunks into the ice. This solid, physical connection to the world causes the fear to recede . . . first from the arms, then from the mind . . . then even more gradually fear's fingers release the heart, which eventually slows and quiets. The intensity is replaced with warm, smooth, flowing beats. The rhythm takes hold, and the dance begins again.

The last two pitches of the climb cascade out of the notch like an enormous wedding gown. Today's brides approach slowly, touched by the mystery and majesty of the place. We are filled with our fear and our audacity. We encourage each other; we push each other. Our vows are strong, but it is April, late in the season for ice climbing. The ice is rotten; the climb is falling down. Time melts and falls away along with great chunks of ice as I rail and pound against it. The dance becomes a struggle.

The entire world shrinks to a section of frozen water in front of my face. The ice is dripping wet and soggy. The rhythm has been broken. I force myself to breathe, to generate my own flow, to create my own beat. But nothing feels right. A chasm fifteen feet wide opens up between Barb, my partner, and me. Impossible to return. I fight. I hit hard to get good placements. A big block of ice disengages itself; my tool is embedded in it. Time stops, and in slow motion I swing onto my other ice axe. I "barndoor" open and the block of ice topples over my shoulder. I look down to see the ice explode beside Barb, who suddenly looks tiny and hunched in her small belay stance.

"I don't know about this, Barb," I shout down, hoping she will offer an easy way out. I reason to come down. But she calls back, "It depends on how much you want it." Indeed. How much do I want it? Doubt slides in with spaghetti arms and little shivers that evaporate my courage.

But desire, commitment and an incredible dislike for down climbing drive me. Up. One move at a time. Filled with solemn focus, I proceed. The final veil is gently torn away. The great Goddess reveals her face of frozen water. I witness her dark, foreboding pinnacles, her places of silent, quiet peace, her vistas too vast to contain in a single glance. Tingling, shivering, we arrive at the summit notch at 4 p.m., a happy marriage of fear, sweat, intelligent strength and smiles.

The vast mystery that spreads before us causes us to stop and look and take it in for heartbeats of silence. Endless jagged peaks. The silent contract, the ceremony is almost complete. We rappel down the climb. The ropes pull, snagging a few times just to remind us that it's not over yet. A climb is never over until you are back at the car. And even then, the journey that we are all on keeps going. As we descend, night overtakes us. We turn on our headlamps, tiny pins of light in a blanket of darkness.

The April fools, married with fear and laughter on Polar Circus, return to the car, smiling in the darkness, two tiny fireflies humming and buzzing softly.

Surfing

Ellen Phethean

> Recklessly she plunges in
> swims out to meet the tidal wave
>
> sick with excitement
> she strains to crest the monster
> before it topples
> crashing her beneath
>
> each wave comes on inexorably
> will she ride it
> or be ridden into the ground
> round and round rasped onto the gritty floor
>
> she treads water
> gently floating breathing easy
> as she watches the next giant
> approaching
>
> detached and calm she can ride them
> easy so big and powerful
> lifted over the top
> if she stays in control
>
> if she mistimes the rhythm or panics
> muscles tired with swimming
> she'll drown she knows

The Tournament

Merril Mushroom

I was hugging myself with joy, heart singing with excitement, as I ran up the front steps and into my house. I looked around the living room, checked the kitchen, delighted to find no one else in sight. Quickly I closed myself into the sanctuary of the bathroom, there to savor my triumphant pleasure in private for a few delicious moments more and to rehearse the way I'd tell my family, practicing the words I'd use to announce the news—that I had won in the individual semifinals, and I would be in the finals! After years of mediocrity, I was a winner at last!

This was the dream of a lifetime come true for me, and I felt full to bursting with the satisfaction of my achievement. From the moment of my first awareness of the magic of winning (which came at an indeterminate but early age), one of my primary desires in life was to be a winner myself; was to be, myself, one of those proud, athletic girls, one who excelled in sports, who was the focus of all eyes after the contest, who received the applause of the crowd. I enjoyed sports. I loved to play the game. I thrived on the physical and mental exercise, the feeling of moving my body. I loved team play as well as individual contests, and I craved to be included in the tight camaraderie of the group of girls who were the best athletes at school.

Alas, this was not to be my lot. Always I had aspired to be proficient at physical contests, to be good at sports. I tried, but I lacked the ability. I just did not have the innate talent some other children had. I was big, but I was not very strong for my size. I was slow. I was not graceful. I was nearsighted. I was agile enough, but not exceptionally so; and I was, at the very best, passably adequate at some events, but never consistently outstanding at any.

However, in spite of my general mediocrity, I did manage to excel at a few games. When reach and dexterity counted more than strength and speed, I was in my element. I was able to hold my own in badminton, Ping-Pong, pick-up-sticks, and jacks.

Actually, I showed a good bit of ability at jacks—enough to be able to dream of possibly becoming a winner. And so I practiced, learned the skills necessary to be proficient, and, gradually, I developed my game until I became one of those girls who hogged all the jacks, one of those who other girls hated to play with because her turn was never over, because she was so good. I could play on and on and on, through one throw after another, fancy after fancy, controlling the fall of the jacks, the bounce of the ball, rarely missing my scoop.

Reprinted, by permission, from Merril Mushroom, 1994, *Sportsdykes*, edited by Rogers (St. Martin's Press).

Even so, I was not as good as the girls who regularly played tournament jacks. Every summer from the age of seven, I had competed in my local playground's Jacks Meet toward District semifinals and Citywide finals, and every summer I was defeated early in the game. But as time went on, my game improved. This was my second year to make the semifinals, and, this time, after years of being eliminated, today I had won my matches one after another, until I had won them all! I had made the finals! At last I would have my time in the limelight. At last I would experience, as had countless other athletes before me, the satisfaction of the payoff for all these years of hard work and perseverance. And it was none too soon—I was eleven years and seven months of age, and this would be my last year in the junior division. Seniors could be tournament spotters, but they did not play competitive jacks in the recreation department leagues. It was now or never for me!

The semifinals had been held at a park an hour's drive from home. The girls from my park met at the playground early that morning. There, we crammed our excited, giggling selves into a recreation department bus. I was disoriented by having to rise at an earlier hour than usual, and by the time we arrived, I was excited, distracted. My senses were overstimulated by the unfamiliar surroundings, by the different placement of courts and sand and bathrooms, by the different vegetation. The very air felt strange upon my skin, the sounds different, smells different, people I didn't know. We girls from home clung together in a knot, seeking solace in the closeness of each other, as we waited for the tournament to begin.

And begin it finally did, and then the day seemed to rush by so quickly—the events, the eliminations, the winning. I bravely faced each opponent, aware of all eyes on us as I waited my turn, blocking out everything except the game. I knew that I was playing my best and that my opponents could not match my skill. And then, before I knew it, the tournament was over; and we were back on the bus going home; and this time I had made the finals.

Now, sitting in the bathroom, I rereheared what I'd tell my folks: They'd ask how it went. I'd respond casually, "Oh, okay," then add, almost as an afterthought, "I made the finals." I'd be very cool about it all. At least I'd try to be cool. But even now I couldn't keep that bubble of excitement in my belly from swelling until I was sure it would burst forth in a long, loud hoot.

The morning of the finals was cloudy. I prayed that it wouldn't rain. My neighborhood park would be hosting the event, so I would have the advantage of playing on my own turf, on familiar floors. I knew that I played best on the outdoor concrete and asphalt basketball court. If it rained, we'd have to play indoors, under the shelter. Part of that floor was wood; and I couldn't get as good a bounce to my ball on the wood as on the harder surface of the outdoor court. The rest of the floor was poured concrete, rough, finger-tearing stuff—a floor that could take the skin off a girl's knuckles down to the bone. No, we *had* to play outdoors! I did every childhood ritual against rain that I knew of, hoping to stave it off for as long as possible.

I had practiced my worst fancies one last time before I left home that morning, easily flipping those elephant jacks—ten of them—over to the backs of my hands, then ringing them into my palms again without a single piece of metal detaching from the whole of the clump. Immediately, I'd tossed the ten jacks onto the floor so that they practically lined themselves up by twos, waiting to be scooped into my ready hand. I skipped to the first required fancy, one that I had only recently completely mastered, one that had been especially difficult for me—"cherry in the basket," also affectionately nicknamed "baskets." I made it to ninesie before missing, a personal best for me. Then I went on to "poison," using one hand only, holding all the jacks in the same hand I used to pick them up and hoping each time I tossed the ball, that the jacks would not fly out along with it like they were *supposed* to do in the "dutchman" fancies. Finally, I worked on "double poisons," where the ball was tossed, the jacks picked up, and the ball caught from out of the air on the fly *before* it bounced.

After practice, I ate a good breakfast, then put on my whites while Mom packed my lunch. I ran the three blocks to the playground and arrived in time to see the buses from the other parks arrive and the lines of girls disembark. I saw their expressions of trepidation and the way they clung to each other as they looked around. I recalled the way I had felt on strange turf during the semifinals, and I was happy to be on my home ground now for this competition.

At last the park director blew her whistle. It was time to start. The air was thick with excitement. We were matched against our first opponents, and, together with a spotter, moved to our assigned places on the courts. The spotters were senior division girls who would mark our plays and make sure we followed all the rules. They would also settle disputes about near-misses and moving jacks. We had five required fancies to do, and these were changed as we moved up through the levels. The girl who finished each fancy first after the required ones could choose the next fancy. We'd play as far as we could get, turn about, until each girl had missed three times. Then we'd report to the director for our next competition assignment. I won my first rounds easily, and almost before I knew it, we were breaking for lunch, sitting on the playground and digging into our paper sacks of sandwiches, fruit, and cookies, while we chattered about the events of the tournament, congratulating the winners and consoling the girls who had already been eliminated.

That afternoon my name continued up the ladder until there was only one line left blank—the one at the top—and I had only one more competition to win in order to see *my* name filled in there. I was to play Sharon Bishop, a girl from Northshore Park, a girl I'd lost to year after year every time I played against her, a girl who was snotty and unfriendly and stuck-up. She had won the championship last year and the year before that, and she had told everyone that three was her lucky number, and she would win this year also. She was three months older than I was, and this would be her last summer to play tournament jacks, too. I knew she wouldn't mess around.

But before the round began, the clouds, which had been gathering all afternoon, finally massed to the spilling point; and spill they did, first in large drops and then in smaller but increasingly thicker and faster streams. We girls scrambled up and raced to the shelter where rainy day activities took place. Our spotter was talking with the director. Finally she came back and motioned Sharon and me over to a large area on the concrete part of the floor. *Uh-oh*, I thought. I knew this floor well. There was a place in it where tiny shells were imbedded in the concrete—almost invisible little shells but sharp and prominent enough to shred the last joint on a girl's pinky finger should she scoop a careless forehand over it.

I glanced sideways at Sharon Bishop. She was strutting through the shelter, aware that all the girls crowding in to watch the playoff or finish their own games for their ranking knew who she was, aware of her fame as a two-time winner. I wondered if I should warn her about the floor. It could certainly swing the competition in my favor if she was unaware of the potential hazard before us. But I couldn't do that. Not only would it be poor sportsmanship on my part to withhold this sort of information, but Sharon might actually end up hurting herself.

Taking a deep breath, I addressed my opponent. "Um, Sharon?" The look she turned on me was enough to curdle fresh milk, as though I might presume to address *her*, perhaps, but she did not owe me the courtesy of a response. Undaunted, I continued, "Um, to be perfectly fair, I, um, need to tell you that the floor we're playing on has some really bad places. . . ." My voice trailed off, as Sharon's sneer grew wider and wider.

"Don't think you're so great just because we're playing on *your* turf," she spat. I could tell that she would have none of my advice, so I shrugged and found myself a spot where the floor was the least abrasive and where my ball would not hit any pocks that might cause it to bounce unevenly.

We sat down. Sharon was one of the few girls who could sit flat on her butt with both knees bent and both legs turned back behind her—a real killer position. This gave her the advantage of being able to play to her front with a maximum of reach and balance. I couldn't sit this way at all. I couldn't even sit the way most of the other girls sat, mermaid-style, with both knees bent in the same direction and one leg turned backward, the other bent in front with foot against thigh. My tendons stretched the other way, and I preferred to sit with both legs spread wide and turned out with the sides of both knees on the floor. This formed boundaries inside which to gauge my throw, but it had the disadvantage of creating a hazardous area for the ball to bounce against leg or jacks.

Sharon and I both played well, moving rapidly through the easy fancies and into the more difficult ones. I was aware of the girls crowded around watching us, the admiring eyes, the sighs of appreciation at skillful, difficult plays, the groans when either of us missed.

We had two misses each and were on our last round when Sharon got into the shells. She was leading, but not by much. We both were in "baby on the back fence," a particularly difficult fancy where we had to place all ten jacks on the back of our left hand by appropriate numbers, then flip them over and catch them without letting any fall to the floor. She had missed on fivesies, I'd missed on threesies, and this would be the deciding round.

Sharon tossed the jacks, and I could tell by the way they spread when they hit the floor that they were on the shells. She tossed the ball, picked up the first five jacks in a clump with her fingertips, and expertly deposited them on the back of her left hand. The last five jacks were spread out, and Sharon tossed the ball and scooped them together, scraping the top knuckles of both her pinky and ring fingers along the shells. I must say that she was cool. If I didn't know the floor as well as I did, I would not have guessed that she had just grated the entire skin off the last two joints of her ring and pinky fingers clear down to the nerve endings. She bit her lip slightly, and a flash of pain showed in her eyes, but she immediately covered up, acting as if nothing had happened. I looked at her hand and saw the exposed pink flesh that lay beneath her flayed skin. I saw the blood slowly well into the scrape, and I knew that she was hurt bad.

She missed on sixies, and then it was my turn, my last chance to beat her and claim the championship. I selected my spot, tossed the jacks. Taking a deep breath, spreading my left fingers out just far enough to contain the jacks without allowing them to drop through, I bounced and caught the ball, carefully placing three, three, three, and one jack, on the back of my hand. Expertly, I flipped them into my palm, catching them all. Again I tossed the jacks, completed foursies, fivesies, and, miraculously, sixies. I missed on sevens, but it didn't matter. I had won! I had beaten Sharon Bishop for the all-county recreation department jacks championship! I was a winner at last!

Posting-Up

Stephanie Grant

My senior year fourteen girls showed up to our first practice. The year before the team had been only half as strong: not enough bodies to scrimmage even. Which didn't bother our coach, Sr. Agnes, who had spent thirty of her seventy-odd years as a cloistered nun and who confused basketball with dodgeball. Sr. Agnes had retired at the end of last season. My dad said it was A Blessing In Disguise. Rumor was that our new coach, Sr. Bernadette, had gone to college on basketball scholarship. She was late getting to the first practice though, so we all stood around shooting baskets and checking each other out. I counted four, maybe five, point guards.

Every player in the city knew Kate Malone, if not by sight—she was six feet tall, with a mass of bright red hair—then by reputation. She led the Catholic league in total points scored for both boys and girls, and she had been kicked out of five Catholic schools in three years. Whatever school she ended up with, she took to the Catholic League Tourney; I'd watched her win with a different team all three years. Kate was the only new student at Immaculatta in 1973 who wasn't fleeing a court order: Immaculatta was her last hope for a parochial school education. The school before us—Sacred Heart—was in Dorchester, but not the Irish part. Kate had been the only white starter for Sacred Heart, which seemed more incomprehensible than her eighteen or nineteen points per game.

She stood at one end of the gym, shooting. Two other new girls waited beneath the basket for her to miss. Basketball etiquette required them to pass back the ball whenever she sank it. They looked pretty bored.

At the opposite hoop, Irene Fahey was practicing lay-ups. The rest of us stood in a rough semicircle around the basket, taking turns with the remaining ball. Irene wove in and out of us, charging from the left, then right, retrieving her own rebounds—whether or not she scored—dribbling out and flying back in, all the while asking questions about Immaculatta and the team.

"What was your record last year? I mean are you guys the losingest team in history? Who's your new coach? Is she a million and one years old like your last coach? I can't imagine losing all the time. I mean did you guys like to lose, or what?"

Irene was the second best basketball player and biggest mouth in the Catholic league. The year before she took Perpetual Faith to the playoffs with a 13-and-2 record. They lost to Kate's team in the next-to-last round by three points.

"You got a team this year, that's for sure. I've never seen so many freaking guards in one place before. I wonder who she's gonna start?"

Irene left Perpetual Faith, she confided in us at the top of her lungs, because her mother felt "the quality of education was deteriorating." Eventually I learned what that meant: Irene left because Perpetual Faith was one of the few Catholic schools in Boston that had black students, and it had accepted more blacks since the busing crisis began. Not only white parents took their children out of public school after the court order became final. Most of the black families removed their kids because they were concerned for their safety, which was exactly what the white parents said. Even I knew that the black people had real reason to worry. The first day of school a busload of black second-graders got stoned by white parents in Southie. We watched it on the news. My mom and dad were so disturbed they shut off the TV.

"Couldn't wait to get outta Perpetual Faith, that's for sure. Goin' downhill, you know what I'm saying?" Irene stomped on my toes on her way to the hoop.

Her lay-ups became so disruptive to our shooting that we were forced to join her. The girls who had been shooting with Kate (or hoping to shoot with Kate) left her to practice with us. Kate didn't budge, and Irene didn't ask.

Irene made me anxious. She sighed loudly at each of our mistakes, like somehow we were personally disappointing her. I missed every lay-up because I knew she was watching. We kept quiet during the drill and grew bored, but we were afraid to say anything. A tiny, dark-haired girl suggested we scrimmage. She was very serious looking. I had never seen her before, which was weird because I went to all the league games, Catholic and city, and I knew all the ball players. Irene was irritated.

"Ya, and who are you? Where'd you play? Not in this league, I don't think. Not too many guineas in this league. Not that I have anything against Italians. Don't get me wrong. Just never seen them play any kinda b-ball."

"Assumption," the girl replied, unflinching. I stared at the gym floor, nauseated; we didn't use words like *guinea* in my house.

"Assumption?" Irene looked puzzled. "Never heard of it. Where's Assumption?"

"Springfield," she responded, still indifferent. Her voice was low and steady.

"Ya, then how come I never heard of it? I got relatives in Springfield, and I've never heard of Assumption. You wouldn't be lying to me, would you? I hope not, lying is a cardinal sin, you know; it'll put a black mark on your soul, and guineas start out with half-black souls because of the Mafia. You can't afford too many cardinal sins."

"No, I wouldn't lie to you. You haven't heard of Assumption because it's not a high school. Assumption College." Ice edged the dark girl's words.

"I don't get it. What's your name?" Irene lost some of the color in her face.

"Bernadette. Sr. Bernadette. And you're Irene Fahey. That right?"

Irene nodded, ash-grey. All of us looked a little ill, except Kate, who was still shooting baskets. The bounce bounce of her ball kept time.

"Why didn't you tell us who you were?" Irene choked. "And how the hell old are you, anyway?"

Sr. Bernadette shrugged. "I just wanted to see you play relaxed, without knowing the coach was watching. And it's none of your business how old I am. Just graduated from Assumption last spring and took my vows at the same time. Any more questions?"

Silence. Then Irene: "Don't they have a height requirement for nuns, for Christ's sake?"

There was a collective gasp. Everything I'd ever heard about Irene Fahey was true.

"No, but there are requirements for being on this team." Sr. Bernadette took a step toward Irene. "One of them is respect. If I get any more lip from you, your behind is going to be warming the bench all season. I don't care who you are or how good you play. Got that?"

"Got it," Irene smiled a big, fake smile. "Got it, got it. I mean you're the boss, right? You're about as big as my kid sister, but you're the coach and whatever the coach says, goes."

I was sweating. Irene lived by the axiom that the best defense is a good offense.

Sr. Bernadette fixed Irene with a glare so cold that every girl within ten feet hugged her arms to her body. I remembered what I had heard in school about Italians and the evil eye and was instantly ashamed.

"Kate, come down here, will you? We're gonna scrimmage. I'd like everyone to introduce herself first. Tell us your name, what school you played for last year, and what position."

There did seem to be something sort of otherworldly about Sr. Bernadette, I had to admit. Like how come she already knew our names?

Everyone shifted her weight from leg to leg as we went around the circle. There were six new girls.

"Maura Duggan, Dorchester High, point guard."

"Frances Fitzgerald, Southie, point guard."

"Peggy Gallagher, Charlestown High, forward."

"Pat Gallagher, Charlestown High, forward."

"Irene Fahey, Perpetual Faith, point guard."

"Kate Malone, Sacred Heart, point guard."

Point guard is like quarterback, only for basketball. She's your best player. She controls the ball. My dad says point guards are born, not made, that it's their disposition more than their skill that a coach looks for. I had never seen so many in one room.

Sr. Bernadette bounced up and down on the balls of her feet. All the guards stared at their hightops: only one of them would get to play point. Kate and Irene never looked at each other.

I started playing basketball because my dad wanted me to. He used to coach boys basketball at Most Precious Blood and coached my brother Tim when he went there. It was sort of like a dynasty, Dad and Tim together for four years. *The Meagher Dynasty* people called it. Dad insisted I play because of my height: I'm 5-foot, 11 ^{1}/$_2$ inches tall, and have been since eighth grade. My brother is 5-foot-7. Tim played guard at Most Precious Blood, but was too short for college ball. I think it made him crazy that I got the right body for basketball but didn't know how to use it. Of course, if Dad had given me one-fifth the attention he gave Tim growing up, I'm sure I'd have been a lot better. For a while I was hoping Tim and I were going to be the dynasty— *The Tim and Theresa Meagher Dynasty.* But it never worked out.

When I enrolled at Immaculatta in 1969, it was a small, egg-heady parochial school for girls who would rather read than do just about anything else. Our basketball team had had thirty-seven consecutive losing seasons. My senior year, everything changed. Busing doubled the enrollments of Boston's Catholic schools. Even though we were technically outside the neighborhoods designated for desegregation, we were close enough to absorb the shock of white students leaving the public schools. Not counting the incoming class, seventy-one new students matriculated in 1973. Six of them were basketball stars. The Sisters said it was God's will.

The whole first week of practice was like tryouts. Sr. Bernadette tried every possible combination of players. She ran very serious practices. The first hour we did drills: ball handling, lay-ups, shooting, and passing. The second hour we broke into teams and scrimmaged ourselves. When boys did this the two teams were called shirts and skins, because one team played bare-chested. When we scrimmaged, one team had to put on these horrible green smocks called pinneys. Everyone complained when they had to wear them. Irene said they looked queer. Sr. Bernadette called the team wearing pinneys "green" and the team without "white." Kate was always on the white team.

Tall people like Kate usually don't play point guard because more often than not they're lousy dribblers. The ball has so far to travel to get to the ground that it's easy to steal from them. Taller girls like me play underneath the basket, as forwards or centers. We spend most of our time fighting for good position and pulling down rebounds, so we don't get a lot of experience dribbling, faking people out, or setting up plays, which is what guards do. We mostly get a lot of experience hitting people. The few tall players who dribble are often so awkward that you don't have to guard against them very closely. Their Own Worst Enemy, as my dad would say. But Kate was not like that. She had a very low dribble for someone her height, and it was almost impossible to steal from her. She never seemed to crouch or bend over when dribbling, which left me with the impression that her arms were abnormally long. In fact, I would have sworn that her hands hung down past her knees. Though, when I saw her off the basketball court, her arms were normal: long, but in proportion with the rest of her.

Irene was built a lot more like your average high school point guard than Kate: short and skinny. Really skinny. No hips and breasts that were all nipple. (A terrific advantage on the basketball court, as in life.) In fact, if it weren't for her long, Farrah Fawcett hair and accompanying makeup, Irene could easily have been taken for a boy.

There were two schools of thought on eye shadow when I was in high school: some girls meticulously matched it to their outfits, being sure that their highlights—above the lid and below the eyebrow—corresponded to the contrasting color in their clothes. Others matched make-up with eye color, varying only the intensity of the shade. Irene was a renegade, defying both traditions, insisting on sky blue—despite her brown hair and eyes and rainbow assortment of J Crew polos. Irene's rebellion stopped here; in all else she was the standard bearer and enforcer of the status quo.

Irene also played more like your average high school point guard than Kate did. She was completely self-absorbed and unconscious of the rest of us. Irene shot whenever she had the ball. She dribbled too much (even if well) and she wouldn't pass. She tried endlessly to go in for lay-ups. She didn't think. Irene played like a one-person team, dribbling and shooting, dribbling and shooting. Of course she got good at both because she had so much practice, but she was lousy to play with.

Friday afternoon after our first week of practice, Sr. Bernadette told us who would play where. We sat, as we had all week, far apart from each other on the bleachers of the gym listening to her comments about our play. She read without looking up from the notes she had taken on her coach's clipboard. We each had a towel and were conscientiously wiping away the day's sweat. Only Kate was still. She sat with her endless legs apart, one planted—knee bent—on the bleacher on which she sat, the other stretched out in front of her, ankle resting on the next, lower tier. Her freckled arms wrapped around the near leg, securing it to the seat. Sr. Bernadette looked up when she got to the end of her notes.

"Starting lineup will be as follows: Pat Gallagher, forward; Peggy

Gallagher, forward; Theresa Meagher, center; Irene Fahey, off guard; Kate Malone, point guard. These are not lifetime memberships. If you play well, you keep your spot, if you don't, you rest a while. It goes without saying that everyone will play."

Before Sr. Bernadette finished her last sentence, Irene was in the showers. Her little body was rigid as she hightailed it across the gym, but her large mouth was open and slack, mumbling things we all tried not to hear.

Sr. Bernadette was the best coach I'd ever had. And the coolest teacher. Unlike most of the other nuns at Immaculatta, she was post–Vatican II, which meant she didn't wear a habit and she smiled at you when she spoke. But Sr. Bernadette was the most post–Vatican II nun I ever knew. She wore her hair short, but not severe. It was thick and black, stylishly cut in a shag. She had bright black eyes and smooth, almost-brown skin. During the day she wore jeans, and at practice she wore shorts and a tee shirt. Hers are the only nun's knees I've ever seen. She talked nonstop about basketball, and she shouted when she was angry or excited. She said "pissed off." She ran. Her last name was Romanelli, which was a big deal at the time because Irish people dominated the Catholic league then, and because what you were, like which Church you belonged to, mattered.

Her office was at the far end of the girls' locker room, next to the exit doors. Its walls were half wood, half glass, and you could see her working away at her desk as we got dressed to leave. The glass was opaque, with a bubbly texture, so you could see her outline. Sometimes girls went in to talk with her after practice if they were having trouble, or if Irene had said something particularly mean to them. I liked to take my time getting dressed so I could watch her move around her office.

There was a lot of talk about Kate's past. Particularly from Irene. Of special interest was why she had been bounced from five Catholic schools. Kate always left practice immediately, without showering; as soon as the door shut behind her, the discussion began. Irene would parade around the dressing room still pink-faced from practice, wet from the shower, and wrapped in a thick white towel. She would stop at practically every stall, grab onto the chrome curtain rod overhead and swing into our rooms unannounced as we changed.

"My cousin Mary Louise was at Our Lady of Mercy with Kate two years ago and she says Kate was expelled for refusing to go to religion class and disrespecting the nuns. She wouldn't even go to Mass."

Irene would pause, release one hand from the chrome bar to readjust the tuck and tightness of her towel, which was arranged to give the appearance of a bust, and continue talking and swinging one-armed.

"But my mother says her mother's just too cheap to pay tuition. Each year they pay half in September and promise to pay the rest by Christmas vacation. But never do. Can you imagine that, your mother lying to the nuns? Jesus Fucking Christ that's gross."

The first time Irene popped uninvited into my dressing room, I was misstepping into my underwear, damp from a hurried toweling-off. She stared at my body as I fumbled with leg holes.

"What do you think, Saint Theresa?" Irene always called me that. "I heard that our star player did it with black boys when she was at Sacred Heart."

Irene's mouth stayed open in a question mark as she surveyed my nakedness. I pulled on my jeans before answering. Somehow Irene always asked you questions that made you a jerk for just thinking about answering them. Her eyes traveled from my (now covered) thighs to my bare breasts. The stall was too small for me to go anyplace, so I stood there growing red, trying to come up with an answer I could live with. Irene was discovering that I had the biggest breasts on the team.

"Jesus Fucking Christ you've got big tits," Irene said. "Hey, Frances! Maura! Did you realize what big fucking tits Saint Theresa has?" A small crowd gathered. My dad says that people like Irene are a form of penance.

Our first game was against Irene's alma mater, Perpetual Faith. We all were quiet on the bus ride over except Irene; she gave us a pregame scouting report on her old teammates. We learned what everyone's shooting percentage was and who shaved her arm pits.

When we climbed down off the bus at Perpetual Faith we could see the other team watching us, but we pretended not to. They were peering out of the small rectangular windows set high in the walls of the gym. We knew that they had to be on tiptoe, standing on top of the bleachers; we knew because we did the same thing when the teams came to play us at Immaculatta. I could picture their stretched arches as they leaned against the glass. They were sizing us up, gauging their strength, laughing at the shrimpy girls, worrying about the tall ones.

Sr. Bernadette had told us to look at the back of the head of the girl in front of us as we filed into the gym. Kate led the processional, followed immediately by Irene. Perpetual Faith's players were shooting when we entered, spread out in a fan underneath the basket. Most of them knew Kate by sight, having lost to her in the past. You could see them pulling aside the new players to explain.

"No, no, the tallest girl's the point guard. The other one, the next-to-tallest, she plays center. Watch out for the guard, that's Kate Malone."

I was self-conscious, not being the tallest and playing center. I knew I got the job because I was tall enough and because busing had brought us only forwards and guards. I would have been happier hiding out as a forward; I would have felt less responsible. One of the Gallagher twins could have played center, they were good enough, they were better than me. But Peggy and Pat had played as forwards together all their lives. Choosing one as center over the other would have disturbed their equilibrium.

I wished I was a star center, the way Kate would have been. Lots of people thought that using her as a guard was a waste. But Sr. Bernadette knew that if Kate played center, Irene would be point guard, which meant that nobody but Irene (least of all Kate) would touch the ball.

My biggest shortcoming was that I wasn't aggressive enough, wasn't mean. I was taller than most of the centers I played, and I regularly got good position. I was a decent rebounder, although I've never been a great jumper, and frequently got outjumped by some little, but elastic girls. Offensively I was a nightmare. No guts. Most of my opportunities to score came from one-on-one matchups: me versus the other center in the middle of the key, smack underneath the basket. I was easily intimidated. If a girl played me close, if she bumped me or perhaps pushed me a little, just to let me know she was there, I would back right off. I would pass back out of the key, move the ball farther away from the basket. I was exasperating, really. Irene said so, right to my face, at practice. I guess I sabotaged a lot of good plays that way, by panicking.

I got constant advice from my teammates and Sr. Bernadette about posting-up, which is hoopster language for these one-on-one battles I kept avoiding. I got advice about staying firm, and wanting it bad enough, and going straight up or going up strong, and even, mixing it up with the big girls. But it was useless; the language alone confused me. Mixing what up? With whom? People assumed I couldn't post-up because I was afraid of the other girl, afraid she would hurt or humiliate me. But it wasn't true.

I played the entire first quarter on the verge of puking, praying no one would pass me the ball. Defensively, I was solid enough: mostly I just stood there and let girls run into me. Irene and Kate shot from everywhere. Swish, swish, swish, went the ball through the hoop. I didn't come close to scoring until the second half, when they substituted in a new center.

Kate and Irene had brought the ball up, and were weaving in and out of the key. I was directly underneath the basket, hands up, my back to the other center. She looked familiar, but I couldn't quite place her. I heard nothing but the sound of my own heartbeat and breathing. Sr. Bernadette waved wildly from the sidelines and I could see her mouthing directions. A play and then several plays unfolded around me. I tried to stay focused on the ball. My opponent and I do-si-doed for position. Finally, I heard a sound that didn't belong to me: the chink chink of Mary Jude McGlaughlin's cross and Virgin medallion hitting against each other.

Mary Jude was a friend of my cousin Anne, and from what Anne used to tell me, she was shy, devout, not overly intellectual, extremely sweet, and oppressively pretty. She had been warming the bench for Perpetual Faith for three years, and had scored twice during brief cameos, once for the opposing team. Mary Jude touched my soaked back lightly, just above my hip, with the tips of three fingers on her right hand. Her breathing was soft and even, and although I couldn't see her face, I knew she was smiling: Mary Jude never didn't smile.

I sighed. Here it was again. How could I possibly compete against such goodness? How could I fake left, all the while knowing that I would be moving to my right, digging my shoulder into Mary Jude as I pivoted, and lightly pushing the ball into the basket? How could I leave her standing there, as people had so often left me, mouth agape, embarrassed, wondering what had just happened? How could I press my advantage knowing the punishment she would take from her teammates, punishment I knew only too well? Worst of all, Mary Jude would smile through it all. This registered as sin to me. Something I would have to purge from my soul in order to receive communion next Sunday. Something, if left unattended, I would burn in hell for. So I didn't.

When the ball finally came to me, I was a knot of anxiety. I turned and faced Mary Jude. I held the ball high, above her head, and discovered I was right about her smile. She beamed at me. I smiled back. She had huge brown eyes. In the half second before I was going to pass the ball back to Kate, one of Mary Jude's teammates whacked the ball out of my hands and into the hands of their point guard. They scored before I turned around.

Irene was all over me.

"Jesus Fucking Christ, what was that? You plan to just give them the ball all day? Whose side are you on anyway?"

I blanched. The one legitimate basket Mary Jude had scored in the last three years was against me: I let her. It was as if I had no choice: it meant so much to her. I was terrified that Irene had figured it out; that she would tell about Mary Jude and the others like her. And there were others. Lots of others. I guess I knew the other centers wanted to win as much as I did, and I couldn't stand the thought of taking that away from them. It wasn't that I liked to lose; I hated to lose. But I guess I hated making other people lose worse. And besides, I was used to it.

I knew that this weakness was ten times worse than plain cowardice. I was My Own Worst Enemy. And now, potentially, the team's.

We won anyway. The first in an endless season of wins. We beat Perpetual Faith 59 to 36. Kate scored 23 points; Irene hit for 19. The team was ecstatic. Sr. Bernadette lectured us on the bus on the way home. I sat as far away from Irene as possible. Sr. Bernadette crouched in the aisle between the seats, pivoting left and right, facing each of us directly as she spoke. Sr. Bernadette had a custom of grabbing your shoulder or your knee or whatever was handy when she talked to you, so she was impossible to ignore. That day on the bus she got so close to me I could feel her breath on my face. I didn't hear a word she said, but I remember how she looked up close. Her hair was damp and limp from all the perspiring she had done during our game, her face glistened and the muscles on her neck stood out. Her black eyes were as black as her missing habit, and luminous.

Usually I hated the bus rides. If I could have, I would have sat right by Kate, who took the seat directly behind the bus driver and across the aisle from Sr. Bernadette. I was dying to be included in their conversations, to listen to Kate talk basketball, and to be on the receiving end of Sr. Bernadette's intensity. They sat at a slight angle to each other so that their knees touched, and Kate held the playbook on her lap. Sr. Bernadette gestured from the book to the air in front of them, with one hand going back periodically to Kate's shoulder to confirm her understanding. Kate stared closely at the invisible drawings in the air between them.

Irene occupied the very last bus seat by the emergency exit; the rest of us were staggered in the seats just before her. The cooler you were the farther back you sat and the closer to Irene you positioned yourself. I sat alone, as far away from Irene as I could get without leaving the group entirely. She talked nonstop about Kate. My ears burned red as I slumped forward in my seat pretending not to hear her, pretending to read the book in my lap, stealing glances at the front of the bus.

But I was, I knew, as guilty as Irene. Like her, I was obsessed with Kate. I wanted to know everything: what her family was like, why she kept changing schools, where she learned to play so well, whether she liked us, whether she liked me. In retrospect, I was infatuated with her, and it was my first big, stomach-wrenching infatuation. But I didn't know to call it that. I didn't even know enough to be embarrassed. Although, thank God, I knew enough to keep it from Irene.

I listened very closely to the horrible things Irene said. Each day she had a new story explaining Kate. Kate was on drugs; she was a kleptomaniac; her mother was a prostitute; her family was on welfare; they were really Protestant Irish; her father was a Jew; Kate was on the Pill; and, the worst possible slander for our immaculate ears, she had had two abortions. Everyone knew that Kate lived alone with her mother, and this in itself was extremely suspect. Some kids at Immaculatta had as many as ten brothers and sisters; most of us had at least four. I had never met an only child; Sr. Agnes said they were sins. And Catholic families were not families without fathers.

If Kate knew about the rumors Irene spread, she never let on. Kate rarely spoke. She had no friends on the team, or at Immaculatta, as far as I could tell. When Kate spoke it was b-ball talk. At practice she doubled as Sr. Bernadette's assistant coach, showing us moves and illustrating plays. One week Kate was assigned to demonstrate posting-up to the centers and forwards. That Monday we gathered around her underneath one basket, while Sr. Bernadette hollered at the guards at the opposite end of the court.

"First you have to find out where you are. Establish some territory. Take up some space. Back your butt into the other girl. See how much room she'll give you. Once you know where she is and how much she'll take, then you're ready. The first rule in posting-up is wanting it. Even if your hands are up like this for the ball, no guard's gonna pass it unless your face says you want it. The second rule is not thinking about it too much. Get ready and go. The longer you wait, the more likely it'll be taken away."

Was she talking just to me? Did she know? Had Irene told her something, or was I that transparent?

"Get out of your head, Theresa," Kate said on Tuesday. "I can see you thinking. Get out of your head."

"How?" I asked. "How can you see me thinking?" And to myself: *What can you see me thinking?*

"I just can," she shrugged. "And if I can, so can they. So lose it, whatever it is."

I struggled to empty my face. I struggled to eliminate Mary Jude and the others from my consciousness.

"Well you don't have to look like an idiot." Kate smiled at my vacant expression. The other girls laughed, and I was giddy with the attention. Emboldened, I asked her how come she knew so much about basketball.

"I don't really know," she said, completely serious. "It's like I was born knowing."

"Did your father teach you?" I ventured. "Or your brothers?" Heads turned; ears pricked expectantly.

She shook her head, No. Now her face emptied. End of conversation.

But I couldn't let it go. After practice, I followed her to her locker. She hadn't heard my footsteps over the noise of the girls taking showers, so she jumped when I said loudly into her left ear, "Uncles or cousins?"

"Uncles or cousins, what?" She looked angry.

I had never been this close to Kate, and now I saw the details of her face for the first time. Her skin was pale—red-head pale—and a pattern of soft brown freckles ran across the bridge of her nose and splashed onto her cheeks. Her eyes were clear blue. They widened with shock and anger as I persisted.

"Did your uncles or cousins teach you to play?"

"Why are you so anxious to know who taught me what? Maybe I taught myself. Maybe, like I said, I was born knowing. Maybe I couldn't help but learn. What's it to you?" She crossed her long arms in front of her chest and grew two inches. Her thin Irish lips pursed.

"I was just curious. Thought maybe if I knew what you did to get so good, I could learn a little faster. You know." Sweat collected on my eyelids.

"Look, lemme give you a tip, save you some time. The thing you need to do more than anything else is be in your body. I've seen it before. Lots of girls play in their heads. Get back here," one of her extraordinary arms flashed out and smacked me in the roundest part of my belly. The spot she touched burned, and I could feel little waves of heat fan out until my fingertips were warm. I knew the color was draining from my face. I nodded and bent forward a little, in an unintentional bow, and got stuck there. I tried to smile my thanks, but I couldn't move my muscles the way I wanted. Finally, I just backed away. We didn't speak again until Friday.

"Terry, come here."

Terry? No one called me Terry. It was always Theresa. I looked behind me; perhaps there was a new girl I didn't know.

"Yes, you, Terry. Come here. Come guard me."

We had had a week of posting-up lessons—we had practiced both offensive and defensive positions—and it was time to show Sr. Bernadette what we had learned. I couldn't move.

"Quit stalling, Terry. Get over here."

Terry. I said it over to myself. Kate had a name for me.

Slowly, anxiously, I got in position behind her. She grew taller and wider until I could see nothing but her muscled back and clump of braided hair. All week I had practiced against the Gallaghers and lost. How could I possibly defend against Kate?

She inched me back toward the basket with her butt. Her shoulders twisted left, then right, then left again. Finally Kate stepped away from me, turned, and shot. When I could at last see the ball, I started moving toward it, straight up into the air. My shoulder left its socket, released my arm, which floated up to touch the ball, and returned. Before I knew it, we were all three back on the ground.

"Not bad, Terry. Not bad at all." Kate looked surprised, but not displeased. "Now just stay there." She slapped one arm onto my shoulder, retrieved the ball with her free hand, and pumped it into my stomach. "Don't think about what you did, just stay here. In your body."

But I was already out, thinking about my new name, afraid of what I'd just done.

* * *

As we won more and more, I grew increasingly frustrated with my inability to score. I wanted to be part of the team in a way that I wasn't. I wanted to slap hands with everyone, triumphant, after an especially tough basket. Or, more truthfully, I wanted everyone to slap my hand, the way they slapped Kate's and Irene's. I wanted to be sought after. I wanted Kate to congratulate me in the same expressionless, monotone manner in which she congratulated Irene. I wanted the cool indifference of excellence.

So at the halfway point in the season, after we'd won twelve straight games, and we were looking like we couldn't lose, I began practicing on my own, mornings, before school. An hour and a half of shooting and dribbling (I set up those fluorescent orange cones and did figure eights around them) every day. I got a little better and a lot bored. Playing alone had its limitations; it's one thing to shoot from eight feet out, it's another thing to shoot from anywhere with someone's hand in your face. And I had no one to post-up against. So I started looking for a morning pickup game.

All the league stars played mornings. Many of them played nights, too, after regular practice or games, after dinner, under streetlights that had been rigged with hoops. I knew that Irene played early mornings in the school playground with a bunch of girls from Perpetual Faith. Girls-room girls. Smokers. They all wore eye shadow that matched their sweatpants and tons of St. Christopher medals and gold crosses that were constantly being tucked into ironed, white tee shirts. Irene was the best athlete there, and she tenaciously maintained possession of the ball, so after a few wasted efforts I decided to try a boys' game. I went to several boys' Catholic school playgrounds and found as many games. It didn't work. I realized that a girl's ability was always a problem for boys. If I wasn't as good as they were, they humiliated me by never passing me the ball; if I was as good, they humiliated me by never passing me the ball. Only girls who were as talented as Kate could play with boys without humiliation. Finally, I got up the courage to ask Sr. Bernadette. I tapped on the bubble glass of her office door one day after practice, after everyone had gone.

"Come in," she hollered, and swiveled in her chair. The office was warm and smelled of leather from balls and gloves and cleats. I stood with my hands behind my back, one hand still on the doorknob.

"What's up, Theresa?" She smiled. She looked even smaller sitting down; her feet swung an inch above the ground.

"I, umm, I was wondering if you, umm, knew of a game I could play in mornings. Other than Irene's game." I turned the knob in my hand. It was slippery.

"What about my game?" she offered immediately.

"What about your game?" I was confused.

"My game." Sr. Bernadette stood up and jammed her hands in her sweatpants pocket.

"You coach a game? I'm looking for a pickup game, not another team." I leaned back into the door.

"No, I play in a game. A pickup game." She was still smiling.

"You play in a pickup game?" I didn't know nuns could do that. After all she had played in college before she took her vows.

"Theresa, what's the problem? Am I not being clear? I can't imagine being any more clear, really." Sr. Bernadette's smile waned and she seemed a little exasperated.

"No. It's just that, what do you mean, a game?"

"Jesus. I mean I play in a morning pickup game and would you like to play with us?"

For Christ's sake, I had made a nun swear. I opened the office door and took a half step out. "Well, yes, I mean, are you sure it's OK?"

"It's OK," Sr. Bernadette sighed. "Where are you going?"

"Then OK. All right. See you there. Where is it?" I was outside her office now. Only my head stuck into the warmth.

"Dorchester." Sr. Bernadette stepped toward me.

"Dorchester. OK. No problem. See you then. Tomorrow OK?" I closed the door. Then opened it. "How do I get there?"

Sr. Bernadette laughed and sat back down. "You can catch the bus on Randolph Avenue, right in front of Immaculatta."

"No problem," I lied and shut her door for good. I couldn't believe it! Sr. Bernadette invited me to her personal game. Her very own private game. I floated home. Maybe now I could sit in the school bus with her and Kate. Maybe now I would be protected from Irene.

The next morning I had to take two different buses to get there, and I had to lie to my parents about where I was going. Dorchester was off-limits.

I jumped off the bus three blocks too soon. My stomach knotted. It was a big, public school playground with several hoops. A handful of men played at the near corner. I stood by the fence in front of them, hidden by their moving bodies. I could see Sr. Bernadette and her friends warming up at the far end of the concrete park. I had imagined the way they might look several times: last night I dreamed that they played in full habits. My mind pictured every possible combination of athlete and cleric on the court. But I never guessed they would be a mixed group; even in Dorchester. I didn't know any black people, none of my friends knew any black people, so I hadn't imagined them in Sr. Bernadette's basketball game. I waited for everyone to start playing before I walked over.

Kate was there! I gasped at the sight of her, exhilarated and disappointed. Sr. Bernadette had invited another person from our team to share in her private life. I was not so special after all. I wondered how long they had been playing together, and if they had become friends. The knot in my stomach tightened.

There were ten women playing ball, including Kate and Bernie—which is what they called Sr. Bernadette. Two more women sat next to me on a green wooden bench that was rooted into the cement a few feet behind one of the hoops. I was sweating so much that my thighs slid off the bench and little pieces of green paint stuck to me when I stood up. The women at my side watched the game closely, calling out encouragements.

The first play I witnessed was a court-length pass to Kate, who was waiting underneath the basket. It took three seconds. They tried the exact same thing next possession but someone on the other team leapt into the air and stole away the play. I was out of breath just watching them.

They fought hard for rebounds and loose balls, and sometimes knocked each other down. One woman got roughed up three times in three consecutive plays. She was a forward and a very aggressive rebounder. She had the same coloring as Sr. Bernadette; another Italian I guessed. Her dark hair stood out every which way. Each time she hit the cement, whoever knocked her down helped her up. By the third fall everyone was laughing. She even smiled, although you could see she was hurt. Someone said it was a good thing she had so much padding, and they all laughed louder. The well-padded woman walked stiffly around the court, rubbing her behind. The others stopped to catch their breath, bending completely over, resting their hands on their knees so that their elbows jutted out and made shelves of their arms. Everyone's tee shirt was stuck to them.

After a minute or two, one of the point guards approached the injured forward and spoke to her. She massaged the woman's butt like it was her shoulder or something. They walked slowly over to the bench. We all stood up.

"Sub," said the guard, looking at me. "We need a forward."

The injured player lay out flat on the ground in front of the bench. She brought one knee up to her chest and held it there tightly. Her sore cheek lifted off the ground. One of the women who had been calling encouragements hustled onto the court.

"You sure look like a forward," the guard shrugged, letting her eyes travel up and down my full length. I felt that same funny heat wave I felt when Kate touched my stomach that time after practice.

"Center," I whispered.

"No kidding?" She smiled. "You're gonna play against Katie?" She shook her head. "Aren't you the brave one. I'd be whispering that too, if I were you." She sped back to the game.

I hadn't even noticed that Kate was playing center. I wondered if it was because they needed a center, or because there were guards who played better than Kate. I had never seen a guard better than Kate, so I watched the friendly woman play.

She reminded me of Irene—except that she was more friendly and she was black—they had the same build and the same jauntiness. She was everywhere at once. It was the kind of attitude you hate in people you don't like. It didn't bother me so much in her. She stole the ball five times in about eight tries.

I was used to seeing people steal a lot. Kate and Irene did it all the time, but against lesser players. This guard was something else again. The women she stole from were no pushovers; they could handle the ball, every single one of them. Where she edged them out was in speed and desire. Just a millisecond faster: she would attack the ball the instant after it was released from her opponent's hand, but before it touched the ground. She didn't grab the ball with both hands: that would have been too awkward, and too easy to defend against. She just tapped it lightly to one side and was gone. Like that. Desire so overwhelming you couldn't see it happening.

My dad had a drill test for desire. He said that desire was the most important thing in an athlete. Only he called it playing with heart. That's how he picked his starters: the five guys with the most heart played. At home, he would roll a basketball on the ground away from me and Tim. When it was a few feet out, he'd blow his coach's whistle and we'd lunge for it. On the cement driveway. We'd dive and grovel and kick for the ball. That was what I thought desire looked like. Desperation and skinned knees. I had trouble recognizing the smiling guard's desire: desire that left no room for alternatives. Desire that brought pleasure.

She was having a great time. Everyone was.

They were a strange-looking bunch. All different sizes and colors and abilities. I had expected them all to be the same. They were not. The guard who reminded me of Irene was 5-foot, 4 inches tall. The other point guard was equally as small, but had legs the thickness of fire hydrants. She could touch the rim of the basket; she could alley-oop.

There was something peculiar about them. Something I couldn't quite name. They were women, not girls. For the first time I saw the difference. I realized that this was what made Kate stand out so at Immaculatta; and that this, somehow, was why she had been thrown out of five Catholic schools. There was a sturdiness about them, a sense of commitment to life, like at one point they each had made a conscious decision to stay alive. They had made choices.

The longer I watched them play, the more inexplicable they seemed. I had never met women like them before. My mother, none of my friends' mothers, were like these women. Yet deep in my stomach they were familiar. I began to suspect I'd met them before and searched my brain for a memory. Nothing.

Kate was playing against a tall light-skinned black woman named Toni, who was as skinny as she was long. Kate seemed thickset by comparison. They spent most of their time about a hair's width apart, exchanging bruises. Fifteen minutes into the game, Kate elbowed her in the head, accidentally, while pulling down a rebound. It smarted. Toni staggered toward the bench, holding her head in her hands. "Sub," she hollered. Everyone else stopped moving.

"Toni, Toni, you okay? Talk to me, Toni." Kate's face was a mask of concern.

Toni turned to them, fingering the growing lump on her head. "You playing football out there, Malone, or what? No finesse, I tell you, Irish girls got no finesse."

Everyone smiled; a few giggles escaped. Kate tried not to laugh.

"Your concern is underwhelming, Malone, underwhelming." Toni resumed her stagger toward the bench and plowed directly into me. "Who are you? More Irish, I see. I need a sub. Go play against your cousin, will ya. You can beat up each other for a while." She shoved me onto the court.

Irene's look-alike came immediately to my rescue. She grabbed me by the shoulder.

"No problem, no problem. Maureen's here, and she's gonna take care of you. Mo's gonna help you out. What's your name, sweetheart? If you're gonna play with us, we need to know your name."

"Theres—Terry," I said, looking away from Kate. "Terry Meagher."

"Okay, Terry Meagher, it's two-one-two zone." She dragged me over to my new teammates. "You just stand in the middle with your arms up like this, okay?" Mo threw both of her arms into the air, her little body making a giant X. "Me and Bernie are your guards, Merril and Sam are behind you. Got that?" She stood frozen in a half–jumping jack. I nodded.

Everyone grunted hello, and Bernie—Sr. Bernadette—winked at me. Mo flung one arm over my shoulder and pulled me to her. She covered her mouth with her free hand and whispered loud enough for everyone to hear: "Don't let Katie get inside, okay? You're finished if she gets inside. Foul her if you have to."

I looked into Mo's eyes. Dark brown eyes in a dark brown face. Irene came to mind: how like Mo she was. How she would hate that. I thought about Mom and Dad. How grateful they were to have sent me to Catholic school, years ago, before it all started, before yellow school buses meant anything more than transportation. I pictured the busload of black second-graders that got stoned. I remembered the TV news clip my parents had kept me from watching; before they shut it off, I had recognized an Irish flag waving behind the mob of white parents.

Mo's left hand hung pink and brown over my shoulder, an inch from my face. I reached up and pressed it with both of my sweaty hands. "Cold hands," I smiled at Mo.

"They're always that way, even when I play." Mo looked directly at me.

"Cold hands, warm heart," I offered, and was instantly embarrassed. "It's an old Irish saying," I backtracked. What was I doing?

But Mo seemed charmed. "I like that. Cold hands, warm heart. Good for you. I like that. You're gonna do just fine. Well, let's go, Terry Meagher. And watch out for these cold-hearted women with hot shots." She laughed and shook her head.

The rest of the game seemed to go in slow motion. I knew it was faster than any other game I'd ever played in, but I could see every detail like it wasn't, like I was watching it under a magnifying glass.

I kept one eye on Kate, one eye on the ball, and one eye on Mo, who was never far from the ball. Then it happened. I was in the middle of the key, with Kate at my back. Mo brought the ball up and charged around me, into the key, making like she was going in for a lay-up. But instead of shooting, she dropped the ball back for me. Her move drew everyone with her, over to the right side of the key. Well, almost everyone. I was just left of center, with Kate between me and the basket.

So I did what Kate taught me. Fake right-left-right, turn, and up into the air. Kate was there, matching everything. A long, strong arm shot into the air and slapped the ball a second after it left my fingertips. We three thudded to the ground. The ball bounced hard, back into my hands. I held my breath. Kate was huge in front of me. Left-right-left, this time and up again, knees bent, arms stretched. Kate's arm grew longer than mine. She slammed the ball. We crashed down. People began murmuring encouragements. I heard my name. This time the ball dropped to Mo. She fired it back to me. I was shocked. She was closer to the basket than either Kate or me. Mo smiled and rolled her eyes up to the clouds. So I went up again, no fakes, just straight up into the air. Kate following.

She would beat me like this every time, I knew, so without ever having done it before, and a little off-balance, I hooked the ball. I had seen people do it before, mostly smaller players who were trying to get over big girls. Irene could hook, Sr. Bernadette could hook, and I had seen Mo do it once early that morning. But I myself had never tried it, not even in practice. It wasn't really a conscious decision, my right elbow just bent, all by itself, and let the ball go. It cleared Kate's fingers, smacked the backboard a little too hard, and fell into the hoop. This time we both landed on our butts.

From the ground, everything finally made sense. I knew what Kate meant by being in one's body: I was in mine. I looked up at the calves and thighs surrounding me. These women were in every inch of theirs. They seemed completely without fear: of their bodies, of each other, of their desires. I could see that they even liked their bodies, which is what at first seemed so peculiar. I had never met a woman who liked her own body.

I stayed on the ground, not wanting to get up. I knew that being in my body meant choosing myself. And choosing desire. So few women I knew had chosen themselves: Sr. Bernadette, Kate, and in her own evil way, Irene.

Sr. Bernadette walked over to Kate, who was still flat on her back, and extended both of her hands. Kate grabbed hold and Sr. Bernadette yanked her to her feet. Kate seemed about eight feet tall standing so close to Sr. Bernadette. They just looked at each other, and I could tell that they were, indeed, friends. But somehow it didn't bother me so much now.

Kate let go of Sr. Bernadette's hands and stepped over to me. She reached out one hand and pulled me up. She dusted my behind and shrugged, indifferent: "Nice move. . . . Who taught you that?"

"No one," I said. "No one taught me that." And she nodded.

Her Marathon

Jenifer Levin

I was drunk sick, I was bleeding. Not the kind that comes from somebody smashing your face in, but the bleeding inside when you're hurt, when you're down, and this whole damn city's like a bunch of sharks smelling something wounded, circling you to bite, swimming around. Stare in the mirror and you say to yourself: Baby, you look like shit. Which I did. Hell, it was true. Like some piece of worm shit crawled out from under a log, squirming around all white, all stripped of the natural color God gave her, crawling in the sunlight. I brushed my teeth. I put lipstick on. Said to myself: Girlfriend, you still got about a ounce of pride left, maybe, so get your ass downstairs and over to the Walgreen's and get some of that stomach-settle shit before you puke all over.

The kid was sleeping. So was Needa and her fucking friends from the grocery shift, snoring, burping beer dreams in a chair, on the sofa, I mean every which place. I tiptoed over bodies. Wrapped keys in a hanky, didn't want to wake them. Then I went down the three flights into autumn, cold sunlight, Sunday.

Usually up here on Sundays you could roll an old empty down First Avenue and it wouldn't touch nothing. Only this day was different. Stepping out of the building was like being wrapped in a big screaming people-circus of arms and shouts. They stayed on the sidewalk, jammed in like fish so you couldn't shove through them to cross the street, you could not hardly move, and some guy's got a radio, and around me every once in a while they're saying, really hushed: "He's coming."

"He's coming."

"He's coming."

There were sirens, red and yellow-white flashes, shadows of light on the empty paved street vivisected by a yellow line, by a pale blue line, and this buzz got loud everywhere around and through me and then, like a Band-Aid, stopped the bleeding.

"Who?" I whispered. "Who's coming?"

"The first man."

"Who?"

"The first runner."

Still, a big sick was in my belly, threatening to lurch out, and there was a part of me thinking: I gotta cross the street, get to Walgreen's. So I started to push, try to make it through the crowd. Some dyke turned to me looking

Reprinted, by permission, from Jenifer Levin, 1996, *Love and Death, & Other Disasters*, (Ithaca, NY: Firebrand Books).

nasty and says, *Mira*, bitch, stay where you are, did your mother raise you in a cave? I mean have some respect! This is the Marathon.

Any other day I would have clawed out her fucking eyeballs. But the sirens, the tires, got closer. Bringing with them the whirling, spattering lights, bright motorcade chrome, October wind, silent feet. And a scream rose up from the whole shark city, from its garbage tins and sidewalk cement, from the sweat and love and hope of human bodies, from my own insides.

Then I saw him.

No, I didn't see him, I caught him with my eyes. But he escaped.

He was tall, and dark, with dark eyebrows and burning black eyes and a fierce young face, and he ran like some great hot flame on the breath of the wind. When he breathed he breathed in the air of the world so that, in that second, there was nothing left for us. His feet were fast, a blur, a howl. He ran like God. Chango, I said silently, here he is, your son. In that second all the air of the world was gone. I choked. I thought I would die. Tears came to my eyes.

"Salazar!" someone yelled.

"It's Salazar!"

"Salazar!"

"Bravo!"

"*Viv!*"

"*Viv*, Salazar!"

He passed, spattering pavement with his sweat.

The sun blew cold, sirens and screams twisted around, wrapped me up into them. Until I fell down into the center of the storm. It blinked up at me, one-eyed, black and fierce.

Woman, it said, you must burn thus. Light a candle. Save your life.

"Help me!" I sobbed. And bit through my lip.

When I opened my eyes the sun had stopped moving. People yelled, cheered, pressed in against me, radios blared, my tears were dry so I yelled and cheered too, and wind whipped leaves down the street as more runners came by, more and more, thousands, until it seemed that they filled the whole city, and that all of us, all of us, were running.

I stayed there screaming for hours. Until the sun started to fade a little, and I lost my voice. Then I stayed there still, way past the time when this guy with the radio said, Okay oye everybody, he won, Salazar won, didn't nobody come close, plus he set a world record.

But here, on our side of town, were still most of the rest of the runners. Fifteen, twenty thousand, someone said. And they all had plenty more to go, more than ten miles, the radio guy said, before they got to the finish.

There were people skinnier than toothpicks running, and a guy wearing pink rabbit ears. Men and girls, both, wearing those mesh shirts so light you can see right through, and men and girls both wearing T-shirts with their names magic-markered on front and back: HELENA, says one; BERNIE'S BOY, says another; and as they went past everyone yells out, "Go, Helena!" and "Attaway, Bernie's Boy!" There were old people running, too, and daughters, and mothers, black and white and every shade in between, from every one of these United States and from plenty of other countries, France and Mexico and Belgium and Trinidad, you had better believe it, so many people, and not all of them real fast, nor all of them skinny—some even looked like me.

I waited screaming with no sound until the crowd began to disappear, lights went on in windows all around, and the sun was going down. There weren't so many runners now but still lots of people walking. Some limping. In the shadows you could see how some had these half-dead, half-crazy expressions. All right, honey, I croaked out about every two minutes to another one, all right, honey, keep going, you're gonna finish. Pretty soon I realized I was shivering and went upstairs.

The kid was watching TV, eating Fritos, most of Needa's scumbag friends were gone, and Needa was pissed. Where you been? she said. You look like something the tide washed in, and how come you didn't get no more beer?

I told her shut up, have some respect, today is the Marathon. The what? she says. The Marathon, I said, the Marathon, and if you didn't spend your weekends being mean and bossing me around like some man, you coulda seen Salazar run. What the fuck, she grumbled. But then she shrugged. We didn't fight after all—even though, truth be told, I was feeling pretty sick of her just then and I wouldn't have minded. I mean, we never even *did* it anymore.

I picked the kid up and danced him around the room a little until he laughed. I thought about how handsome he was—bright smile and big black eyes the girls would all fight and die over some day—and how he was doing okay with the alphabet in kindergarten, too, and the teachers said real nice things about him, and other kids wanted to be his friend. Then I thought, squeezing him close, what a fucking miracle it was, maybe, that such a great kid had come out of a loser like me. Fact of the matter being that neither me nor his father is all that great in the looks department; neither one of us remembered, really, why we ever did that boy-girl shit in the first place—I always did like the ladies better, maybe just got curious. Then first thing I know I'm about to pop, mister father there blows, and later, there's Needa and me. She came on so sweet to me at first, so butch and pretty. Now life was more or less her working and me working, paying rent, keeping things clean, getting the kid back and forth to school, on weekends some videos, arguments, TV, beer. And neither one of us with a nice word or touch for the other. Nights, I'd get filled with a sudden big darkness when all the lights went out. Filled with a power so black and brown and green, Oggun, Yemaya, iron, water, a big washing-over foaming waving ocean sadness. Then plain exhaustion that pressed my eyelids down. Needa would already be snoring. I'd turn my back, start to dream. In the morning, would not remember.

Stop dancing your son around the room, snapped Needa, you'll turn him into a fucking fairy. Come here, kid. We're gonna get a couple movies.

Fine, I told her, look who's talking. Biggest bull I ever knew. Go on, both of you. Get a couple of Real Man movies. Get a couple of Let's-Kill-Everyone-in-Sight things, why don't you. Fill his head with a bunch of real machitos getting their guts blown out.

When they left, I cleaned up Fritos and beer cans. Got some frozen chicken out. Then halfway through soaking it in a pot of warm water, I wiped my hands with a fresh white cloth, lit a couple candles, offered up a plate of half-thawed gizzards. I stay away from the powers, mostly, but that night felt different. Kneeling in front of the plate for at least a little proper respect, red candles, white candles dripping, watching thin pieces of ice melt off the gizzards and the thawing organs swim in remains of their own dark blood, I thought again about Salazar. I wondered if he ran so hard and so fast that, when he won, his feet were crusted with blood. I remembered things my grandma told me, long ago, when I'd walk out laughing into the sun of a hot sweet summer morning. About the happiness of the air filled with voices and smells, joy of loving, the ferocity of vengeance and of hate, how to heal what you care for, how to ruin an enemy. The holiness of sacrifice.

Not that I even did it right.

When they want live roosters, they don't mean half-thawed chicken gizzards. But it was all for the fire, hungry holy fire that doesn't die, even when the world tries to kill it, that stays alive, eating, eating—I offered it truly in my heart—and God sees everything.

The next morning Needa groaned and stuck her head under a pillow when the alarm clock rang early. I tiptoed around, stuck on a pair of sweatpants, socks, old tennis sneakers, one of her used-up sweatshirts. It was cold out, wind coming off the river. Sun wasn't even up yet. I held keys in the space between fingers and balled up my hand like a fist, like a metal-bristling weapon, and when I started to run could feel the fat bobbing around my stomach and arms and hips and thighs, heavy and disgusting, bringing me a little bit closer to the ground each time the skin folds flopped up and down. After a couple minutes I thought I was gonna die. I had to stop and gasp and walk. Then when I could breathe okay I'd run as fast as I could another half a minute or so, stop and gasp and walk awhile, then run again. I did this about fifteen, twenty minutes. Until snot dripped to my lip, and my face was running wet in the cold, blotching Needa's sweatshirt in chilly clinging puddles. I started to cry. Then I told myself, Shut up you. It worked, the tears stopped. I went back inside, climbed stairs with legs that were already numb and hurting, and made everybody breakfast. Needa growled her way through a shower and padded around with a coffee cup making wet footprints everywhere, watching "Good Morning America."

There he is, she grumbled, there's your *man*, your Salazar.

I ignored her sarcasm.

But I was stuck there in the kitchen, making sure the kid's toast didn't burn. I told Needa tell me what they're saying.

They're saying about how he won yesterday. You know, the race. Guy set a fucking world record or something.

I wanted to run and see, but couldn't.

That's how the weeks went: me getting up early in the dark, going to bash my fat brains out trying to run, getting breakfast for everyone, showering when they were all finished with the bathroom, getting Needa to work and the kid to school and then getting myself to work too. My eyes started hurting bad from being open extra long. My legs were sore, thighs feeling like they were all bruised and bloodied on the inside, calves with pinpricks of pain searing through them. Needa noticed me limping around all the time, and laughed. What's with you, girl? You think you gonna be in the Olympics or something? You think you gonna run that marathon?

Finally, one Saturday, I went to see Madrita.

She took out the cards and beads and shells, there in her little place in the basement, pulled all the curtains closed so everything was cozy and safe like your mother's womb. Outside, it rained. She was trained the old way, did everything absolutely right, took her time. After a while I asked her, Well, how does it look?

"Sweetheart, you gotta lotta obstacles."

Hey, I told her, that ain't exactly news.

She sighed. "You gotta stop worrying about the home. Home's gonna take care of themselves, you be surprised. Lots of rage and pain but lots of love too. See, sweetheart, you can do what you want, only it's difficult. First, purify yourself."

"Purify? Myself?"

"What I said."

She wrote down all the stuff I had to get, white and red roses and violet water and rose water, mint, coconut, a bunch of sunflowers and herbs and things, and made me memorize how to do the bath right. Then she told me go up to the little shop the Jew man has, here's the address, he's one of them from Spain and he knows the right things, even *babalaus* goes there for supplies. And while you're there get a couple pieces of camphor, sweetheart, and some fresh mint leaves. Put them in a little bag, pin it inside your bra, it'll keep you healthier. You got a cold coming on.

Needa wasn't too happy about the bathwater sitting all night, reeking herbs and flower petals, before I got into it—first!—the next morning. Yaaah, she grumped, you and that devil shit. Ever since the Marathon. Makes me feel like I'm living with some fucking boogy. But listen, woman: Don't you go casting no spells on me.

I was stripping sweaty sweats and socks to bathe. Caught her staring, out of the corner of my eye, and bared my teeth. Then she rubbed my naked butt, friendly like, and the both of us laughed.

The mornings got darker, closer to winter, but every once in a while I'd wake up easier when the alarm hit, sometimes even with a feel of burning red excitement in my chest and throat, like the running was something pleasurable, good, a gift. Truth is that it did feel good some mornings. I'd breathe splendidly. Thighs move like water, arms pump rhythm. The feet did not want to stop. Those days I'd stay out longer—half an hour or more—with happy buzzing like music in my head.

Celia, one of the girls at work said, just before New Year's, I been meaning to tell you, you are looking really terrific these days.

It was true.

I circled around the file cabinets all afternoon, putting things away, singing.

That night, after picking the kid up and dropping him and his cousin off with his grandma for a couple hours, I skipped grocery shopping and just went home, changed into some sweaty old things, and I went outside into the wind and dark and I ran again, very sweet and happy and like music, the way I had that morning, running off and onto curbs, twisting around cars and garbage cans and people, I didn't care. I hummed and sang going back upstairs. Needa opened the door for me, mad.

"Where the fuck you been? I feel like I ain't got a lover these days."

"Oh you got one, honey. Whether you want one or not."

"What's that supposed to mean?"

"Whatever you want it to, girlfriend."

She moped around the rest of the evening, drank about a six-pack of Ballantine and fell asleep on the sofa. Later I went to pick up the kid. Walking home he said how big he was getting, how he was gonna be in first grade next year and could take gym, and run at the school track meet next spring.

That's good, I told him, it's good to have a plan.

We ordered pizza, watched TV and drank Coca-Cola while Needa snored away on the sofa. I was feeling different, lighter, happy-headed and full of fresh cold air from running again, but at the same time dark and warm inside. I put the kid to bed and left a kitchen light on for Needa, then turned in myself, breathing full and deep, sniffing camphor, mint, letting some calm, clean-burning soft red feeling wash over me, droop my eyelids shut, wrap me up all safe and bright, and soon I dreamed.

In the dream I was running on dirt and grass through trees near the Reservoir in Central Park—quick, effortless, light, my toes and ankles bouncing and strong—and next to me a man was running, and we breathed in perfect rhythm. I looked over. It was Salazar.

Alberto, I said, I want to run the Marathon.

Listen to me, Celia, he said, you're not ready yet. You gotta do some shorter races first.

Okay, I said.

Then we stopped running.

He faced me, hands on hips, fierce dark flame face, slender and serious and young. I noticed he wore a collar of beads, scarlet-wine red and white. Oh, I laughed, I thought so, you really are a child of Chango. So am I.

It's fire Celia, he said. But everyone has a power. Use it for running. Use it for loving. Use it for God.

I woke up smelling rotten beer breath. Needa was sitting slumped over, head in hands on my side of the bed, crying.

"What is it, honey?"

"Lost," she sobbed, "I got lost."

I put my arms around her. Her cheeks were all soft and smelly, but there was that nice odor to her too, one it seemed like I remembered from long, long ago, woman smell, soap smell, a crumply warm feel of her hair and clothes.

Lost, she sobbed.

No, honey, I told her, holding her, rocking the both of us back and forth. No, honey, no, sweet woman, my Needa, don't you cry. You didn't get lost, you been found.

Help me, Celia, she said. Help me, God. Gotta work harder, keep up with you. I am so ashamed of my life.

I remembered the dream. I pulled her down alongside me on the bed, held her, rocking, whispering true things to the back of her neck. Telling how I was proud of her, and of our child, and our home. How hard we had worked. How far we had come. How, before taking on the whole rest of our lives, we had to do the small, obvious, necessary tasks, one step at a time.

"Like how I'm not gonna just jump in and run the Marathon right off, honey. I gotta do some shorter races first."

"Huh," she sniffed, "get you, the expert. Who you think you been talking to, the angels?"

But she pulled my arms tighter around her when she said that, and I didn't want to fight, or let her go.

It happened like this: no more booze. No more videos. No more shit food.

I shifted the force of the power to purifying myself, for real. And, like magic, once I did that, Needa and the kid came around. Maybe one or both of them would make barf sounds whenever I dished up some brown rice shit for dinner. But Needa's belly flab was littler, and she even started going after work a couple days each week to pump iron with her buddies at some smelly old gym. Those nights she came back fresh from the shower, cold air in her face, smelling of powder with a warm skin glow. Have to keep up with the little lady, she said, but in my own way, love, understand? I mean, running, racing, turning into some skinny fag, that is *not* your Needa's style.

End of May, I was going to run the Women's Mini-Marathon in Central Park, a little more than six miles. I laid down the law at home. No fucking up and no messing up between now and then. Cold weather, warm, and warmer, rains and damp hot sunlight and hazy mist of all the city seasons started floating past, through us, like we were nothing but thin vessels that for a moment could catch a whiff of the breeze and the universe, then lose it, let it go. I kept running, every day. The kid did okay in school. Needa and I started making love again some nights, oh so nice, rubbing back and forth. Oh, so nice, to feel her touch around inside me again. And then, late spring.

How it was, the night before: I'm sitting around, we had some of them buckwheat noodles with vegetables for dinner, everybody's quiet, no TV, thinking about how I'm gonna run the race tomorrow with about nine thousand other women and how they, the family, they have got to cheer us and watch, and I look at Needa and the kid and see how slender they are now, and healthy, how beautiful and handsome and slender, and start thinking how much they are mine—just that, they are mine. And I look down at my own bare feet and see that they are skinny, too. Bumpy with callouses and with veins. Bashed a little bloody around the big-toe edges. The littlest toenail on my left foot is dead and black. All from running through the mornings and the nights. From running in my dreams. We got changed, poof. Just like that. Thought we were gonna change ourselves, maybe even the world. But, poof. The world changed us. Through work, love, sacrifice.

Holy, I thought. This is holy.

I chewed cinnamon sticks for dessert the way Madrita recommended, went to sleep with a hint of fire inside. Morning I got up scared, scared. Too scared to notice how Needa was being so sweet, feeding the kid, making sure I drank water because it was looking to be a hot, hot day, pinning my racing number on my T-shirt straight with safety pins, #6489-F-OPEN. Too scared to notice we were leaving—leaving our home, taking the subway, walking, silent, through the heat and the morning.

There we made it, finally, to the West Side, into the park. To hear music play over loudspeakers. Announcements blaring, half-heard. Reminders about some awards ceremony later. On a lawn. The lawn. Some lawn. To hot bright light crystallized through the trees, sunlight, damp blazing air, water stacked in paper cups on tables, and tables, and the laughing, crying voices like in my childhood, so many people. A banner, a big blinking magic electronic clock, zeroed out, waiting. And runners, waiting—women, all shapes and sizes and ages and colors, thousands of them, of us, just thousands.

Baby, says Needa, I'm proud of you.

The kid'd made friends already. Some other woman's twin sons, about his age. I catch sight of him, out of the corner of an eye, his half-smiling, half-serious little handsome face, glowing under the rim of a baseball cap. Yeah, he's telling them, my mom's fast, too. My mom's gonna run the race. Me and my other mom's gonna watch.

Some things are forever inside us. Some things cannot get said.

That's why, when the gun went off, it was like this piece of me fell deep, deep down inside, into the big dark well of myself—this was the piece of me that recorded, in absolute detail, every moment of the race—and lodged there, safe but never recoverable, at least not in words. I can say that the different-colored crowd of thousands moved in a big shuffle at first, all together; then, little by little began to unwind into space, like it was some light-stitched vast fabric coming apart at the seams—so that first, we were all the same, then some of us swayed forward, some back, some to one side or another, and the tarred hot surface of the road melted uphill into trees, green, brown, into a hot misty blasting summer air running blue and gray and yellow under sunlight. I can say that my heart popped right into the base of my throat and stayed there for the first mile or so that I staggered along, sweating after the first few yards, gasping to breathe; then something inside me let up—or gave up, yes—and my heart settled down into my chest where it belonged, I was sweating and suffering but could breathe again, and the elbows and bouncing breasts and shoulders and hair and flesh of women was all around me, smells of bodies and of the city and the trees and sun, and I drank water from somebody's paper cup, kept running, tossed it like a leaf to the cup-littered ground. I can say that in the second mile, once in a while, sweating and running, avoiding veering hips and limbs, I saw some girl run by with a Sony Walkman, wearing sunglasses with mirrored lenses, closed off to the world; once in a while, too, conversation filtered into the sponging soaking deep-down fallen-off piece of me, women's voices in English and in Spanish and in other languages, too, trying to laugh, muttering encouragement; but by the third mile, fact is, there was not anyone chatting.

What there was, was the breathing. Hard and uneven, or measured, controlled. I kept the feet moving, slow, steady, like the pace I did each morning, the pace I did some nights—but never as fast and light and easy as my dreams. Still, it moved me forward. Clumsy. Slow. With a little fat bobbling, yet, around hips and belly and thighs. Around me, all shapes. Like crazy soldiers in some war. The sweat gushed down me. It was hotter than I'd thought. At each mile, you heard them, calling out the time. Time? Time? I never thought of it before. How much it took to do one mile, or one block, or twenty—each morning, some evenings, even in my dreams, I ran by the minutes. Thirty-five, thirty-six minutes. Into the fourth mile. Now it was feeling like forever. Now it was feeling like one more hill would be the last. My fat, bouncing thighs and sweating, gushing body would never be things of beauty, like maybe in foolish moments I'd imagined; and maybe in my stupid dreams I talked about marathons—but here, here was a little stupid miniature marathon, and it hurt so bad I could not ever imagine doing this again, much less running anything longer. But more water, more flesh around me, slipping on paper cups in my flopping old tennis shoes with this number safety-pinned right under my tits, over flabbing belly, every slight upgrade of road sending sunlight searing through me, stabbing thighs and ankles, making me gasp and hurt and, without killing myself, I ran as fast as I could. Clumsy. Fat. Slow. But the heart settled back down, pounding with breaths, with mint and cinnamon and camphor. Sunlight shot through the leaves of trees. Hose spray cooled our skin, drenched our socks. More sunlight shot through, blinded me. Fire, I thought. For your husband, your child, your God. To hell with that, Celia. For your own living self. Okay, man, fuck everything. Fuck the whole sunlit sweat-smelling cinnamon-smelling fucking shark-circling world. Whiff of Chango. Fire in the belly. Fuck even your world of dreams. Because this, sweetheart—this, here, is real.

Then, for a mile, I knew what was real. All this, steeped in the miserable sweat and sacrifice. I knew it without knowledge of the mind, only the sure unlying knowledge of the body that can run and love, give birth, sob, suffer. And knowing what was real, and that this, this, was it, now, only this, and it was enough, and that I lived now, really lived, and knew now what it was to breathe—knowing this, blind with pain, sweating and gasping and almost dead, I stared down and saw that there was a little hole in the tip of my right tennis shoe, near the little toe; it had rubbed the toe raw and, around the little hole, the dirty white fabric was soaking through with blood. Then I felt all the dried-up pieces of me come to life and, suffering, I ran on the breath of the wind. Until, after a while, the wind deserted me. Just before six miles. Left me, one faulty woman, in a mob of suffering moving flesh, to finish the last few hundred yards alone. It was all uphill, there were people watching and I was ashamed, people screaming around me, I was running so slow, nearly dead of exhaustion and of shame, stomach in spasms, drenched with sweat, crying. Until I heard someone yell out *Mom* with a voice, among all the other little voices, meant only for me. And I heard Needa, laughing, crying, yelling, and heard that her voice was hoarse, a croak, almost gone: Attagirl, baby! My baby! My lady! You can do it youcandoityoucandoityoucandoit! Break an hour breakanhourbreakanhourbreakanhour!

Fifty-nine minutes and fifty-nine seconds. But I was not lost, and I was not last.

Girlfriend, I said, get some pride.

I did.

Then I staggered under the big heartless blinking clock, the yellow sun, dripping water, my shoe spraying blood.

I got a medal. They gave everyone medals. Slipped around your neck, in the finishing chutes crowded with beaten, grinning women, a silvery goldlike medal on a red and blue ribbon, like a necklace, just for finishing. Then they gave you a carton of Gatorade. A free Mars bar. And a plastic egg-shaped container full of mesh tan pantyhose.

Needa hugged me. So did the kid.

They were all over me, screaming, proud and happy.

Runners were still finishing, running, staggering, walking. I moved through the crowds. I lay on the grass. Closed my eyes, with Needa sitting on one side and the kid on the other, each holding a hand, and I fell down into the deepest, blasted-off piece of me that had come apart and wedged down inside with the explosion of the starting gun, that would never, ever be the same. It was so dark, falling deep down there, full of iron and of water, musty brown and wet wet green and the still malignant air; but also, it was red like blood, and bright, and filled with a bubbling, smouldering, surprising color. It was filled with this work and this imperfect love, and with chicken gizzards, sacrifice, camphor oil, rainbow light.

Something blared over a loudspeaker.

"—And now, a special treat for all you ladies! To present the awards, we have with us here—"

I fell into a place of half-dream, half-sleep.

Needa poked my ribs.

There he is, Celia. There.

Who!

Your Salazar.

I turned my head in the grass. Salt was full in my sweat, salt on my lips, I licked it with the air and it tasted real, good, sweet. Opened my eyes to see the young, slender, serious man standing above me, body and clothes of a runner, his eyes in shadow, fierce face gazing down.

He nodded. Saying softly, politely, Good for you, Celia.

Alberto, I said, can I stop now?

No, Celia. He said it gently. Then he smiled. Not until you die. And even then—who knows?

I opened my eyes.

There was an awards podium, in the sun on the grass. Women, slender and beautiful, gifted young magnificent runners, walking up, intermittently, when their names were called over fuzzy loudspeakers, accepting the bright gold and silver statues they gave for awards. And there, with famous men and women athletes and politicians behind the podium on the stage in the sun and the park, there he was, handing out each statue, shaking each woman's hand. Salazar. There was no collar around his neck, no red and white of gods or saints of fire, as in my dream. Not running, he seemed different. Quiet. Humbly human. Pale and young, and far away.

I started to cry.

Needa held me in her arms.

The kid crawled into my lap, laid his soft little cheek against my drenched, floppy chest.

"What is it, sweet?"

"It don't stop, Needa."

"No, my love."

"I gotta do some more of these."

"Okay, baby."

"And then, in a few years I think, I gotta do the Marathon."

Yes! Alberto muttered, through a microphone, and shook some woman's hand. I squeezed the hand of Needa, and of our child. The fire poured down. It kissed me. It moved in to stay.

I wrote this story for Julie DeLaurier.

All events herein are fictional, except for the New York City Marathon and the Women's Mini-Marathon (once sponsored by L'Eggs, now sponsored by Advil, under the auspices of the New York City Road Runners Club). I have used these events here solely in a fictional context.

All characters herein are fictional, too, with the exception of the great American marathon runner Alberto Salazar. I use him here in an imaginary way, as a dream figment or a sort of divinity—and with all due respect. I have never met Mr. Salazar, and do not know if he is a child of Chango . . .

Women Who Run

Laurel Starkey

yes, they do run.
traces of early morning sweat
trickle down slick backs,
heels tense, ready to let feet fly.

the mountains, mauve and unmoving
poke up in the distance,
rub their shoulders,
brace their stubbly chins against a matte sky;
women run
in the shadows of these mountains.

summer licks their toes
and drapes itself over tanned arms,
as women who run heave breaths
in accord with the banners of triumph.
from many cultures, race and tongues
these free spirits
have found a common foothold
in womankind

because they run;
yes they do, they run.

freely and forever.

Reprinted, by permission, from Laurel Starkey. Originally published under the pseudonym Devon Skye in *Atalanta*, Los Angeles: Papier Mache Press, 1984.

Running

Ellen E. Moore

I enter my room
later than planned
and pull on my favorite sweats,
the grey fleece ones that blend
with night air and pavement.
Stretch my fingers
to the ceiling light,
then lie on my back; extend
my head to my knees;
it's easy tonight.

I don't remember out the door
or even the first block.
Now I'm running past the park,
notice the lights illuminating
the vacant car lot.
I am not afraid tonight.
I keep running,
sometimes counting,
maybe humming,
down the hill, past
the lights, feel
more energy, another block,
reach the corner,
turn around, touch my toes,
touch the stars--I'm running
home now. It's the same way back.
The hill rises now,

but I am all
powerful tonight.
I reach the crest
breathing hard, two blocks left,
my legs kick in--
I'm flying.

Swimming

Svava Jakobsdóttir
Translated by Dennis Auburn Hill

An unusual busyness reigned over the house, filled with a silent tension. She sat alone at the kitchen table and was an outsider amidst all the activity. Forgotten. Her mother paid no attention to her, but stayed for long periods with grandma. Sometimes she heard her mother going into the bathroom and although she did make quick, brief visits to the kitchen, they were just to fetch a spoon or a glass, or medicine from the refrigerator, not to speak to her. Grandma was very sick. The girl knew that papa was expected home from work soon. And the doctor was to come.

She was undecided whether she should go to her swimming class or appear to have forgotten about it. She never went to swimming class unless her mother forced her on her way. You have swimming today, her mother was used to saying, and early on she had accustomed herself not to hear this. Most effective was losing herself in a book, letting the plot take control of her, neither seeing nor hearing anything outside it, until her mother snatched the book out of her hands, pushed her swimsuit at her and ordered her to get going. Objections were pointless. Nevertheless, she went through the same rigamarole every time: her back hurt or her throat was sore and then all that chlorine in the water was so unhealthy. She recited this as she crawled into her coat and boots and didn't stop until her mother said she ought to be grateful to get to learn to swim. Her mother had never learned to swim and there was no logic to dispute the fact.

Dusk had fallen over the kitchen corner, but she didn't turn on the light. There wasn't a sound coming from grandma's room. Maybe grandma was dying. As long as she could remember, she had known that the time would come that someone would die. This knowledge dwelled within her, living its own life there, which she had no control over, since it always stirred at the worst possible moment—in the dark as she was about to fall asleep. And now when it had come to that, that someone was about to die, she sat paralyzed as if the slightest movement might call forth some misfortune that couldn't be undone. She stared at the salt and pepper shakers that stood on the table as if she were trying to memorize their shape and configuration forever. Would that be a good enough excuse for skipping swimming, if your grandma was dying?

But no one had said she was dying. And she hadn't dared to ask. She tried to put out of her mind what she had seen a little earlier when she sneaked into grandma's room. Grandma had sat halfway up in bed with many big pillows behind her back. Her face was so strangely white, and then suddenly she lifted her head from the pillows, her eyes wandering restlessly about the room and an endless stream of words coming out of her mouth: she has to help with the haying, it had to be raked up, but just look, I have all this wash to rinse, oh, it's so cold, the water . . . But she didn't hear any more because her mother pushed grandma back down, stroked her forehead with a damp washcloth, shushed her like a child and said she needn't have these worries, she wasn't hired help in the country out east any more. Grandma calmed down for a while, but then started suddenly and lifted up her decrepit hands with so much force that her bent fingers seemed to straighten themselves as she called out: in a minute . . .

She slipped out of the room and felt she had seen a totally different woman than the grandma who had sat for so long with a blanket on her lap so that her arthritis wouldn't get worse, often with a book from which she looked up now and then and said to the household as they were running about, that oh, she was now nothing but a lazy . . .

The girl shoved the salt and pepper shakers hastily out to the edge of the table, stood up all of a sudden, fetched her swimsuit and left the house. She stopped outside on the sidewalk and looked around as if she didn't understand how she had gotten there, then headed in the direction of the swimming pool. She dragged her feet as if she were still undecided whether to go or turn back. The more she moved forward the more she felt her anxiety about swimming overcome her: she sensed the tension in her body, as if she had already entered the water in which she couldn't see the bottom, struggling and splashing with neck outstretched, head raised above the water, and mouth constricted, and when she opened her eyes wide, the goal was far in the distance where the swimming instructor stood with his stopwatch, she couldn't see the other side of the pool, there was nothing to hold on to, nothing . . .

She stopped. She had reached the corner and now Baron Street lay before her. The swimming hall was in sight. Maybe it wasn't proper to go swimming if your grandma was dying. She could still turn back. But maybe she wasn't dying. She hadn't asked. And now she was gripped by the same feeling as before at the kitchen table, when she didn't dare move for fear that some misfortune would take place. She firmly resolved not to look back.

With nearly superhuman effort she emptied her mind. Think about nothing. Her feet bore her all the way to the swimming hall and her body carried out all the routine movements automatically. Complete silence reigned in her head. Even the chatter and clamor of her classmates as they were undressing in the changing room didn't get through her. The sound of the shower was that of a distant waterfall. Slowly she walked up the stairs, counting the splinters as she went. Then the pool came into view. For a moment she stood on the edge of the pool and looked expressionlessly out over the water. Then she went in.

It took a while before she became aware that she was floating. She was floating! She knew how to swim! All that fuss was unnecessary. The secret was knowing how to breathe, to breathe deeply enough and to hold your breath long enough. She became filled with an indescribable joy. She took in a deep breath, then put her face into the water as she kicked her feet vigorously and cleared her way forward with her arms and then she lay dead still and let herself float like a log until the air in her lungs was exhausted. She then repeated the same performance. Each time she tried to breathe more deeply and to let herself float longer and longer, slowly and still. And not to make a stroke unless her life depended on it. All the time she was floating she was aware of the depths beneath her, where she directed her inner vision as the water bathed her body and she perceived that if she could just manage to continue like this, just float united with the water, she could then drown without a struggle. If that was what lay ahead of her. When her legs had become tired and her arms stiff, she would slowly and calmly glide down into the depths in harmony with the water. Without having to struggle. Without having to struggle with the water and death.

Then she was struck in the back unexpectedly. She looked up in terror and lost control of her swimming. She caught a faint glimpse of the hairy legs of the swimming instructor on the edge of the pool. The stick that he had hit her with pointed at her with one hand and held the stopwatch in the other. She couldn't hear his shouts; terrified she struggled about in the water, kicking at the depths and when she saw her clenched fingers rise helplessly up out of the water she could hear the echo of her grandma's voice: In a minute . . .

Mary Bacon Loses Her Final Race

Joan Ryan

Nine years before jockey Mary Bacon put a bullet in her head at a Motel 6 in Fort Worth, Texas, she had already begun to die. It was the fifth race on June 9, 1982, at Golden Gate Fields. Bacon's horse clipped the heels of another horse on the backstretch. She crashed to the ground and a trailing horse stumbled over her. When the ambulance attendant reached her, she was motionless, bleeding from her skull, nose and mouth. He thought she was dead.

Bacon was in a coma for 11 days, in intensive care for 23.

When doctors told her the blows to her head were so severe she would never regain the balance she would need to ride again, she found new doctors. She had come back from worse spills than this, she said. Once she was clinically dead for three minutes after a fall in 1973. Another time a horse pinned her against a barn wall, crushing her pelvis and rib cage and rupturing her spleen. She once spent four days paralyzed from the waist down. By the early 1970s, when Bacon was still in her mid-20s, she figured she already had broken 39 bones in all.

Nothing had ever kept Mary Bacon from riding. She was abducted at knifepoint in 1969 by a crazed stablehand at Pennsylvania's Pocono Downs, escaped and raced three horses that night. She rode when she was seven months pregnant. She rode a week after giving birth. When it became clear that tracks would enforce a rule (now rescinded) prohibiting spouses to ride against each other, she divorced her first husband.

"I want to ride," Bacon once said. "That's all that matters. Riding is living."

Bacon was one of the first notable female jockeys. She came to prominence in the late 1960s at the New York tracks, drawing attention as much for her private life as for her riding. She was beautiful, cocky and tough as a new saddle. She modeled for Revlon cosmetics and posed nude for Playboy. When her fellow female jockeys criticized her cheesecake image, Bacon retorted, "They're just jealous. Most of them couldn't tie a knot in my reins."

Publicity was Bacon's constant companion. In 1975, she was taped by two television stations in Walker, Louisiana, speaking at a Ku Klux Klan rally. Later, she said she went to the rally out of curiosity after seeing the movie *The Klansman*. But it cost her the Revlon contract and a TV campaign for Dutch Masters cigars. Not long afterward, she stirred up another

Originally printed in the *San Francisco Examiner* on June 23, 1991. Reprinted by permission of the *San Francisco Examiner*.

controversy when, without presenting any evidence, she accused tracks in Louisiana of drugging and mistreating thoroughbreds.

"We used to say she had one tap too many on the head," said Phyllis Wuerth, who was a nurse at Golden Gate Fields when Bacon rode there. "But she was as tough as they come. No one put anything over on Mary. No one, no one, no one."

Ten months after the Golden Gate Fields spill, Bacon still had not received medical clearance to ride. "To say she is depressed is an understatement," her second husband, jockey Jeff Anderson, told reporters as he prepared to ride Billy Ball in the 1983 Cal Derby. "She's not complete unless she's on a horse."

For five years, Bacon traveled from state to state and track to track searching for a doctor who would give her an okay. Anderson describes those years as "living with a wildcat." Finally, in 1987, a doctor at the fairgrounds near New Orleans gave her the all-clear. Bacon rode a few races there, but trainers were reluctant to give her mounts. Why hire a 40-year-old woman when they could get a 20-year-old man?

So Bacon kept moving, looking for rides. She found her way to Texas, to what racing people call "the bushes." Jockeys work horses in the morning for the opportunity to race them in the afternoon. The purses were almost nothing. Bacon didn't care.

"Mary ended up winning a race in September of 1989," Anderson said by phone the other day from Kansas City. "It was the biggest race of her life. She had the biggest smile I ever saw. It didn't matter to her that this wasn't Belmont. She was so happy just to be riding again. She'd ride anything with hair."

A month later, Bacon was diagnosed with cervical cancer. It wasn't terminal, but the radiation treatments left her too weak to race. Traveling with Anderson, who was by then a jockeys' agent, she got jobs exercising horses. Anderson could see she was struggling to control the horses. He kept telling her to give it up, but she refused. Predictably, a horse threw her last year, breaking her arm in three places.

"Finally, she came to the conclusion she couldn't ride any more," Anderson said. "The truth is, she never fully recovered from the accident at Golden Gate Fields. She was never the same after that."

Anderson and Bacon spent the past winter in Hot Springs, Arkansas, then moved on to The Woodlands Track in Kansas City. While Anderson went to the track, Bacon spent her time grocery shopping, cooking, jogging. She was miserable.

"She won most of her battles early in her life, but in this battle there were very few winners," Anderson said. "How much can a person take?"

On Wednesday, June 5, Bacon told her husband she was going to Trinity Meadows near Fort Worth. She had heard there might be opportunities there. She packed the car and drove off. She checked in to the Motel 6 off Interstate 35 on Thursday. At about 11:30 Friday morning, a maintenance worker saw Bacon walk to her car, retrieve a small-caliber revolver and walk back to her room. She had bought the gun when she arrived in Texas, and, Anderson later guessed, must have had someone else load it for her. "She didn't know anything about guns," he said. Thirty minutes later, a maid found her on the floor with a bullet in her head. She was still alive.

When Anderson got the call from the hospital, his first reaction was, "I wanted to beat the crap out of her." He flew down and was at her side when she died at 1:45 the next morning. She was 43.

"I went through her things at the hotel room and I never came across her saddle or her helmet or any of her jockey clothes," Anderson said. "She went down there to die.

"Mary had so many battles in her life and she just got tired of fighting them. She went to the place she loved more than any place to end her life."

There will be a memorial for Bacon in the winner's circle at Belmont Park in New York Monday. Her ashes will be scattered near the grave of Ruffian, one of her favorite horses.

A few years back, Anderson was in the hospital recovering from a fall, and Bacon was visiting him. A reporter surveyed the toll racing had taken on them, the broken bones, broken backs, pinched nerves, blood clots, concussions, ruptured organs. What, they were asked, would it take to make them quit riding?

"Death," Anderson said.

"That's right," Bacon said. "I'd have to be dead."

Margarethe "Gretel" Bergmann
from *How She Played the Game*
A One Woman Play

Cynthia L. Cooper

(Margarethe "Gretel" Bergmann is rather ordinary-looking, with dark hair and eyes, strong legs ,and a solemn, but not strident, appearance. She sits on a bench speaking with a distinct German accent.)

Sometimes, I think, the hardest thing to be an athlete is not to be an athlete. We do not so much choose to be an athlete. It is just what we are. And the times when we are what we are—an athlete—everything comes together— the body and the soul, the heart and the mind—as we race across the dirt of a track, blood rushing, feet flying. And the times when we are not an athlete, when we *cannot* be an athlete . . . it . . . what shall I say? . . . it bristles against the bones.

There is no other way to explain it. It is like the other things we are. We are born a woman or a man. We are born with blue eyes or brown. We are born a Gentile or a Jew.

I know this because I am an athlete. Oh. I am not someone you have heard of. My name is Gretel—Margarethe—Bergmann. See, it is no one you know. I am not in a record book or almanac you keep on a shelf somewhere. And I am a Jew. So. You are saying how does it matter that I am born a Jew? To that, I have no answer because it is something I myself do not understand.

But what a thing it is to be born to sports! When I was a little girl in Lauphein, Germany, in the 1920s, my life was all soccer and field handball . . . I played on the boys' teams. In 1930 I won six track and field ribbons! Do you know, I used to even do my chores on ice skates in the winter? I loved sports so much. I decided I would become a physical education teacher. To do that, one had to go to the University—in Berlin. It was a big city, Berlin, compared to Lauphein, but I applied anyhow.

(GRETEL speaks to an unseen school administrator.)

"Guten dag. I am Fraulein Bergmann. I have looked over the list of registrants for the university, but I do not find my name."

"Yah. I have my acceptance letter right here. It is from the dean. I am to be in the department of physical education."

"I do not understand when you tell me something has changed. My record is good."

"So. Yes. I am of the Jewish faith. That is true."

"Chancellor Hitler has said not to admit Jews?"

"How long must I wait for the 'climate' to change? I wish to continue sports. Now. In my best years."

"Yah. Yah. I understand there is nothing you can do."

I could not give up athletics so easily. I went to England. And it was a very good thing. I won the championship high jump for my college! 1934. And my father was there on business to see it happen.

(The next sequence is a dialogue between Gretel and her father.)

"Papa! Hug me! I am the champion in all of Britain!"

"Gretel," he said to me. "We must speak. I am not here on business."

"What do you mean?" I asked.

"The Americans, you must know, have said they will not come to the Olympics in Germany because Chancellor Hitler is discriminating against Jews. The Chancellor has made the Olympics of 1936 very important, and so he is seeking all of the German Jewish athletes for the Olympic tryouts."

"But I have left, papa. They would not even allow me to play on my own soccer club. It is not a time to be Jewish in Germany. The bars and restaurants do not even serve a Jew. How can I return to be an athlete for the Chancellor?"

"Gretel. I am not here for the Chancellor. You are perhaps the best Jewish athlete in the country . . . male or female. You can win the high jump, as you did today. The Nazis all paint the Jews to be overweight and bowlegged. If we can show that a Jew can be an athlete, too, it will break down the barriers of discrimination. I am begging you to return, Gretel, not for yourself, or for Hitler, or even for myself. I am begging you for all the Jewish people in Germany."

We did not know, our people did not know. I returned to Germany. Twenty-one Jews were invited to the Olympic camps. And so I went. I tried to train, but I was not allowed to compete at the camps—only members of the track and field association were permitted, and they, of course, did not allow Jews. Of the twenty-one, two of us were left on the Olympic team in 1935. I was one. Helene Mayer, the fencer, who had a Jew as a father was the other. It is so funny that by the religion, a Jew is one with a Jewish mother. To the Nazis, anyone with Jewish blood was a Jew.

And then the newspaper stories came:

"Change in Nazi philosophy to admit Jews, prompts U.S. vote to join Olympics. High jumper on women's team . . ." We had heard rumors about the arguments in the United States. One of the college coaches was quoted. "It is one thing to say you are opposed to political things in Germany," he said, "but don't shoot your own boys in the back and say they cannot have their birthright of competition in the International Games."

But I really had little time for the news. Getting the highest mark on the high jump was most important. In June of 1936, only two months before the Olympics, I equalled the German high jump records! Five feet—three inches. The whir all around the camp was that I would win a gold or a silver. There was an air of excitement everywhere in Germany about the Olympics that summer.

In July—July 13, it was—two weeks before the Olympic Games—I received the letter from the German sports authorities. "Fraulein Bergmann. This letter is to advise you that your achievements at the Olympic training camp have been inadequate, and we have found it necessary to remove you from the German Olympic team. Please depart from camp immediately."

I came to the United States. I had ten dollars, for that is what I was allowed to take with me. An athlete with no place to compete . . . no 'birthright of competition.'

So. I have said it is hard to be an athlete and not to be an athlete. But sometimes one must live by another thought, too. Helene Mayer won in fencing a silver medal for Germany. I have heard that during the medal ceremony, she wore a swastika on her sweater and raised her arm in a Nazi salute. She even said the words, 'Heil Hitler.' So, I said to myself, "Margarethe. Perhaps it is sometimes better on the conscience not to be an athlete, after all."

Contest

Florence Victor

Back from the kill
They sat drinking tea,
Studying Audubon.
I, the eccentric neighbor,
Said no, I'd rather not see
The pheasant,
Or admire the woodcocks.
I gave no lecture
Praised the brew
And was generally pleasant.
Still, when someone suggested
That fresh air might be good for me
I made it clear
This was no gossamer poet here
But a former first-baseman
Hiker-in-the-woods
And recent rock-thrower.
Bragging proceeded to exercises
And of three girls, I clearly was best.
Having antagonized everyone
(Except the silent male cleaning his gun)
I went home
Not murderer,
Just winner.

The Uni-Gym

Anne Rouse

> At a shout to a disco drum, the women dance
> In sorbet cotton knits. Sweat darkening
> On spines, they bend and reach.
>
> In the stone chill of the gym downstairs,
> Weightlifters howl, as if for sex,
> Or pace, furtive in the room-sized mirror,
>
> To meet gingerly in bed. His density
> Helps him feel safer from the likes of her—
> Whose heart is stronger now, and unforgiving.

Early Morning Swim

Vicky Darling

> Sometimes, gliding smoothly along the slow lane
> we touch, and recoil in shock
> as this is a solitary and private affair
> though we know each others' bodies so well.
>
> Watching each other with covert glances
> in familiar rituals of dressing, undressing,
> each mole and scar, sagging breasts, scrawny arms
> are recognised like old friends
> by the sisterhood who meet silently
> each morning.

There are men, certainly, young blades
with hairy chests, tattoos, mouths grimacing
splashing violently down the fast lane.

We women are different,
stately as swans we glide
up and down, up and down,
arms circling, pushing away encumbrances.

Part VI

Beyond Gender, Space, and Time: Dervish Rhythms in the Games of the Gods

... we have found
This place where the gods play out the game of the sky
And bandy life and death across a summer ground.

A Game of Ball
Muriel Rukeyser

In this last part, authors are in search of the very essence of sport and the human attraction to it. They explore the abstract and inviting perceptions that dancers, soccer players, ice skaters, and ancient Aztec ball players alike seem to have. It is as if these authors have discarded questions about exclusion, the body, nature, and personal experiences with others or even encounters with sport in search of more abstract, subjective, and universal meanings of sport. And in their search they have written some of the most insightful and engaging works in this collection. With great artistry these authors relinquish their hold on language to the abstraction of metaphor. In attempting to tell us what sport is, their voices have confidently disappeared while the essence of sport seems to reveal itself independently of the authors. In so doing, these authors alter our perceptions, as all great artists do, and open up the sporting world, revealing its marvelous and compelling complexity. Through language, sport becomes evocative, bringing forth from within us the human in sport.

Sport is the place "where the gods play out the game of the sky" and where the human mind "searches for perfect order." It is a world where Martha Graham dances "not with lyrical hands / but with / the nervous system," a world where movement is stillness—a stillness that holds the moment in "a lozenge of impeccable clarity." In this world runners ache for savage breath with hot, "empty" teeth; people are pawns "in the game of another"; and there is only "One short step from eternal art into artificial eternity." It is at once a human world and a world of the spirit. It is a world bound by space and time, yet free from space and time—a world of perfect order. It is the female experience of sport, but it is also an experience beyond the confines of gender.

In this sporting world are the struggles of the human soul, the pain of loss, the longing for a God who will take "the rat inside of me, / the gnawing pestilential rat" and "embrace it." Here, the dancers are mortal but inspired by "cosmic energy." Their dancing is sacred, ethereal, but they feel it "in the bone" as "the deepest, the only joy." Here, swimmers are "at the center of life," blank . . . griefless," and "without error." And runners are as constant as the speed of light. Here, competition and victory lose their traditional meanings on athletic fields that spin according to the rhythms of the universe. Here, black queen and white king, "Dark player and bright," can "bandy life and death across a summer ground" and turn "ceremonial violence / to the mercy of a workable peace."

Golden Section, Giants Stadium

Diane Ackerman

I

The mind wakes to a whistle
blown in the flesh, whose pea the mind is,
wakes and flows down being's slipway,
then *knows* the sheers of river light,
bridge-rivets and factories,
and raw, panting jungles so humid
the snakes hang straight down, ghettos,
and parkways where dogs salute trees
and picnickers laze on gingham squares
under the lightly buzzing stars.

O the mind, the spidery mind
on whose web the flies of meaning walk.
Nature neither gives nor expects mercy,
but the mind quests to be fit, to be seemly,
and fears second (dying is first)
to become just as plural as all it surveys.
So the autos of habit pull up
to each club at the prescribed hour.
So tidy moments of rapture unfold in the dark.
So the moon rises like a fat white god.

II

Who can know the dervish rhythms
of the mind that whirls for truth

in odd ports-of-call: a New Jersey stadium
whose dry surplus is autumn, late at night,
when the Morse code of the galaxy
pales behind the fainter lights,
and, gifted with the breezy rhetoric
of his legs, a tall, willowy Beckenbauer
swivels, bluffs, and floats long passes,
running upfield among spoon-hipped Latins
playing soccer as if their sun could never cool.

Those tense men in mild weather
who hive and swarm, flying dense circles
around the ball's white flower
to ply the queen of wins with the honey
of their fatigue—for them, defeat lies
in the open scream of a goal-mouth,
and cheers rush like surf breaking
on the bony shoulders of their private sea.

Speak to me, Beckenbauer, about the rhythm
of the mind that searches for perfect order
in imperfect places: art galleries and polling booths,
books, sin-bins, and churches:
and can turn even ceremonial violence
to the mercy of a workable peace.

Frozen Motion

Wislawa Szymborska
Translated by Baranczak and Clare Cavanaugh

This isn't Miss Duncan, the noted danseuse?
Not the drifting cloud, the wafting zephyr, the Bacchante,
moonlit waters, waves swaying, breezes sighing?

Standing this way, in the photographer's atelier,
heftily, fleshily wrested from music and motion,
she's cast to the mercies of a pose,
forced to bear false witness.

Thick arms raised above her head,
a knotted knee protrudes from her short tunic,
left leg forward, naked foot and toes,
with 5 (count them) toenails.

One short step from eternal art into artificial eternity—
I reluctantly admit that it's better than nothing
and more fitting than otherwise.

Behind the screen, a pink corset, a handbag,
in it a ticket for a steamship
leaving tomorrow, that is, sixty years ago;
never again, but still at nine a.m. sharp.

Dancers Exercising

Amy Clampitt

Frame within frame, the evolving conversation
is dancelike, as though two could play
at improvising snowflakes'
six-feather-vaned evanescence,
no two ever alike. All process
and no arrival: the happier we are,
the less there is for memory to take hold of,
or—memory being so largely a predilection
for the exceptional—come to a halt
in front of. But finding, one evening
on a street not quite familiar,
inside a gated
November-sodden garden, a building
of uncertain provenance,
peering into whose vestibule we were
arrested—a frame within a frame,
a lozenge of impeccable clarity—
by the reflection, no, not
of our two selves, but of
dancers exercising in a mirror,
at the center
of that clarity, what we saw
was not stillness
but movement: the perfection
of memory consisting, it would seem,
in the never-to-be-completed.
We saw them mirroring themselves,
never guessing the vestibule

that defined them, frame within frame,
contained two other mirrors.

Martha Graham

Elaine Equi

1.
In 1923
for the Greenwich
Village Follies

you performed
three dances
one Oriental
one Moorish

and one
with a large veil.

You said:
"Grace is your
relationship
to the world"

a deep-rooted
inclination
to converse

and just as poetry
is not about words
nor math about numbers

so too the dance
is not about its steps.

2.
With your spooky
Franz Kline makeup
and adolescence
of Indian maidens

the daughter
of Dr. George Graham
a specialist
in nervous disease

you dance
not with lyrical hands
but with
the nervous system

capricious and sterile
as a guillotine
for swans

dark fins
circling the white
of the eyeball.

Breaking the Speed Record

Cristina Peri Rossi
Translated by Psiche Bertini Hughes

He had begun the fourteenth lap. He was a good runner: the papers announced him as the favorite and even forecast a new record. They had been waiting for a new record for several years, one always waits for this kind of thing. And now this theory of a Brazilian physicist, a madman he thought: that the speed of light does not always remain the same. What could this mean? he asked himself. The papers had said that he was in condition to beat the record. So, had Einstein made a mistake? Or was light also trying to beat a record? In his fifteenth lap the crowds gathered around the track; already he had a good lead, a considerable lead, for he was born to run . . . in the warm sunshine, and how warm it was! What did it mean to be born to run? Those lap two-thirds through the race, and still keeping up a wonderful pace . . . long distance runner . . . controlled rhythm, when he set off he didn't hesitate a moment in separating himself from the rest and establish from the start who would be the winner. If they thought that he was going to hold himself back, that he would not sprint away from the team in order to save his strength and leave the final pitiless conflict to the last meters, they were mistaken. He was now running, away from the elbows of the other runners, with nobody coming in his way and with all the track empty in front of him, as fast as light, if light is still moving through space at a constant speed. Somewhere else—beyond the oval racing track around which he was running over and over again, as in a tormented dream—his trainer would be anxiously looking at his stopwatch. To think that the speed of this ray of sun shining across the track was not constant! As constant as his pace. Seventeenth lap, only seven more to victory . . . this ray of sunshine racing like a breathless runner. The rest had remained behind, he had passed them several laps before; now it was the case of beating someone else, the legendary runner who had established the last record, the final record up till now, if only the speed of light would remain constant. At the twenty-first lap he began to suspect that he would accomplish what had been forecast; in spite of being tired, his rhythm was excellent, he was running along the track with a steady step, his movements were elastic and light, "as light as a gazelle," as the announcer put it, "elegant, as if running did not cause him any problem." He had a confused glimpse of the faces of the spectators; there was no need to see them more clearly, only the track turning in his

"Breaking the Speed Record" by Cristina Peri Rossi is reprinted with permission from the publisher of *Short Stories by Latin American Women* edited by Celia Correas de Zapata (Houston: Arte Publico Press-University of Houston, 1994).

| 295 |

mind... and his trainer would keep his eyes unremittingly fixed on the stopwatch; now he was passing the young runner with red hair and blue shorts whose breathless panting did not bode well, next runner number seventeen, completely outpaced by the rest, several laps behind him in one of the laps which he had run earlier on, with the brightness of the sun on the track. Everyone's eyes were clouding over, blinking through the drops of sweat; there remained only three more laps according to his calculations, three more laps before the little man with the flag designed like a chess board would let it drop at the moment he crossed the finish line, the end of the track, the ribbon which meant that the mad race was over . . . and then he heard a shout, a single shout, it was his trainer calling out assuredly that he was about to accomplish what had been forecast, that he was about [to] establish a new record, the best in the world in the ten thousand meters on the level as flat as a pan.

It was then that he felt an enormous desire to stop. Not that he was tired; he had trained for a long time and all the experts felt that he would succeed; in fact, he was only running in order to establish a new record. But, now, this irresistible desire to stop. To lie on the side of the track and never get up again. Attention: it is forbidden to touch a runner once he has fallen. If he gets up under his own power, he can continue the race. But no one is allowed to help him stand up again. This uncontrollable desire to sit at the side of the track and look up at the sky. Surely there would be trees, he thought. Interwoven branches, quivering leaves and at the top, perhaps a nest. The smallest leaves shaking in the breeze, this same breeze which alters the speed of light, no longer constant, according to the Brazilian physicist. "I am nothing exceptional," he had said a few nights before to an elderly admirer, "I am just somebody who knows how to organize time."

His trainer waved to him excitedly: only one more lap. Only one. And his speed had not diminished. He passed a runner who was panting with his hand on his ribs. That dry pain under the ribs, the tightness that makes it so difficult to breathe. Once it begins, the race is over and you might as well get off the track—although one does not do so out of a sense of pride. That discomfort in the spleen, as he had learned during his years of training. An organ of which we are rarely conscious because it only troubles us when we have made an unusual effort, when we have run too much. And now this unknown and uncontrollable longing to stop, to rest by the side of the track, look at the trees, breathe deeply. The laps are all the same, they merge in one's memory and one no longer knows whether it is the twenty-third or the twenty-fourth, the sixteenth or the seventeenth, as it happened to that boy who thought he had finished and threw himself on the ground. Some-body—most likely his trainer or one of the judges—went near him and without touching him, informed him that he was mistaken (he had figured it wrong) and there were still three laps to run. And the poor chap with his muscles in a knot. Unable to get up. And if he did get up, it would be only to start running again, unless he fainted beforehand. But nothing like this would ever happen to him. He ran with ease, as if it were the most natural thing to do, as if he could run forever. With a rhythm which was constant, with an unvarying stride, unlike light which had deceived him and which now, it seemed, was moving at uneven speed. He was about to beat the record. But what now of the indescribable pleasure of stopping, sliding gently towards the side, the side of the track, a few meters away from the end, just a little before the finish line, slipping slowly to the ground and lifting his head up . . . the tall trees, the blue sky, the slow-moving clouds, the curly, bunched-up branches . . . the leaves quiver, he looks upwards and watches the rhythmic flight of the birds . . . he does not hear the hubbub of the people crowding around him; undoubtedly they are reproaching him, insulting him, his trainer is furious . . . to see the rest of the runners go past him, see their shorts, some are panting heavily, one is raising his hand to his chest, you will not finish, you will not reach the end; but high up the trees float in the air, in an unreal atmosphere, unseen by anyone else; now comes the blond fellow suffering from a cramp and beginning to limp . . . have I seen that bird before? . . . and the announcer describing the unexplainable event. His speed had been constant but suddenly, as that of light, it longed to stop. And he raised his eyes to the sky.

Amateur Athletic Meeting

Elizabeth Smither

A green ouija board that will not turn
Though the runners are running, the Western roll
Is shouldering itself into sleep in the sky
And the javelins are aimed, the discus flies
To pierce and fall and flatten the ground.

It is too slow, too lacking in polish
Though the breathing of the sprinters comes like jockeys
And many who do not race are running importantly
Outside the lines in their training suits.

Still it is charming. The falling dusk
Over the antics, the starter's calls
The pistol barking, the small result
The possibility that the field might spin.

The Runner

Erin Mouré

Not to stutter the amnesia of the chest
while the body is still running!
Not to stutter now or the amnesia will close,
close up its forgotten chest
& the alphabet will stop its tumbling
The amnesia in which everything awakes like a soft
tread of the running figure.
Who knows this woman?
Who knows her breast is full of remembered water!
Who knows what her chest will say to us if only
it keeps up its terrible running . . .

Don't stop, now, chest . . .
Chest that touches no one . . .

Listen . . .

Reprinted, by permission, from Erin Mouré, 1985, *Domestic Fuel*, (Ontario: House of Anansi Press).

Dance Memories

Denise Levertov

> *Plié,* the knees bend,
> a frog flexing to spring;
> *grand battement,* the taut leg
> flails as if to beat
> chaff from the wheat;
> *attitude,* Hermes brings
> ambiguous messages
> and moves dream-smoothly
> yet with hidden strain
> that breaks in sweat,
> into *arabesque* that traces
> swan-lines on vision's stone
> that the dancer not seeing
> herself, feels in the bone.
> *Coupé,* the air is cut
> out from under the foot,
> *grand jeté, glissade, grand jeté, glissade,*
> the joy of leaping, of moving by
> leaps and bounds, of gliding
> to leap, and gliding
> to leap becomes, while it lasts,
> heart pounding, breath hurting,
> the deepest, the only joy.

Song for Girls or Balance Beams

Zehra Çirak
Translated by Gerald Nixon

Prologue

At the end the beam gets narrower
Having once climbed up
There is nothing more splendid for the body
Than to stay on top for a while
Although moving forwards and backwards
It would prefer to move upwards—
Anything but falling for the ground.

Compulsory singing

Fallen girls need no wings
No backward arches without support
Their hands reach out in directions past
Their feet touch the hardness of new times
Their heads do not wish to fall
Alone without the body
And it doesn't fall far
Into the most devoted heaven
Fallen girls tremble their way to the ground

Free singing

The girls' bosoms sing soprano
Their eyes sing alto
From their golden cat's throats

From "Fremde Flügel auf eigener Schulter" by Zehra Çirak © 1994 by Verlag Kiepenheuer & Witsch Köln.

Flows the eternal woe of the genders

Epilogue

The balancing beam ends in many ways
Once you have climbed up

Greek Dances I

Simonne Jacquemard
Translated by Patricia Nolan

> In a line, their arms held high, joined
> like rushes, like winged battlements
> and oars stretched high on the horizon,
> the Greek dancers as one body, in a single surge
> silently advance, swept along by the thrill
> of unknown.
>
> This stillness moves like the swings
> of a pendulum turning on its axis
> yet suspended
> by the threads of destiny, like puppets
> jerked by spurts of cosmic energy,
> it sweeps them along in orgiastic thrall
> making their cry hoarse
> and stifled, a call that carries
> them to forbidden realms.
>
> Music, swift as winged horses
> pipes sounds, vibrations
> elusive as foaming waves,

Danse de l'orée by Simonne Jacquemard © Éditions du Seuil, 1979. Permission for the use of the translation from the French by Patricia Nolan.

suddenly all together
the black booted figures
descend to earth again,
the ethereal travellers stamp
the earth with their heels
sending a titan shock to its core
where the sounding gong, the mortal
sacred celebration of volcanic
eruptions is about to begin.

Greek Dances II

Simonne Jacquemard
Translated by Patricia Nolan

Who summons them, in a ferment
of bitter honey and spiralling flutes,
who leads them in procession
on these high summits where none
but the cloven hoofed initiate may follow.

Stitch by soldered stitch, following in profile
they stretch out in their slow adventurous
dancing procession, behind the leader
whose arms upraised, climbs the first slopes
and shows them high above
the hovering eagle,
menacing like the gods' desire.

Danse de l'orée by Simonne Jacquemard © Éditions du Seuil, 1979. Permission for the use of the translation from the French by Patricia Nolan.

Muscle Like Metaphor Pulls Thin and Tough

Vivian Jokl

Running strips my nerves,
like fungus curling off old wood.
I stride, aching for a savage breath
but my hot teeth are empty.
I think of death by not breathing
as I run myself rigid,
straining for a wildness
that is not in me.

A woman running after roads,
I attract the bark
of a dog
ignorant of running pain.
A rabbit in berry bushes
hears the hound,
huddles frozen
and I run faster.

I rarely get out of my body,
but when I do
the top of the forest flies.
I run no longer knowing
where the earth is.
Birds burst from stems,
pound the air like my feet.
They soar. I am an airplane,
tacked together with flaps
for folding up or down,

my stress points reinforced.
I stretch my muscle like metaphor
until it pulls thin and tough.

African Chess 1977

Tessa Ransford

The Black Bishop
moved setfaced
towards his Jerusalem
where, in this game,
the Black King
dealt him death.

The White Bishop
edged diagonally
this way and that
until the White King
edged him off the board.

White Castles stand siege.

Black Castles make threatening moves.

The Black Queen fractures
into millions of mothers
who try to nourish life
when every move is against it.

The White Queen
manoeuvres with all the misery

of her privileged
powerlessness.

Who are the opponents?
What fingers touch the pieces?
Whose mind works out the next move?

What are the rules?

They play the game like beginners,
but others are standing
behind them
leaning heavily on their shoulders.

In this game
the colours mean nothing.
It is the strong against the weak
while each one is always
a pawn
in the game of another.

Between Hard Rocks and Savage Winds I Try

Vittoria Colonna
Translated by Muriel Kittel

Between hard rocks and savage winds I try
the waters of this life in fragile craft;
no longer have I art nor skill to steer:
it seems no help for my relief comes nigh.

Muriel Kittel's English translation of Vittoria Colonna's poem "Between Hard Rocks and Savage Winds I Try" is reprinted, by permission of The Feminist Press at The City University of New York, from *The Defiant Muse: Italian Feminist Poems from the Middle Ages to the Present*, edited by Beverly Allen, Muriel Kittel and Keala Jane Jewell. Translation © 1986 by Muriel Kittel.

Spent in a moment by harsh death is he
who was my star and my direction clear:
now 'gainst teeming air and wrathful sea
I've no more aid, but everywhere more fear;

Not fear of wicked sirens' sweetest song;
not fear of shipwreck between these lofty shores;
not fear of foundering in the swirling sands;

fear only still to navigate these waves
that I have plowed so hopelessly and long,
because death hides from me my haven sure.

Rowing

Anne Sexton

A story, a story!
(Let it go. Let it come.)
I was stamped out like a Plymouth fender
into this world.
First came the crib
with its glacial bars.
Then dolls
and the devotion to their plastic mouths.
Then there was school,
the little straight rows of chairs,
blotting my name over and over,
but undersea all the time,
a stranger whose elbows wouldn't work.
Then there was life

with its cruel houses
and people who seldom touched—
though touch is all—
but I grew,
like a pig in a trenchcoat I grew,
and then there were many strange apparitions,
the nagging rain, the sun turning into poison
and all of that, saws working through my heart,
but I grew, I grew,
and God was there like an island I had not rowed to,
still ignorant of Him, my arms and my legs worked,
and I grew, I grew,
I wore rubies and bought tomatoes
and now, in my middle age,
about nineteen in the head I'd say,
I am rowing, I am rowing
though the oarlocks stick and are rusty
and the sea blinks and rolls
like a worried eyeball,
but I am rowing, I am rowing,
though the wind pushes me back
and I know that that island will not be perfect,
it will have the flaws of life,
the absurdities of the dinner table,
but there will be a door
and I will open it
and I will get rid of the rat inside of me,
the gnawing pestilential rat.
God will take it with his two hands
and embrace it.

As the African says:
This is my tale which I have told,
if it be sweet, if it be not sweet,

take somewhere else and let some return to me.
This story ends with me still rowing.

The Swimmer

Sharon Olds

The way the seed that made me raced
ahead of the others, arms held to her sides,
round head humming, spine
whipping, I love to throw myself
into the sea—cold fresh
enormous palm around my scalp,
I open my eyes, and drift through the water that lies
heavy on the earth, I am suspended in it
like a sperm. Then I love to swim slowly,
I feel I am at the center of life, I am
inside God, there is sourweed in skeins like
blood beside my head. From the beach
you would see only the ocean, the swell
curling—so I am like a real being,
invisible, an amoeba that rides in spit,
I am like those elements my father turned into,
smoke, bone, salt. It is one of
the only things I like to do
anymore, get down inside the horizon
and feel what his new life is like, how
clean, how blank, how griefless, how without error—
the trance of matter.

A Game of Ball

Muriel Rukeyser

On a ground beaten gold by running and
Over the Aztec crest of the sky and
Past the white religious faces of the
Bulls and far beyond, the ball goes flying.

Sun and moon and all the stars of the moon
Are dancing across our eyes like the flight of armies
And the loser dies. Dark player and bright
Play for the twinned stiff god of life and death.
They die and become the law by which they fight.

Walls grow out of this light, branches out of the stone,
And fire running from the farthest winds
Pours broken flame on these fantastic sands
Where, sunlit, stands the goddess of earth and death,
A frightful peasant with work-hardened hands.

But over the field flash all the colors of summer,
The battle flickers in play, a game like sacrifice.
The sun rides over, the moon and all her stars.
Whatever is ready to eat us, we have found
This place where the gods play out the game of the sky
And bandy life and death across a summer ground.

Reprinted, by permission of International Creative Management, Inc., from, *Beast In View*, 1944, by Muriel Rukeyser.

About the Editors

Susan J. Bandy and Anne S. Darden share a common interest in the literature of sport, particularly the work of women writers. *Crossing Boundaries* is a result of their combined efforts and the culmination of five years of research.

Bandy was a competitive basketball player in high school and college. She earned a PhD in the history and philosophy of sport at Arizona State University. She is currently a Fulbright Scholar to Hungary, where she teaches courses devoted to sport history as well as women and sport at the Hungarian University of Physical Education.

Darden has published and presented papers on women's sports literature. She earned a master's degree in 19th and 20th century American literature from East Tennessee State University. She has been an editor at *Aethlon: The Journal of Sports Literature* since 1992. Darden lives in Johnson City, Tennessee.

Explore the Female
Sport Experience

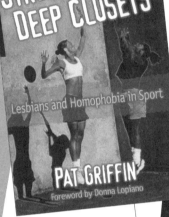

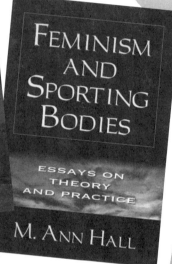

Item BGRI0729
ISBN 0-88011-729-X
$19.95 ($29.95 Canadian)

This book is the first to explore the lesbian sporting experience as well as examine homophobia and heterosexism in women's sport. Engagingly written, the work brings to light the experiences of lesbian coaches and athletes in their own words. Author Pat Griffin lists obstacles lesbian athletes face and details numerous personal and political strategies for leveling the playing field.

Item BHAL0969
ISBN 0-87322-969-X
$22.00 ($27.95 Canadian)

Ann Hall, one of the leading authorities on gender relations in sport traces her 30-year journey across the feminist terrain—from liberal, radical, Marxist, and socialist feminism to more recent trends in contemporary cultural theory in sport. It focuses on the debates over these positions within feminism, illustrating their relevance to sport and physical education.

HUMAN KINETICS
The Premier Publisher for Sports & Fitness
P.O. Box 5076, Champaign, IL 61825-5076
www.humankinetics.com

2335

For more information or to place your order, U.S. customers call toll-free **1-800-747-4457**. Customers outside the U.S. use the appropriate telephone number/address shown in the front of this book.